BUSHRANGING TALES

First Printing, 2022

ISBN print edition: 978-0-6489572-5-6
ISBN eBook edition: 978-0-6489572-6-3

Cover image: Attacking the mail (Bushranging, N.S.W. 1864.), by S. T. Gill. [Courtesy: State Library Victoria; 2395195; is006721]

BUSHRANGING TALES

Volume One

AIDAN PHELAN

Australian Bushranging

Dedicated to my dad, Keith, who indulged my youthful fascination and continues to inspire me every day despite his earthly absence.

A Guide To

Est. 2017

Australian Bushranging

Contents

Foreword: What is a bushranger?

A "bushranger", in the most concise definition, is a criminal who takes refuge in, and operates from, the wilderness (usually heavily forested areas). Other terms used to describe this class of criminal includes bandit, fugitive, outlaw and bolter.

In popular understanding, bushrangers are considered to be criminals who commit highway robbery and associated criminal acts (murder, assault etc.) in the Australian bush. While this refers to the modus operandi of *most* bushrangers during the peak period of the 1850s to 1870s, it is not a complete depiction. In fact, the earliest crimes committed by those labelled as bushrangers were typically stock theft, home invasion, murder and arson. The highway robbery aspect only became commonplace as a result of the gold rush, which saw gold being shifted on the roads from the diggings to the towns and made for lucrative targets. Prior to this, most bushrangers stole what they needed such as clothes, firearms, horses and supplies, and those were usually taken during raids on farms or stores. Many of the early bushrangers were seen as champions of the convict class for their rebellious behaviour, just as later bushrangers came to be seen as champions by those who felt the law was unjust and those who upheld it were crooked.

The term dates back to the early 1800s and describes a class of criminal unique to the Australian colonies at the time, though it was subsequently used to describe similar criminal types in places as far apart as New Zealand and China. Early bushrangers were also frequently referred to as "bolters" if they were escaped convicts rather than settlers that had gone rogue. Over time the terminology fell out of favour, but many modern fugitives fit into the definition surprisingly well. You will often see these people referred to in the media as a "modern day Ned Kelly".

References to "outlaws" is complicated in this context as it can either be a colloquialism for a person that lives outside of the law or it can refer to those people who were declared an outlaw under the Felons Apprehension Acts introduced into New South Wales in the 1860s and Victoria in the 1870s. The latter definition is a legal term that encompassed those who had been declared exempt from the protection of the law by the government. People declared outlaws had thirty days to turn themselves in before the declaration took full effect, after which time they could be killed without provocation and the killer would be entitled to the reward offered for the outlaw.

Not all bushrangers fit cleanly into the traditional definition of the term, however. For example, Musquito was a bushranger and also an Aboriginal guerilla fighter during the frontier wars of the 19th century, therefore classifying his acts as merely criminal or acts of war are difficult to establish. For this reason some people even question whether the term bushranger really applies to people like Ned Kelly and Paddy Kenniff, but it is clear from the aforementioned terminology that they are. Bushranging is not merely an Australian equivalent of highway robbery in the times of Dick Turpin, but a result of criminals adapting to the terrain of the colonial frontier.

For ease of classification here we will stick to the concise definition [a criminal who takes refuge in the Australian wilderness] with a particular emphasis on the colonial era, 1788 – 1901. We will also include

Post-Colonial bushranging such as the outbreak of "boy bushrangers" in the 1920s and modern examples where applicable. It is interesting to imagine how bushranging could manifest in the information age where people have access to cars, high powered firearms, the internet and cashless shopping.

"The Mudgee Mail Arrives At Its Destination(!)"
Melbourne Punch, 19/11/1865, p.4

I

The Hunter Becomes the Hunted

It was September 1817, and the bushranger gang of Michael Howe had finally fallen apart. Since 1814, they had terrorised Van Diemen's Land by raiding farms and even the residence of Lieutenant Governor Thomas Davey. Recently Davey had been replaced with a new figurehead in the form of Lieutenant Governor William Sorell, and Howe had attempted to test the legitimacy of his offer of a pardon for turning himself in and helping authorities catch the other bushrangers.

Howe handed himself over to the authorities and gave them information that seemed to be useful on the surface, but lacked any helpful details to actuate a capture. Howe would go on to claim that Reverend Robert Knopwood had personally escorted himself around Hobart Town. An indignant Knopwood denied the accusation and it was not pursued any further. Still, Sorell was as good as his word and had written to his counterpart in New South Wales about Howe's pardon.

As Howe waited in Hobart Town for news of his pardon, occupying his time by knitting items for sale, his former associates, still at large, were gradually captured or killed independent of his supposed information.

His right-hand man, Peter Septon, had been murdered by one of their newer recruits – a man named Hillier – by having his throat slashed while he slept. Their friend Richard Collier, who had been beside Septon, barely escaped alive, with a slash across his own neck and a hole in his hand where he had been shot by Hillier, only to end up on the gallows in Hobart Town.

Meanwhile, having been told by a messenger that his pardon was rejected and there was now a noose and a gibbet waiting for him on Hunter Island, Howe absconded from the gaol and returned to the bush. This time, however, he was alone.

Despite being on his own, Howe still had harbourers to help him get by. One of these was William Drew, also known as Slambow, who was a shepherd in the employ of a grazier named Williams, near New Norfolk. Slambow had no particularly strong sympathy for Howe's plight, but offered his support for whatever he could get in return, which was usually items of use that Howe had stolen.

Slambow was Howe's unofficial messenger, relaying information to him and conveying letters that he had written to their destination. Now, a month after Howe's escape, Slambow had just received another one of Howe's letters intended to be sent to the Lieutenant Governor. He didn't bother reading it as Howe's messy writing was usually difficult to decipher, and he himself was more or less illiterate anyway. He had speculated that the missive was in relation to Howe's absconding from custody. Howe, discovering that he had been lied to about the pardon, was keen to attempt to negotiate with the government to get what he was promised and start fresh. It was a magnificent display of optimism, and misplaced given that the government had officially decided that the door on that option was now permanently closed.

Slambow had no particular fondness for Howe, seeing their relationship as purely transactional, so when another bushranger he was harbouring, named George Watts, approached Slambow with a proposition to capture Howe, he was all ears.

Under cover of darkness, Watts approached Williams' hut. He had often come this way and gained some food and drink to tide him over, but never when Howe had been present. He went to the door and knocked three times upon it. After a moment, Slambow opened the door and granted the bushranger entrance.

As Watts sat at the table ripping a lump of bread apart with filth-encrusted fingers he looked up at his young confederate.

"You seen that Howe 'round here lately, boy?"

"Aye, about six weeks ago. Came with a letter for the Lieutenant Governor."

"A letter, eh? Didn't know that Yorkie beggar could write."

"He's been here about two or three times," Slambow explained, "Always on his own; always at sunrise. He waits on the other side of the river where the boss keeps most of his sheep, then I have to meet him in the scrub."

An awkward silence fell over the pair as Watts mopped up some dregs of stew from his bowl with the bread and pushed it into his mouth past his overhanging moustache.

"'Ere," said Watts, "how'd you like to earn yourself a bit of coin, m'lad?"

"How so?" Slambow replied.

"The government wants Howe. They're offering a hundred guineas for him. If you and I work together, bring him in, we could split the reward and I'd get me a pardon."

"How much of a split?" Slambow asked.

"About half sounds fair, don't you reckon? Fifty guineas could get you on the way from being the shepherd to being the grazier, and I'd have me freedom."

Slambow stroked his chin thoughtfully. "Howe's due back on Thursday or Friday. That would be the best time to take him," he said. Watts grinned.

***

Watts had arrived as a convict in Australia via the ship *Coromandel* in 1804. After marrying in 1811 he slipped back into a life of crime. He was tried with William Clark, William Field and Thomas Garland on 28 September 1813, for stealing promissory notes from John Ingle to the value of £4 10s., £6 10s., and £7 17s. 6d., respectively. While the others were acquitted, Watts was sentenced to transportation for seven years to be served at the Coal River penal settlement, Newcastle. In November of that same year he absconded and made his way to Van Diemen's Land. By 1815 he had gone bush with Thomas Garland. They were joined by another runaway, James Whitehead, who abandoned them after they began setting fire to haystacks and barns. Whitehead had then joined up with Michael Howe, but had since been killed in a skirmish with redcoats.

On 5 July 1817, the reward for Watts was Proclaimed at eighty guineas, and he was suspected by the authorities of being one of Howe's associates. Howe himself, though, deeply mistrusted Watts after hearing what Whitehead had to say about him and Thomas Garland.

***

On the appointed day, Watts arrived at the meeting point and took a small boat belonging to a man named Triffit and rowed across the river Derwent. On the opposite bank, he hid out of direct view along a path to wait for his accomplice, William "Slambow" Drew, who was due to arrive at sunrise as per his arrangement with Howe.

Meanwhile, Drew had gone about his usual work for the day, then borrowed a musket and hunting dog from his employer, Williams, who had come up to the farm to tend to his sheep.

He headed out in the dark and met Watts at the rendezvous point. The bushranger noted the musket and furrowed his brow.

"What are the dog and musket for?" Watts asked.

"If we're going to catch an outlaw, I need a gun. The dog will make sure he doesn't give us the slip. He's a swift little beggar; he can run down kangaroos in no time flat."

"We're not hunting kangaroos, boy. If Howe sees you with the musket he'll get the wind up him. Leave it here."

Slambow placed the musket near Watts' campfire, but the bushranger kept his own weapon close to hand and primed, reasoning that Drew was the lure and he would stay secreted in the bush until the time came to pounce.

They camped out until sunrise then headed to the meeting place, a spot known as Long Bottom, and Slambow called out, "Howe!"

They were met with silence, so Slambow called out again, "Howe!"

This time there came a reply from across the creek. A low voice with a Yorkshire accent boomed, "Slam-boh!"

Michael Howe emerged from the dawn gloom and crossed the creek, attempting to stay as dry as he could. He was dressed in rags, with kangaroo skin moccasins, a kangaroo skin cloak, and a calico knapsack slung over his shoulders. His black hair and beard were long and matted, and he rested his musket on his shoulder to keep it high and dry.

As Howe came within ninety yards of Slambow, Watts emerged from the bush with his gun levelled at the outlaw. Howe quickly levelled his own piece at the arrival, only just discerning Watts through the early light. Williams' kangaroo dog began to bark.

"Hey, up," Howe growled.

"Stop there, don't come up until you've knocked the priming out of that gun," Watts hollered back.

"And leave myself defenceless against you?" Howe replied.

"Alright, I'll do the same," Watts answered, "I'm going to knock the priming out. Watch."

Watts did as he said, flipping the musket and opening the frizzen to tip the black powder out of the pan. Howe did the same with his own weapon and approached Watts and Drew.

The trio travelled quietly about forty yards and set up a camp, preparing a small fire.

Watts patted his pockets. "Anyone got flint and steel?"

Slambow shook his head. Howe grumbled and took his own out of his knapsack.

As the outlaw crouched and began striking the stone against the steel ring over the kindling, Watts nodded to Drew, who returned the gesture, then leaped and bowled Howe over, grabbing his collar. As Howe struggled to grasp Watts and throttle him, Drew planted a foot on his throat to keep him pinned. Howe gurgled as he snatched at the muddy boot clamping his airway shut, which only served to give Drew the access he needed to bind Howe's wrists with a length of rope.

They rolled Howe onto his belly, and Watts stomped between his shoulders to keep him down. Drew searched through Howe's pockets frantically, confiscating two knives. Once Drew confirmed that Howe was disarmed, Watts allowed him to sit up.

"I'll cook t'pair of yers alive for this, yer bastards," Howe snarled.

Watts smirked, "Good luck cooking with your hands tied, old man."

Howe lurched forward and grabbed at Watts, but could not get a grip, so instead swung his arms at his captor's head like a mallet, knocking him to the ground. Drew grabbed Howe's musket and clubbed him in the head with it and the bushranger was finally subdued.

Howe came to, as Drew and Watts sat by the fire eating breakfast. The smell of burning wood and frying ham mingled with the taste of dried blood in his mouth. Watts turned as Howe sat up.

"Want some breakfast, old man?"

Howe simply scowled in return.

"Suit yourself."

Howe moved his wrists to test the rope. The rope was rough and worn down, and the knot that Slambow had tied was poorly made - Howe would know, being a former sailor.

As the others ate and gloated, Howe continued to stretch the rope, and surreptitiously rub the knot against whatever hard surface he could find to loosen it.

After breakfast they began the long walk to Hobart Town, where Howe was to be hanged and Watts and Drew would receive their rewards. Drew suggested he should take the kangaroo dog and musket back home before they get to town, in case his boss missed them while he was out. Begrudgingly, Watts agreed.

They returned to the farm where Williams had been searching for Slambow all morning. The shepherd apologised and explained that he had captured Michael Howe. The grazier was incredulous, but Slambow showed Williams the knives he had taken from Howe's pockets.

"How did you manage that?" Williams asked.

"I had some help," Slambow replied.

"You might need some more help in getting him into Hobart Town. It's quite a journey on foot."

Slambow shook his head with a smirk.

"Trust me, I have it under control. Not only did I get his knives, I have his gun too."

Williams remained doubtful. Slambow, in his experience, was full of self-confidence but tended to rush head first into situations he had not fully weighed up. He implored him to be careful and allowed him to leave, asking him to try and make it back before nightfall.

When Slambow returned, the trio began walking, Drew in the rear holding Howe's unprimed musket and Watts in front, leading with his own gun now reloaded and primed.

"It's nothing pers'nal, mate," said Watts, "we all do what we have to so's we can get by."

Howe remained silent. He kept an eye on Watts, but would occasionally look over his shoulder at Drew. He saw his knives tucked into Drew's trousers and took note.

When they had walked about eight miles, Howe decided to free himself. The ropes, worn down as they were, provided no resistance as he wrenched his hands free.

He spun around like a whirling dervish, snatching a knife from Drew in one clean motion.

Drew screamed.

Watts turned to see what the commotion was and was stabbed in the stomach by Howe. Stunned by the wounding, Watts staggered backwards and dropped his musket, pressing his hands to the freely bleeding puncture. Howe seized the fallen musket and cocked the hammer. Watts, still reeling, made for the bush and hid behind a wattle tree. He slumped against the trunk and tried to catch his breath.

Howe turned once again to face Drew. The outlaw's face, which always had a roughness, now took on a most terrifying appearance as it curled up into a wolfish snarl. His grey-green eyes seemed to go darker and deeper, hypnotic in their fury.

Drew turned and bolted.

"I'll settle your business," Howe growled as he lifted the musket and shot Drew in the back. The ball struck by the right shoulder blade and pushed straight through the thorax and out of the breast bone in a burst of gore.

Drew staggered as he lost momentum, then plunged face-first into the dirt. There was no more movement, only a faint death rattle gurgling from his throat as his life was extinguished.

Howe waited a moment to assess his handiwork, then stopped to pick up Watts' discarded knapsack. He fished around and snatched up the powder, wadding and ball he needed, then proceeded to the scrub.

Watts remained concealed, but began whimpering and shuddering as shock set in. He leaned out and saw Howe reloading the musket with the machine-like precision only a military man would have.

He couldn't see Drew.

"Is... is he dead?" Watts asked weakly from his hiding place.

"Yes, and I'll serve you t'same as soon as I can load my piece," Howe replied coldly. The rod clanged ominously as it slid all the way down the musket barrel to tamp the ball and wadding paper. Howe raised the musket and began to scan the bush, his eyes were hard and piercing like an eagle searching for a mouse.

Watts, in extreme pain from his stomach wound, broke from cover and ran. Howe whipped across and fired in the direction of the fleeing prey. The shot went wide of its mark.

Watts made it about two hundred yards before collapsing from loss of blood and exhaustion.

Meanwhile, Howe collected his things, and whatever he could use from the kit Watts had dropped, before checking on Drew's lifeless form, where it lay in the dirt. He shook his head, retrieved his musket and began to return to the safety of the bush on foot.

***

As he regained consciousness, George Watts looked around, but could not see Howe. When he was convinced he was in the clear, he took off again, heading for a hut a half a mile from where Drew lay dead. The hut was the residence of a Mr. James Burne.

He stumbled to the door and banged on it to get the occupant's attention, wailing for help. The wife of the owner answered the door and, upon seeing the bloodied bushranger, let out a shriek.

"Help me, I'm dying," Watts gasped.

The woman helped him inside and guided him onto a bed. The helpless marauder looked up pitifully at the woman.

"Fetch... the constable..."

"Constable Waddle?" the woman asked.

Watts nodded.

"Take me into... town... make... a statement..."

Watts passed out, leaving the overwhelmed woman to organise to get the constable out to the house.

When the constable arrived, Watts was barely able to speak and only managed to give his name, which immediately raised alarm bells. Watts was allowed to rest, with the constable arranging to return in the morning to finish taking the statement.

The following day, Watts was still struggling to speak, only imparting the detail that William Drew had been shot nearby. A search in the surrounding area resulted in the retrieval of Drew's body.

An inquest was held and it was deemed that Michael Howe was guilty of the murder of William Drew. Watts was taken to the general hospital in Hobart along with the corpse. He died three days later.

Michael Howe was now the most wanted man in Australia. The previous reward of 100 guineas was increased to include a pardon and free passage back to England for any convicts who helped the authorities capture him.

Howe became more reclusive and grew suspicious of his harbourers. He was terrified that Aboriginals would murder him or that at any moment a party of redcoats could cross his path and riddle him with lead. He rarely slept, and what sleep he had was troubled by nightmares.

It would not be long before fate caught up to him.

Michael Howe

> *"We will stand it no longer. We are determined to have it full and satisfactory, either for or against us, so we are determined to be kept no longer in ignorance, for we think ourselves greatly injured by the country at large."*
>
> **– MICHAEL HOWE**

Michael Howe was born in 1787 in Pontefract, Yorkshire. Life during this time was rough on lower class families thanks to the Industrial Revolution, and poverty was rampant. For a young man of the lower classes there were really only two options to earn a decent living: join the armed forces to fight for Crown and Country, or become a rich man's servant. Howe's choice out of these two options indicates a very important aspect of his nature. He briefly enlisted in the army before joining the Royal Navy on a man-of-war, then on a Merchant Navy vessel. Howe absconded, however, by jumping overboard. Evidently the harsh treatment inflicted upon him as a sailor and soldier had pushed him to the edge and he had decided to take his chances elsewhere. He is reputed to have vowed from this time forward to be no man's servant.

Now looking for a means of supporting himself, while also due for punishment if he was caught after absconding, Howe became a highwayman. He was convicted at York assizes on 31 July, 1811, for robbing a Miller on the King's highway, and was transported to Australia for seven years in late 1812.

Howe was sent to New South Wales on the *Minstrel*, where he was transferred to *Indefatigable*, then taken to Van Diemen's Land. As part of his sentence, Howe was assigned to the wealthy merchant and grazier, John Ingle, who had a reputation as being harsh and overbearing. Howe resented his enforced servitude and took to the bush. No doubt the horrific treatment of convicts was the driving factor in Howe's rebellion.

He joined up with a gang of bolters led by Peter Mills, the former Acting Deputy Surveyor of Lands at Port Dalrymple, and George Williams, former Acting Deputy Commissary of Stores and Provisions. Mills had run up significant debts, and rather than deal with them he took to the bush. The gang raided farms and camps for supplies, even stealing herds of sheep and cattle for their own purposes. Most of the men in the gang were rather quiet and level-headed, but some others tended to be outspoken and volatile.

Lieutenant Governor Macquarie issued a proclamation on May 14, 1814, in which he listed the gang members and gave them until the first of December to return to their assignments. If they returned on or before that date they would receive a pardon on the crimes committed during their absence.
Howe turned up at a spot called "The Ovens" in August 1814 – nearly four months later to the day of the proclamation – with other members of the gang, and bailed up a party of soldiers who were escorting prisoners from Port Dalrymple. This would be the earliest recorded appearance of Howe as a bushranger.

An oft-repeated fallacy is that Howe joined a gang of bushrangers led by a legend-ary rogue called John Whitehead. These accounts state that Whitehead had one of the largest bushranger gangs ever recorded with a purported member count of at least twenty eight, but it was not the case. The Whitehead that Howe joined up with – whose actual name was James Whitehead – was simply one of the many convicts that joined the ever-growing gang with its ill-defined hierarchy. Prominent members were Richard McGuire, Hugh Burn, Richard Collier, Peter Septon, George "Bumpy" Jones, James Geary, and an Aboriginal woman named Mary Cockerill, nicknamed "Black Mary".

The gang operated mostly around New Norfolk, raiding farms. They tended to have the bulk of their members remain at camp, while a pair or small group would head out to get to work at the targeted farms. Interestingly, many of the attacks seemed to not simply be targeted at farms that looked likely to yield decent takings. It appeared that the bushrangers would attack based on information supplied to the them by harbourers, in particular a well-known figure around Van Diemen's Land named Edward Lord, who was at the time described as the richest man in the colony. It seems the outlaws were possibly being used as a tool by their harbourers to cause grief to people in the region that they were in conflict with, as part of an ongoing, unofficial land war between settlers.

One farmer who had repeated run-ins with the bushrangers was Dennis McCarty. On one of these occasions, he had spotted some of the gang on the outskirts of his property making mocassins and opened fire. The gang bolted for cover and a battle ensued, during which one of McCarty's servants launched into attack against the bushrangers with a sword. In the fight, most of McCarty's men were injured, and when Howe saw another member of his gang make a move to shoot one of the men dead, he intervened to stop him. In direct consequence of this battle, Charles Carlisle died and the charge of his murder was laid upon James Whitehead, Peter Septon, Michael Howe, Richard Collier, Hugh Burn, James Geary and Mary Cockerill.

Such affrontery was unacceptable and on 25 April 1815, Lieutenant Governor Thomas Davey controversially declared Martial Law in an effort to contain the elusive banditti. It did not produce the desired effect and on 10 May the gang raided the house of Adolarius Humphrey, a notorious magistrate.
The Humphreys were not home when the bushrangers arrived, but they went straight to work plundering the place and mouthing off about what they would do to their opponents if they came upon them. When Howe, Geary and McGuire were ransacking the place they found leg irons in the house — a clear indication Humphrey had been ill-treating his servants. In response to this they went on a rampage and destroyed everything they could.

The gang launched a revenge attack on Dennis McCarty on 18 May 1815. Such a move, however, had been anticipated, and a party of soldiers from Hobart Town had been stationed in the homestead while McCarty and his wife were out of the house.
While James Whitehead scouted the perimeter of the homestead a soldier fired on him, killing him. A battle ensued, during which, Whitehead's body was decapitated in order to prevent the soldiers from claiming the reward on the head. Most versions of the story state Whitehead ordered Howe to, "Take my watch," as a code for the decapitation, upon which command Howe cut the head off and brandished it like a trophy at his attackers before escaping. The headless corpse, dumped on the doorstep, greeted McCarty when he arrived home. The head was later found dumped in the bush and the rest of the remains were gibbetted on Hunter Island in Hobart.

Howe soon stood up into more of a leadership role, his calm and commanding presence keeping the wilder inclinations of his mates under control. Howe took much pride in his position and referred to himself as the "Governor of the Ranges" (as opposed to the "Governor of the Town" which was what Howe called the Lieutenant Governor.) Under his watch, however, the gang's numbers began to dwindle.

Hugh Burn and Richard McGuire were apprehended in a hut after a shootout with soldiers of the 46th regiment, and subsequently hanged. When the remaining gang undertook a raid of Richard Fry's farm at Elphin, near Port Dalrymple, in September 1815, it was reported that they now consisted of only a half dozen members.

On 5 July 1816, Howe, Septon, Collier, Geary and "Bumpy" Jones bailed up Thomas Seals in his hut. They baked damper and shot one of his cattle, which they butchered and ate, leaving the scraps for the dogs. They stayed for several days. When they left they took Seals with them and committed several robberies. They let Seals go in the evening.

On 8 September, 1816, the gang raided the property of Lieutenant Governor Davey. During this audacious robbery, Howe fixed himself some eggnog, and Peter Septon gave a sick servant a drink made from wine and milk, a popular remedy for gastric illness at the time. Before they left, Howe borrowed a dictionary and promised to return it.

At this time, Howe's gang consisted of himself, Peter Septon, Richard Collier, James Geary, "Bumpy" Jones, Matthew Keegan, John Brown, John Parker, John Chapman, Thomas Coyne, Thomas McCaig and two Aboriginal girls, one of whom was Mary Cockerill, the other's name is unrecorded.

After months of easily evading the soldiers sent after them, Howe and Mary Cockerill were ambushed by soldiers from the 46th regiment in April 1817. Howe darted off and fired back at the redcoats before dumping his gear, including his knapsack and firearm. While it is generally stated that Howe shot Mary either accidentally or because she was slowing him down, it is not clear from contemporary reports whether Mary was even shot at all. Assertions that she was pregnant with Howe's child are also untrue. In his kit, retrieved by the soldiers, were his musket and a stolen gardening book bound in kangaroo skin filled with hand-written notes.

Mary immediately began to help the police track the rest of the gang to their camp by the Shannon River. When the soldiers came upon the bushrangers, Howe and company mocked them and bolted into the bush. Mary also helped the authorities reclaim sheep the gang had stolen, and was rewarded for her assistance with clothes, food and accommodation.

At this time, the new Lieutenant Governor of Van Diemen's Land, William Sorell, issued a proclamation promising harsh penalties for the bushrangers and their harbourers, but an amnesty was also on offer in an attempt to bring an end to the lawlessness. Howe saw this as an opportunity to give up the outlaw lifestyle he had come to detest, and intended to negotiate his surrender by writing to Sorell.

The negotiations were managed carefully by Howe, who agreed to give the authorities information on the condition that he be given a Royal Pardon. He was taken into custody in Hobart on 29 April 1817, to await confirmation of the pardon. During this time he claimed that the esteemed magistrate, Reverend Robert Knopwood, was one of the associates of the gang, and had even personally escorted himself and a fellow bushranger, George Watts, through the streets of Hobart. He mostly occupied himself with hawking items he had been knitting while awaiting news of his pardon.

Howe's incarceration did not last long as he took advantage of the relaxed security he had negotiated and fled to the bush once more. It is believed this was a response to receiving information from an associate that the pardon had been refused, though in actuality it had been approved.

Reports that Howe had murdered his friend Peter Septon and attempted the same on Richard Collier are completely incorrect, as he was being guarded by soldiers at the Hobart Town Gaol at the time. It was, in fact, a new member of the gang named George Hillier who had committed the deed.
Several other members of the gang had been captured or killed by soldiers in Howe's absence including "Bumpy" Jones, who was shot and decapitated by soldiers.

Howe now found himself on the run again with no gang to go back to. Shortly after Howe's escape, George Watts conspired with a stockman named William Drew to capture Howe. They lured him to a camp, captured and restrained him. The next day Howe broke his bonds and stabbed Watts, then took his musket and shot Drew. Watts was not dead however and struggled back to town where he told of what happened before dying of his wounds.

As Howe lived a solitary life in a hut by the Shannon River, his clothes disintegrated, his firearms ran out of ammunition and he could not readily find nutritious food. More significantly, his waking hours were spent in terror of the Aboriginals, who were very active in the area launching spear attacks on white people as a response to colonisation.

During this time he was ambushed by bounty hunters, one of whom was an Aboriginal tracker named Musquito who would later earn his own infamy as a bushranger and leader of the Aboriginal resistance against the colonials. During this struggle, Howe lost his supplies again, including a journal made from kangaroo skin in which he had written about his most intimate thoughts and ominous dreams.
Howe was now more vulnerable than ever. He clothed himself in a cloak of kangaroo skins, and his dark beard grew long and bushy. He was afraid to sleep for fear of death or capture.

Howe's associate, a kangaroo hunter named Warburton, conspired with a farmer named Worrell to kill him for the reward of £200 on his head and free passage back to England. Warburton managed to track Howe down and told him there was ammunition and food in his home on the Shannon River. In actual fact the hut was concealing Worrall and an infantryman named Pugh who were waiting, poised with rifles.

On 21 October 1818, upon arriving at the property, Howe hesitated to go inside but eventually did so with a pistol drawn. Howe was ambushed, but ran away as fast as his feet would take him, musket balls whizzing past him. The bounty hunters chased Howe down to a muddy inlet. Howe was shot in the back and tumbled down an embankment. He wrestled with Worrell before Pugh caught up and stabbed Howe through the ribs with his bayonet. Howe fell and then Pugh began to smash his skull in with the butt of his musket, finally killing him.

Howe's head was cut off and displayed on a spike over the gate of the Hobart Town Gaol as a warning to other would-be bushrangers. The body was buried in a shallow grave by the river.

Mere months later, a pamphlet was printed by Andrew Bent, supposedly based on a manuscript by Thomas Wells, declaring Howe to be the "last and worst" of the bushrangers; it was a declaration that did not age well.

CORONER'S INQUEST.— An inquest was taken on Monday last at the County Gaol in this town, before A. W. H. HUMPHREY, Esq. Coroner, upon the body of William Drew, whose death we mentioned in our last.

The first evidence was Mr. Assistant Surgeon Hood, of the 46th regt., who deposed that the death of the deceased, William Drew, seemed to have been occasioned by a musket ball passing through the thorax, by entering the back a little below the right shoulder, and shattering the breast bone in its passage; he did not perceive any other injury about the body.

The next witness was Mr. W. Williams, who stated that the deceased was his servant, and employed in looking after his sheep in the vicinity of New Norfolk. It appeared by the testimony of this witness, that he left Hobart Town on the Wednesday prior to the death of the deceased on a visit to his flock; and that when he got to the First River, he found Drew in the hut there. The next morning, Mr. W. went to his grazing ground for some sheep, which he brought back and sheared himself; and on the following morning, soon after daylight, he sent Drew for some more to the same place. Drew being absent for upwards of 4 hours, witness became alarmed, and went to look for Drew; and when he arrived at the place where he had sent him, he walked about for nearly an hour before he found him, who was then running towards witness with a gun, and a dog; upon his coming up, Mr. W. asked him what was the matter, to which he replied, "George Watts was stopping with Howe, whilst he came to acquaint him of it," and delivered his musket to Mr. W. saying "he did not want it as they had got Mich. Howe's gun, and that Watts had one of his own." During their conversation Drew shewed Mr. W. two knives, which he said he had taken from Howe; and upon Mr. W. asking him if he could be of any assistance, he replied "no, as Howe was secured;" he then ran away; Witness and the deceased had previously agreed to take Howe the first opportunity.

George Watts deposed, that after Mich. Howe had been to Drew, at William's hut, with a letter for the Lieutenant Governor, about six weeks ago, he (Watts) went to Drew, and enquired of him whether he had seen Howe; he replied he had a or 3 times successively, and was again to see him on the Friday following at sunrise; he said should he come on Thursday or Friday, they could take him.

On the Thursday night Watts went to New Norfolk, took Triffit's boat and proceeded across the river, and concealed himself along-side of a path, near the place Drew appointed to meet him, till daylight. About sunrise Drew came, and told him he was to meet Howe at a place called the Long Bottom, where William's sheep were. Watts told Drew to leave his gun, as he thought Howe would not come up to them if he perceived it; Drew left it hidden; they then both proceeded to the place where they expected to meet Howe; upon arriving there, Drew called two or three times, which Howe answered, from the opposite side of the creek. When Watts came within ninety yards of Howe, he told him to knock the priming out of his gun, and he would do the same, which both parties did; they then went about 50 or 40 yards and began to light a fire. The first opportunity, Watts caught Howe by the collar and threw him down; Drew tied his hands, and took two knives from his pocket; Watts and Drew got breakfast, but Howe refused to eat; they then were about proceeding to town, when Drew proposed to take his master's musket and dog back, which Watts agreed to, desiring him not to inform his master of any thing, which he promised. Upon Drew's return, they all proceeded towards Hobart Town, Watts with his gun loaded walked before Howe and Drewe behind. When about about 8 miles on the road, Watts heard Drew scream and on turning round received a wound in his stomach from Howe; but how he got loose, he did not know, excepting by cutting the cord. Howe said, that "he would settle Drew's business," as he had by this time got possession of Watt's musket; he immediately fired at Drew; Watts being amongst some wattles did not hear him speak or see him fall; he enquired if Drew was dead? Howe replied "yes," and "he would shoot him as soon as he could load his piece." Drew carried Howe's musket previous to being shot, but it was not primed. Watts dreading being shot, ran about 200 yards, and lay down a few minutes from cold and loss of blood. Upon being able to walk, he made all haste to a hut belonging to James Burne, and on being put to bed he told Mrs. Burne that he was stabbed by Howe, and requested her husband to get Waddle the constable to take him to town; by the time Waddle arrived he was hardly able to speak; he only informed him of his name, and, when able to talk next morning, he told him Drew was shot. The testimony of the other witnesses merely relates to searching after, and finding the body of Drew, and conveying it to town.

The Jury, after a short deliberation, returned a verdict that the deceased, William Drew, was murdered by Michael Howe.

II

⚜

The Valleyfield Siege

On 7 June 1824, a gang of convicts made their escape from the penal settlement on at Macquarie Harbour. After years of brutal and inhumane treatment at the hands of their overseers and masters, and having seen other convicts try and fail to escape through the forest, these men gathered under the leadership of James Crawford. The group consisted of fourteen men in total, and on the fateful day they seized a boat and attempted to escape by sea. Crawford was an old seadog from Liverpool, short of stature at only a smidge over five feet tall and possessed of an indomitable spirit hardened by years of experience as a sailor and a convict. Among the men was a Mancunian named Matthew Brady, who stood only two inches taller than Crawford and had a burly frame. It was Brady who had prevented the other men from viciously flogging the surgeon that they had kidnapped in their bid to seize a vessel, and his calm, disciplined demeanour seemed to provide a needed counterbalance for Crawford's coarseness and boisterousness. AS the fugitives threatened to lash Dr. Garrett to a tree at Farm Cove to flog him, Brady attested to

Garrett's kindness towards him when he was recovering from one of his own many floggings. The men had relented and let the doctor go free.

After landing at an estuary of the River Derwent, the convicts went ashore and headed inland, robbing dwelling places as they went. In short order they earned a reputation as a fierce band of outlaws when they engaged a party led by the indefatigable Scotsman, Lieutenant William Gunn, in a gun battle. Following this fracas six of the gang were recaptured, and the reward for the rest was set at £10. The last hurrah for the banditti under the leadership of James Crawford was to be enacted in July of 1824 in spectacular fashion near Epping Forest.

Crawford's remaining gang comprised of Matthew Brady, James McCabe, Charles Ryder, Henry McConnell, Jeremiah Ryan, James Bryant, and James Baines. If Crawford had a grand plan, he wasn't letting the others in on what it was, and it certainly seemed he was more inclined toward the aimless procurement of whatever currency and sundry items they could use to survive and pay harbourers, rather than devising an escape from the colony. Perhaps the others had also adopted this mentality, and maybe that was why they set their sights on a much larger target than they had previously attacked.

On 15 July 1824, the bushrangers began the day by robbing the widow Smith in Longford. It was a robbery devoid of bloodshed, and the widow was treated rather civilly excepting the purloining of her material goods and the odd threat or cursing from Crawford. Without any mounts to carry their cargo, Crawford took three of Smith's servants as prisoners and made them carry the booty they had liberated from the woman as they moved to their next target, which was the main aim of the day. The bushrangers and their prisoners travelled by foot to Epping Forest, in the vicinity of the Macquarie River, where the property of George Taylor, *Valleyfield*, sat.

Valleyfield was a grand estate for the time, and was an excellent example of the Georgian architecture that was popping up throughout the fledgling colony. George Taylor was in his mid-seventies, and had lived prosperously enough since arriving in Van Diemen's Land from Scotland in 1823 with his wife, two sons, daughter and various servants. They prided themselves on being hard-working, God-fearing and resilient. Certainly it had been tough to establish such a successful farm between adapting farming techniques to the Australian conditions, and trying to foster positive relations with the local tyrrerenotepanner people, but so far it had been a success. It had been less than a decade since Michael Howe and his colleagues had terrorised the area, but the Taylor's had not yet experienced the unpleasantness afforded by a visit from bushrangers. That was about to change.

The bushrangers and their captives arrived at *Valleyfield* at dusk and were greeted by Taylor's youngest son, George junior, who had been meekly leafing through a Bible while shepherding his father's flock back to their paddock. He was approached by the freebooters, and Crawford levelled a firearm at the young man. He was duly informed that he was now a prisoner of the bushrangers and they gave him a portion of their loot to carry.

"You live here?" Crawford asked.

"I do," answered Taylor.

"So, this is your old man's place?"

Taylor nodded.

"Will he put up a fight?"

"Of course," said Taylor.

"Oh, then, we will give you the post of honour. Go to the front and let him shoot you first."

As darkness began to fall, the family were in the homestead awaiting young George's return. Their attention was roused by the sound of their dogs barking outside. George senior tried to see what the commotion was but could not make out anything in the gloom. He sent his servants out to investigate and suddenly the bushrangers were spotted approaching the house heavily armed, accompanied by their prisoners, walking into the amber light cast from the windows of the homestead. The servants rushed back inside and informed Old Taylor of what was coming their way.

Old Taylor had to think fast, and though he was quite advanced in years he was still as sharp-witted as a young buck. His immediate inclination was to resist the incursion, and he gathered his family and servants to him.

"We must repel these brigands," Taylor stated firmly with a Scottish burr, "I will take up arms. Who among you will join me?"

All of the company agreed to fight alongside Taylor, except for the farm's carpenter, John Lowe, who flew into a panic and ran outside to seek a hiding place in one of the outbuildings.

The occupants of the house rounded up every weapon they could find – muskets and fowling pieces, anything that could be fired or wielded – and any ammunition that was freely to hand. They took positions by the doors and windows and awaited the arrival of the bushrangers. As they stood at the ready, they heard George junior call out.

"Listen," he began, "Everyone is in danger! Do not fire on me, please!"

The tension suddenly snapped and one of the servants fired at the bushrangers. The ball whizzed past James Crawford's head, causing him to reel back. This created enough of a distraction for Taylor to throw aside his load and bolt for cover. He reached the safety of the house just in time for a battle to break out.

Gunfire erupted all around the property, cracking apart the serenity of the night with each blast. Lead balls zipped around like angry mayflies, buzzing as they went past ears, but did not strike their intended targets for the gloom was too profound for the defenders to get their enemies in sight as they scrambled for cover. Not only were the men of the household engaged in the repulsion, but the ladies stood shoulder to shoulder with them, loading and priming the firearms as if they were trained soldiers themselves.

As Old Taylor stood reloading his piece, Crawford saw the outline of his form in the window and took aim. George junior spotted the fiend raising his firearm and pounced on him, pinning him to the ground. As they grappled in the grass, one of the servants fired in their direction, striking Crawford who howled like a wounded bull. Brady and McCabe attempted to reach their comrade but were kept back by the firing from the house, which churned up the lawn at their feet. They accepted that it would be folly to continue to attempt a rescue, and they resumed cover behind the trees and fired off as many shots as they could from their own weapons in the direction of the house.

Another servant saw Crawford and Taylor wrestling on the ground and attempted to shoot the brigand, but the shot missed its target and accidentally struck young Taylor in the chest. By a stroke of luck, the shot merely wounded him thanks to his heavy winter clothes, which had padded him up, but the injury rendered the young man momentarily helpless.

The battle continued to rage, and as the bushrangers surrounded the house attempts were made to break in. John Lowe's hiding place was discovered and though he cowered, he was stabbed fatally with a bayonet. The assailant was impossible to recognise in the dark, but as Lowe's bloodied form slumped over, James McCabe, Charles Ryder and James

Bryant were spotted making tracks from the spot, though nobody was looking in that direction at the time, with all fire being directed from the front of the house.

With Crawford subdued, the bushrangers continued to fight without any directions, darting from tree to tree and occasionally stepping into the light where they became targets. It was as he stepped into the light that Jeremiah Ryan was struck in the head, a lead ball taking out his left eye. He collapsed, screaming uncontrollably and clutching his face as blood gushed from the wound. It was not fatal, and he was dragged clear by Brady and McConnell. Ryan continued to wail and whimper as Brady took his cravat and tied it around the injured man's head, covering the wound.

Another of the gang was now taken prisoner, with James Bains pinned down by a servant and subdued as he attempted to gain entry to the house. Realising that they were fighting a losing battle, Brady, McCabe, Ryan, Ryder, Bryant and McConnell took off, retreating into the night.

Finally, once the sound of gunfire ceased the family and servants were able to relax. They remained vigilant in case the bushrangers should return for Crawford and Baines, but no such rescue effort materialised. The two captured bushrangers were bound and kept under guard until morning when an alarm could be raised with the constabulary.

Word of the gallant conduct of the Taylors and their staff soon spread, and they were lauded for their bravery. Even Lieutenant Governor Arthur wrote to them to express his admiration, and to offer his commiserations should George junior's wounding prove fatal, as had been reported. A silver plate was offered to the family as an award, though the family would never claim it. George junior, upon his recovery, was also granted 500 acres for his courageous conduct.

Elsewhere, the surviving bushrangers were licking their wounds. With Crawford out of the picture, discussion turned to who would assume his role as the head of the gang. It was not a long discussion as all of the bushrangers had taken note of Matthew Brady's calm demeanour and humanity throughout their time on the run. Crawford had been a bully, and his ruthlessness had resulted in his own capture, but all of the men had remembered the way that Brady had intervened at Farm Cove to protect Dr. Garrett from the flogging that others had desired to inflict. It was a simple gesture, but one that resonated with the men, who had been oppressed by the convict system so long that they had begun to turn into the very vengeful beasts that the authorities had accused them of being. They felt that if Brady could maintain that kindness and dignity, maybe he could bring out those qualities in them also; but more importantly they knew that Brady was not likely to be so brash as Crawford was and lead them into a death trap unprepared for resistance. Brady accepted the decision graciously. It would be a month before the bushrangers would again appear to raid a farm owned by David Wedge at Oyster Cove, and this time they would get away with a large haul of weapons and tools before departing by boat. The Oyster Cove raid would be just the first in a long line of daring exploits that would seal Brady's name in the history books as one of Australia's most notable rogues.

Matthew Brady

> *"I take leave to inform you that I am Brady, the bushranger, who you have heard of before, for I've robbed above half the settlers of the country already, and mean to rob the other half before I've done with them; and now, Sir, I'll trouble you for your money."*
>
> — MATTHEW BRADY

The charismatic and daring Matthew Brady is one of the most renowned of the bushrangers for his fearlessness and chivalrous behaviour as much as his prolific criminality. Few outlaws in Australian history have been viewed so favourably, most being referred to in quite overblown and pejorative language. While it is indisputable that, generally, Brady exercised much discretion and relative gentleness during his exploits, he was responsible for innumerable robberies and, irrefutably, committed one cold-blooded murder. Unfortunately, many details of his story are lost to time through both poor contemporary records and scant reports in the press, meaning that very little of what has been handed down is verifiable. Yet, what is verified demonstrates a tale at least as worthy of recognition as those later outlaws that have gathered so much public recognition and sympathy such as Hall and Kelly.

Born in Manchester, England, in 1799, Matthew Brady was employed as a gentleman's servant before being nabbed on a charge of forgery in 1820. In his records, his name is recorded as "Mathew Bready", though this is likely the result of a record taker trying to spell the name phonetically from it being delivered in a Mancunian accent. At Lancaster Quarter Sessions on 17 April 1820, he was found guilty and sentenced to seven years transportation.

On 3 September that year, Brady was sent with 159 other convicts to Van Diemen's Land on board the *Juliana*, arriving 29 December. In his records, he was described as standing at 5'5½" tall, with dark brown hair and blue eyes. He was also tattooed with images of a man and woman on his left arm, a fish and the letters TB on his right arm.

He was assigned to work in the employ of William Brest, but soon found himself sent to Van Diemen's Land's harshest prison of the time: Sarah Island in Macquarie Harbour. Here, from 1821 through 1823, he was flogged repeatedly for infractions ranging from neglect of duty to absconding, enduring a cumulative total of 525 lashes.

He joined a gang of convicts led by James Crawford who successfully escaped from Macquarie Harbour in June 1824. The men succeeded in absconding from their duties, taking the surgeon from the penal settlement as a hostage. During their efforts to procure a boat, the convicts threatened to flog the surgeon, but Brady reportedly stayed their hands as the man had treated him well on the island when he had been recuperating from his own floggings. They successfully stole a whaleboat and traversed the stormy waters off the southwest coast of Van Diemen's Land. They were pursued at sea by the authorities but were able to evade them by pulling into a cove, out of sight, long enough for the pursuers to pass them. They reached the Derwent River after nine days, and upon going ashore became free-booters.

The gang stole firearms from a settler and took to the bush, raiding homesteads to take what they needed. Over the next few weeks, the number of gang members dwindled as members were either captured or killed, the Valleyfield raid being the most devastating to them. During one this raid, the gang were met with resistance and a gunfight broke out. After gang member Jeremiah Ryan lost an eye during the fight, he was intercepted while wandering aimlessly in the bush on the verge of death from dehydration. Eventually the only two men left from the initial band of escapees were Brady and Irishman James McCabe. McCabe was a young man with sharp features and a pockmarked face, whose impulsiveness and temper tended to almost get the better of him on occasion, but Brady's influence seemed to keep him from suffering the fate of their erstwhile companions.

The pair began making connections and developing a network of harbourers around the Tasmanian midlands, occasionally collaborating with new accomplices but never for long. One of these harbourers was a former constable named Thomas Kenton. He would plan robberies with Brady and McCabe, though never actually took part in them himself, merely taking a cut of the takings in exchange for giving the bushrangers a safe haven. Kenton would put out a white sheet to signal the coast was clear to the men, who were soon joined by a boy named Samuel Hite.

Unbeknownst to the bushrangers, Kenton had been conspiring with the authorities and in early March 1825 he arranged a meeting with Brady, McCabe and Hite as a cover for an ambush. When they reached Kenton's hut they were pounced on by soldiers. McCabe bolted, Hite was taken easily, and Brady was severely bashed before he could be subdued. Their hands were bound, and Hite was taken to town to be lodged in the lockup. Brady was to be kept in Kenton's charge until the soldiers returned.

Brady, badly concussed and bleeding from the head, requested a drink. While Kenton was out of the hut collecting water, Brady freed himself from his bonds, allegedly by thrusting his hands in the fire to burn the rope. He then took up a musket, and when Kenton returned Brady threatened to shoot him. He relented but informed Kenton that one day he'd get revenge, before escaping.

Brady and McCabe met up again and established the region around the Central Highlands as their base of operations. They added a bolter named Plumb to their number and on 12 March, the trio were surprised by two constables and a soldier in bush clothes at Wood's Lake. Brady attempted to avoid a conflict be pretending to be a plainclothes constable who thought the newcomers were bushrangers, but a gunfight broke out, during which Plumb was shot and captured by Constable Dutton. Brady and McCabe evacuated under cover of darkness.

A raid the following month was spoiled by the arrival of a party of soldiers who surrounded the hut they were in. When the owner of the hut ran outside begging the soldiers not to shoot he was fatally bayonetted by one of the soldiers while Brady and McCabe escaped through the rear of the building.

Lieutenant Governor Arthur was greatly vexed by the continued and escalating depredations by the bushrangers and put out a declaration in April 1825 stating:

*His Honour has directed that a reward of £25 shall be given for the appre-
hension of either [Brady and accomplice James McCabe]; and that any prisoner
giving such information as may directly lead to their apprehension shall receive a
ticket-of-leave, and that any prisoner apprehending and securing either of them,
in addition to the above reward, shall receive a conditional pardon. [...] Fifty
acres of land, free from restrictions, will be given to the chief constable in whose
district either McCabe or Brady is taken, provided it shall be certified by the
magistrate of the district that he has zealously exerted himself in the promulga-
tion of this order, and to the adoption of measures for giving it effect.*

Brady himself decided to thumb his nose at the authority of the Lieutenant Governor by issuing his own Proclamation, which was pinned to the door of the Royal Oak
Hotel in Green Ponds:

*It has caused Matthew Brady much concern that such a person known as Sir
George Arthur is at large. Twenty gallons of rum will be given to any person
that will deliver his person unto me. I also caution John Priest that I will hang
him for his ill-treatment of Mrs. Blackwell, at Newtown.*

Brady and McCabe now formed a new gang and their operation quickly escalated,
sending fear and excitement through the colony. Brady had gained a reputation for
treating women with kindness and respect that endeared him to many. He impressed
upon his associates that they should never be guilty of injuring the defenceless or
otherwise harming those who posed no threat to them, as well as the importance of
only taking what they needed. This meant a prohibition on excessive thievery, and
under no circumstances molesting women in any way.

On 9 October 1825, the bushrangers raided George Meredith's property *Redbanks*
at Swanport. They utilised Meredith's boats to transport their booty. After the
victim's servants had scuttled the first boat, the bushrangers transferred everything
to a second one and took one of the servants to direct the boat to a hideaway at
Grindstone Bay. However, during the night the gang got horrendously drunk, and a

brawl erupted, during which their captive was killed. As a result, Brady ordered the remaining alcohol be destroyed and swore his gang to temperance in order to prevent further incidents. The one dissenting voice was James McCabe who left the gang as a result. He was captured two weeks later between Hamilton and Bothwell.

As Brady's notoriety grew, so did his ambition and his audacity. He and his gang desired to ridicule the forces of law and order, and succeeded in October when they were able to freely travel around Hobart Town despite there being armed arties of vigilantes patrolling the streets on the lookout for them. The discovery of this naturally saw outrage in the press, but nothing could be done.

On 24 November 1825, the bushrangers stuck up *Thornhill* station at Pittwater and kept the occupants prisoner overnight. In the morning they trekked into Sorell with their prisoners and stuck up a party of redcoats who had been out looking for the gang in their own barracks. The soldiers had been caught in torrential rain and returned to base empty handed with waterlogged muskets, thus had no defence against the bushrangers. The gang then raided the gaol and attempted to free the occupants of the cells, however the inmates were too afraid to leave. The soldiers and the gang's other prisoners were promptly locked up. They were soon met with resistance from outside, as Lieutenant Gunn had heard of their presence and was determined to take them on single-handedly. Two bushrangers on sentry opened fire on Gunn, who was hit in the right arm, injuring it so badly it was necessary to amputate. Before leaving, the gang built a scarecrow to act as a decoy to allow them escape. Surprisingly, it worked as the locals were convinced there was still at least one bushranger guarding the gaol, albeit while standing very still.

Desperate to escape from Van Diemen's Land, Brady and what remained of his gang managed to steal a brig called *Glutton* on 1 December, and intended to use it to gain access to a larger craft called *Blue Eyed Maid* and make their way across Bass Strait. Unfortunately, the gang hit bad weather and they retreated back to land.

A few days later they would almost be involved in another shootout at another of George Meredith's properties near Swanport. Though soldiers surrounded the building, the bushrangers had already made their escape. The soldiers followed them for twenty minutes before turning back for breakfast.

On 20 December, Brady's gang robbed Francis Flexmore in Green Ponds then went to a local pub where they handed out free drinks to the patrons before leaving town. The local constabulary were alerted and after a brief conflict one of the gang, Samuel Hodgetts, was captured.

By January of 1826, it was becoming harder for Brady to trust his gang members as convicts hoping to be rewarded with a remission of their sentences infiltrated the gang in order to spy and feed information back to the authorities. The reward was now 300 guineas or 300 acres of land for settlers and a free pardon and free passage to England for convicts for bringing in Brady.

Brady also found it hard to command such a large gang, and some of them were becoming reckless, as demonstrated when gang members Bird and Murphy got drunk during a robbery at Lake River and burned the property down.

In March the gang attempted an act of piracy on the Tamar, desiring to hijack the brig *Glory*, but some of the spies convinced the others to abandon the idea. Instead they returned to land and headed to Richard Dry's property *Elphin* outside of Launceston, but sent a messenger to alert authorities as a double bluff.

In the middle of the night, the authorities responded to the news and surrounded the building. Brady warned the women in the building that there would be firing and that the soldiers would not discern between who they were shooting at, entreating them to stay low and hidden. During the ensuing battle, a local surgeon named Dr. Priest was shot in the leg but refused treatment, dying a few days later from infection.

Soon Brady learned of what Thomas Kenton had been up to since their last encounter. Kenton had been gaoled following Brady's escape and since his release had been spreading lies about Brady in order to improve his own reputation. On 6 March Brady tracked Kenton down to a hotel called the Cocked Hat Inn in Breadalbane and rode there with gang members Bryant and Williams. Brady calmly informed Kenton that he would be killed for his betrayal and slander. Kenton was unrepentant and proceeded to goad Brady, who responded by shooting him dead. This was the only murder Brady himself would perform.

A matter of days after Kenton's murder, a posse engaged Brady's gang in a running gunfight at Prosser's Plains, having been tipped off by a spy named Cowen. Brady was badly injured by a bullet that passed through his leg. The gang split up, Brady seeking refuge on an island in the North Esk River with his accomplices Murphy and Williams. Cowen led a posse to the hideaway, and although Brady escaped, Murphy and Williams were shot dead in their sleep by their pursuers, leaving Brady alone in the bush without supplies and badly wounded.

He was spotted soon after by bounty hunter John Batman, after Brady had spooked some of Batman's cattle. Brady was hobbling nearby with a sapling he had cut down for a crutch. Batman challenged him with a musket and Brady surrendered.

After being taken back to Hobart Town, Brady and the remaining members of his gang were put on trial, with Brady pleading guilty to all charges. The bushrangers were inevitably found guilty and duly sentenced to death by hanging. Thereafter Brady's cell was allegedly filled with gifts of fruit and sweets, letters and flowers from admiring women. His last act of defiance was complaining vocally about being forced to share a cell with Thomas Jeffrey, the cannibal and murderer. Brady ranted to his guards that if he was not relocated, he would cut Jeffrey's head off. When guards searched Brady, they found two large knives concealed on his person and promptly relocated him to another cell. Brady also expressed disgust at having to be hanged alongside Jeffrey.

Matthew Brady was hanged in Hobart on 4 May 1826. He was buried in an unmarked grave, though for a time a small cairn had been built on the spot to mark it. By the 1870s this had been removed and the location has been forgotten.

Hobart Town Gazette and Van Diemen's Land Advertiser (Tas.: 1821 – 1825),
Saturday 24 July 1824, page 2

With considerable satisfaction, we announce the apprehension of two more of the fourteen bushrangers, who it may be remembered escaped some few weeks ago from Macquarie Harbour; and with increased pleasure we are enabled to state, that one of the two is James Crawford, their notorious leader. The following particulars of this important occurrence we derive from unquestionable authority:—

About night-fall on Thursday se'nnight, the remaining seven of this lawless gang, after robbing widow Smith, at the Macquarie River, and loading three of her servants with their booty, peremptorily ordered them to walk before on the road to Mr. Taylor's residence, at the Penny-royal creek. On their way there, they fell in with one of Mr. Taylor's sons, who was grazing sheep, and whom, after loading him with their baggage, they compelled to precede them to his father's. In the interim, their movements having been observed by that Gentleman, he very prudently armed his family and domestics, to act on the defensive. When his son saw what he did, from a fear of not being recognized, and therefore of being shot, he cried out, "Father, don't fire !" — so that from Mr. Taylor's anxiety to avoid injuring his son, the ruffians were allowed to go close to the house, when one of the domestics fired, the son disengaged himself, and joined his father's party, other firing took place, and a general conflict followed. Soon after this, one of the villains, levelled his piece at Mr. Taylor's head, but was prevented from effecting his murderous design by the son, who grappled him by the throat, and threw him; when one of the servants shot him in the breast, but without inflicting a dangerous wound, as his cloathing was remarkably thick. This fallen brigand was the leader, to whose assistance another of the gang immediately came up; a servant also came in aid of his young master, but in attempting to shoot his opponents, by some intervention of lamentable fate, he missed his aim, and mortally pierced the beloved object of his zeal! Shortly after this dreadful accident, a second bushranger was secured, after being twice knocked, down by a musket; a third had an eye shot out, but escaped with four of his companions — leaving behind them all their ammunition, stores, &c., and, though last not least, the murdered body of Mr. Taylor's carpenter, whom one of them had run through with a bayonet, which instantly caused death!

When our informant, who was an eye witness of these horrible transactions, left the Macquarie, Mr. Taylor's son was not dead, but we regret with exceeding sorrow that not even the faintest hope was entertained of his recovery. — Thus the abode of comfort has been changed into a house of mourning, through the hardened depravity of wretches, who are neither to be melted by lenience, admonished by Law, nor intimidated by the brandished rigours of retribution. — Thus have two human lives been sacrificed entirely through the wanton aggressions of beings, who only know their God — to blaspheme Him! and their fellow creatures — to ravage and assassinate them! — who are still as resolved as ever to commit crime, though the tree of ignominy was but yesterday oppressed with the convulsed forms of their expiring comrades! — and whose speedy apprehension is no less devoutly to be wished, as a public benefit, than as the, only way by which their souls can possibly be rescued from still deeper perdition.

It is but justice to the much afflicted Mr. Taylor, and his servants, to say, that they are entitled to the warmest thanks of all the Inhabitants of the Colony, for their bold and spirited conduct on this occasion; and as a proof of the high sense which is already entertained of it by several respectable housholders of Hobart Town, we beg to refer our Readers to an Advertisement inserted in our front page, announcing that a Subscription, as a tribute of respect to the meritorious houshold, is opened at the Bank. — We now hope to be soon enabled to announce the speedy apprehension of the other four murderers, who are without arms or ammunition, and who we trust will remain so until they are taken.

Just as these pages were being sent to Press, the following honoured and honouring testimonial was furnished. We are extremely proud to exclude other matter of interest for its prompt insertion:

"*Government House, Hobart Town,*
July 19th, 1824.

"Sir, — I yesterday evening received information that your house had been attacked by the gang of prisoners, who lately made their escape from Macquarie Harbour.; and that, after a very gallant defence, you succeeded in defeating their attempt, seizing two of them, and driving the rest from your premises.

"It gives me much concern to hear that one of your sons has been severely wounded in the contest; — most sincerely do I hope the wound may not prove mortal; but, should it unhappily be the case, every circumstance of alleviation will accompany the mournful event, from the reflection that you were struggling for the common safety of your family.

"The spirited example which you have set, will, I trust, under similar circumstances, be followed by every Settler in the Colony, — which would more effectually tend to put down the lawless attacks of these robbers, than any Military force which could be furnished; and I desire to accompany my warmest approbation of your conduct, with an assurance that it will ever afford me pleasure to testify how much I appreciate your firm and manly behaviour.

"I am, Sir,

"Your most obedient humble Servant,

(Signed) "Geo. Arthur."

To Mr. Robert Taylor,
Macquarie River.

III

꧁꧂

Cash and Company take
their leave

After many misadventures while on the run from the law, Martin Cash had finally been nabbed in late 1842, and to make sure he stayed put he was sent to the notorious Port Arthur penal settlement, a former timber camp. This sprawling complex housed convicts, military and civilians, and was home to great industry fuelled by convict labour. Not the least of these industries was timber, which came from the huge gum trees convicts had to fell and carry on their shoulders in "centipede gangs", so called for the resemblance to the venomous arthropod when walking in formation.

Cash was transported from Hobart Town to Port Arthur on the *Tamar* brig, along with fifteen others. Overnight they journeyed, sleeping on the ballast stones for lack of bedding. All were in irons to discourage any attempt to dive overboard. The following morning the brig dropped anchor in the port, and a launch boat was prepared. The prisoners had plenty of time to become acquainted with their new home as they rowed into Russell Cove. The freezing water lapped at the shoreline, and Cash noted the cylindrical guard tower built over the powder magazine, resembling a mediaeval turret. A smattering of buildings sprawled out uphill behind it and around it — stores, offices, workshops, military barracks, a magnificent sandstone hospital, and the tiny prisoners' barracks. Nearest to the dock was the Commandant's house, which was a rather grand-looking building in the Regency style that housed Charles O'Hara Booth, his family and their servants. A wooden semaphore tower stood on the crest of the hill, it's wooden signal arms flipping up and down to announcethe new arrivals as they landed at the dock. Cash shifted his gaze further eastward and took in the sight of the grand church with a tree-lined avenue leading up to it from the water's edge.

The first stop was the barber, who clipped off Cash's carrotty curls and whiskers. He was then stripped naked as a newborn and every inch of his body scrutinised by clerks, who made notes about his appearance. Once re-dressed he was acquainted with the Commandant, Charles O'Hara Booth.

The new arrivals were lined up in the courtyard of the barracks and Booth arrived in full uniform, all epaulettes and tassels, to address them. He was a severe-looking man, gaunt and balding with narrow eyes that seemed to burn like gimlets when impassioned, and bushy mutton-chop whiskers.

"You will find that I am a righteous man; a gracious man. But you will also find that I will not tolerate any ingratitude of my generosity. Even the slightest infraction can expect to meet with the fullest rigours of the law," said O'Hara Booth. "Gentlemen, there is but one gateway out of Port Arthur, and I hold the key in my pocket."

The prisoners were dismissed and those who were not required to be in irons had theirs struck off. They were, once again, stripped naked, then their uniforms were handed out — one-size-for-all "canary" suits of yellow wool, the colour of disgrace, stamped with black broad arrows — and they were escorted to their cells.

Cash was assigned to the carrying gang under Benjamin Stephens, an overbearing and cruel convict overseer. The gang was tasked with hauling bundles of shingles weighing more than ten kilograms each through the bush to a hill called Tongataboo. Cash's first night at Port Arthur was spent shivering, soaking wet from the rain that they had been caught in on the way back to the barracks.

After a week, Cash sought to see the doctor as his boots had caused his foot to become lacerated and an abscess had developed on his toe. Naturally, this had impaired his ability to walk. He was marched uphill to the hospital where he visited Dr. Thomas Brownell. He was a thin man with a large nose, very thin lips and large intelligent eyes.

After some inspection of the afflicted appendage, Brownell looked up to Cash and remarked, "It's very well you came in to see me. You were in a good way to lose this foot."

Cash spent the next three weeks under Brownell's care in the hospital. This extended convalescence was cut short by his placement into a new work party. His new employment was to assist a centipede gang in carrying large beams from the saw pits to the work sites — a journey of around three miles. After six weeks he was reallocated to chopping firewood. Thereafter, Cash found himself being bounced around to different assignments in the settlement.

As winter passed, Cash devised his escape. When his assignment took him up Mount Arthur, which overlooked Eaglehawk Neck and East Bay Neck, which connected the peninsula to the mainland of Van Diemen's Land, he stood for an hour carefully making mental notes about the placement of everything — the water, the dog line, the guard towers. He dreamt of the sweet pleasure that would come from being free from brutish and bullying overseers who would have a man flogged for so much as breathing in the wrong direction, and he longed to exchange his daily bread and skilley for a full meal with meat and vegetables.

The fateful day came while assigned to a work gang under the oversight of a man known as "Cranky Jack" Smith at Long Bay in December of 1842. "Cranky Jack" had sent Cash into the water to move some boulders that made it difficult to safely bring boats alongside the jetty. Cash did as ordered then returned to muster, but, out of nowhere, "Cranky Jack" began to lay into Cash. Fists flew as the infamous lout thrashed the drenched Irishman. Cash had enough and rose to his full height. His hand balled up and he swung it into the face of his attacker, knocking him flat. He grabbed "Cranky Jack", lifted him to his feet and knocked him flat again, then hurled him down twenty feet into the water. With the overseer in the drink, Cash grasped his opportunity with both hands and bolted into the bush.

As he made his way deeper into the bush, he found an outlook and observed soldiers swarming about Eaglehawk Neck like red ants, with the semaphore tower all a flurry as it signalled the news. Cash scrutinised the lay of the land, making the decision to swim across the water on the Norfolk Bay side of the isthmus.

Night fell, and Martin Cash made his move. He removed his boots to be able to move as silently as possible. He halted when a soldier came close to him, but continued on when the soldier went on his way, oblivious to the escapee just beyond the scrub that he had been sent to look out for. Cash kept hunched as he sneaked out and continued his journey. When he reached the water he removed all of his clothes and bundled them up, placing the bundle on his head. He waded into the icy waters, gasping for air. He prayed that he would not be discovered by sharks as he attempted to stride through the water. A mass of seaweed snagged his legs and he wrestled with the green lashes that curled around him. When he reached land he dressed as quick as thought and pressed on. The bushes snagged and scratched him as he marched onwards. When he became exhausted, he flung himself to the ground and waited for daylight.

In the morning he resumed his trek, passing a probation station with a wide berth. He continued on until nightfall, whereupon he collapsed and fell asleep from utter exhaustion.

The next day he took off, believing he was no more than an hour away from East Bay Neck. He became lost and wasted a whole day looking for the road. That night he struggled to rest; the pain of three days without food or water seared through him.

He struggled on, with a sharp pain near his heart slowing him down. He drank water whenever he found it, but it barely sufficed. He was soon met by a party of troopers under the former convict, turned constable, John Evenden, and taken back into custody after a failed attempt at fleeing.

"Well, Cash," said Evenden as they returned to the barracks, "we thought you'd made it clear, but we finally caught up with you within a mile of East Bay Neck. I don't suppose you realised you were just a mile short of freedom, old man."

The next day Cash was returned to the settlement in darbies, but the news of his daring feat had already spread. That night as he sat in his cell he was smuggled an extra ration of bread and skilley. Cash dreaded the punishment he would receive for his "ingratitude".

When he was tried before O'Hara Booth, the furious commandant sentenced Cash to eighteen months' hard labour in chains. He was then taken to the blacksmith to have irons riveted to his ankles.

"Martin Cash, is it? The devil who got within a whisker of East Bay Neck? Well, I shall have to find the right sort of irons for one such as you."

The smithy was meticulous in choosing the lightest possible irons to attach. As a convict himself, he valued the glimmer of hope that rogues such as Cash could bring by their daring. Many had tried to escape Port

Arthur, but very few had ever gotten so far. If Martin Cash could get within a mile of the mainland in a couple of days, then escape from the Hell on earth that was Port Arthur seemed far less impossible for others.

It was during this renewed internment that Cash was allocated to a gang that carted stones from the quarry. With Christmas approaching, Cash decided to bide his time. He soon befriended Lawrence Kavanagh and George Jones, who were also assigned to the quarry.

Jones, a London cockney, was only a young man, with smooth, round features and a large forehead, dark hair and intelligent eyes. He had gravitated to Cash almost immediately and introduced himself. Cash had responded quietly.

"Cash, eh? I've 'eard of yer," said Jones, "yer was in some bad business in Sydney, yeah?"

"Aye, a bad business with some cattle led to bad business everywhere I went. I've been in and out of gaols a great deal these past few years. What are you in for?"

"Larry and I are in for life. Robbery under arms. Innit right, Larry?"

Kavanagh nodded. He was a tall, lean Irishman with greying hair and long features. The pinky finger on his right hand was missing, but he handled his tools well all the same.

Over the next few days, they built up a rapport and began to talk about their desire to get away from Port Arthur, what they missed about the world outside, and what they would do if they regained their liberty. Thus, the seed was planted.

One day as Cash was waiting for the cart to be loaded, Jones sidled up to him.

"Yer worked as a stock-rider for Mr. Bowman, dincha?" Jones asked.

"I did," Cash replied.

"Ah, I fowt so. In that case I reckon I know yer just as well by reputation as if by person, if yer follow me."

Cash nodded.

"Now," Jones continued, "given we know each avvah, may I speak in confidence?"

Cash shrugged, "I suppose."

Jones gestured for Cash to turn around to avoid attention from the overseer.

"Do yer intend to abscond?" he asked.

Cash paused for a moment, scrutinising the smaller man's face.

"Yes," Cash finally replied.

"When?"

"Now, if you are ready."

George Jones sniggered in disbelief at the Irishman's eagerness as much as his bluntness.

"I say we get Kavanagh in on it. He was the cleverest bushman in New Sowf Wales. He's a Sydney man, too, and he's game to get outta here."

"A great many Sydney men might wish to try their luck getting out of here. If he's so clever, how'd he end up here in the first place?" Cash responded with a smirk.

"He broke out of Hyde Park Barracks, y'know. He'd be a good one to have wiv us on the outside."

"Is he the only one?"

"He is."

"Good, because if you let anyone else into our confidence I'd do better to try my luck on my own."

The trio began to plan the escape in earnest. Kavanagh expressed to Cash that he needed only to point himself and Jones in the direction of the road out of Port Arthur and they would ask no more of him. He then requested that they wait a few days for him to arrange some rations to take with them from his contact, Joshua Roberts, who was the cook for Thomas Lempriere, the head of the commissary at Port Arthur. It was agreed, then, that Boxing Day was to be the day they took their leave.

***

On Christmas Day, the convicts were permitted to fraternise and smoke tobacco. On a stage erected in the courtyard of the prisoners' barracks, musicians performed, as did the famous convict poet Frank MacNamara. It was a welcomed relief for the men, but Cash, Jones and Kavanagh had their minds on other things.

On Boxing Day of 1842, as the carts were being prepared in the quarry, Cash, Kavanagh and Jones managed to peel away from their work party, bounded up an embankment, and hid. They monitored the movements of the guards and other convicts to see if their absence was noted — it was not. Kavanagh took the lead, guiding Jones and Cash to the spot where the rations had been hidden for them. Kavanagh opened the sack and noted the partial loaf of bread and the flour, which would be enough to tide them over for the two to three days trek up to the mainland.

Suddenly the trio heard a great commotion — their absence had been noticed. People rushed around all over the place, the semaphore towers went berserk sending messages across the settlement.

Cash turned to the others, "Follow me; stay low, stay quiet!"

Cash led the others into the bush, following the same route he had taken previously. They kept going until they reached the foot of Mount Arthur. They took cover behind the scrub and caught their breath. Jones and Kavanagh looked at Cash expectantly.

"They'll have everyone they've got searching for us from the Neck to the coal mines. I suggest we stay here until we can be sure they've called off the search," Cash said.

"How long is that?" Kavanagh asked.

"It took them three days to catch me last time. Reckon we have enough rations to tide us over for that long?"

"We can stretch it, I reckon," Kavanagh replied.

"Alright, let's stay here for three days. The scrub will keep us concealed."

***

Three nights elapsed before the trio began moving to Eaglehawk Neck, where they intended to cross through the water. When they emerged from the bush they were at the head of Long Bay. They took a route past Signal Hill, the dense scrub tearing at their clothing until it was little more than rags. Another night's rest and a breakfast of damper baked on a charcoal fire inside a hollow log, allowed them to continue.

The land here was virgin territory, untouched by human hands or feet, and the branches, at times, grew so low the men were forced to crawl on their hands and knees, but after much tribulation they finally emerged at Eaglehawk Neck.

"Look," Cash said, pointing to the region of the dog line, a cordon of savage, half-starved dogs that were tethered close enough to meet each other, but not to attack each other. The spot was swarming with soldiers and constables in convict uniforms.

"Well, what do we do now?" asked Kavanagh.

"We go around to the other side as silently as possible," Cash replied.

So they went, keeping low and walking barefooted, hoping to avoid making a sound. Upon reaching a secluded spot they rested and finished the last of the damper. For the next three hours they laid low, waiting for things to settle down before the final push.

When they resumed the journey, they took extra caution when crossing roads where even the slightest noise might rouse a party of guards. As the sun set they reached the water's edge. The rush of wind blowing in from the sea, the splashing as the waves lapped at the shore, the moon glimmering on the water, everything at that moment filled the escapees with terror and excitement.

To avoid being slowed down and chilled to the bone by wet clothes they stripped nude and bundled their clothes and boots, carrying them above their heads as they waded into the water. They went deeper and deeper until they were only just able to keep their heads above surface. They could see the pontoons in the water where even more dogs were tethered. At that moment the animals were quiet, but still alert. Cash turned to look back at the others and a wave rolling back from the shore bowled into him. As he gasped and spluttered, he felt his bundle wash away towards the ocean away from his grasp. He could not see the others or hear them.

"Jones," he tried to call out quietly, "Kavanagh!"

No reply.

His mind drifted to a recent escape attempt where the swimming bolters had been taken by sharks barely a mile away from where he now bobbed helplessly. He tried to force the idea out of his mind as he struggled on.

Finally, after much graceless splashing and flailing, Cash could feel ground beneath his feet. He clung to the sand with his toes, clawing himself onwards to the shore. When he felt himself rising out of the water, he paused to regain his balance and to listen for his companions. At first there was nothing, but in only a few moments he heard voices and moved towards them.

He recognised Jones' voice; "Martin's drowned..."

Cash took the last of his energy and burst through the bush to find Jones and Kavanagh dripping wet and naked.

"Arrah! Martin," Kavanagh shouted.

"Keep it quiet," Cash chided.

"Martin, you ratbag, we thought you must have gone under," said Jones.

"A wave knocked me off course. I lost my bundle," Cash replied.

"No fooling, same as us," said Kavanagh with a laugh.

The three naked fugitives took a moment to rest, but found the chill of the night more profound on their wet skin. They resolved to keep moving.

They ventured into the bush where thorns and branches slashed, tore and pierced their skin on every accessible place, and harsh lumps of ironstone cut up their feet. Despite their valiant efforts, the injuries were too painful to endure without at least having some notion of where they were walking. They attempted to find ferns with which to make beds, but struggled in the Stygian blackness. Exhausted, they fell into an uneasy sleep, the snarling and screaming of devils echoing in the night as they fought over food.

***

When morning broke the men took much amusement from their nakedness and the peculiarities of their situation.

"Well, we can't go around like this forevermore; we need clothes, boots and food," said Cash, "I suspect we'll find it a short walk from here. Last time I was up here I spotted a prisoners' hut on the road between the necks."

Cash guided the others onwards. Each step on the jagged dolerite with their unprotected feet felt like walking on hatchet blades. Finally they came in view of the small hut Cash had alluded to. They hung back and observed the hut for a few minutes to gauge the risk. Once convinced there were no guards about, they crept up to the building. Kavanagh took up an axe that was resting against the wall next to a log pile and joined the others at the door.

Once all three were ready, Cash shouldered the door open and the three pushed inside, hollering like madmen, Kavanagh holding the axe above his head. The lone occupant, a man named Martin Cope, stood awestruck with his mouth agape at these three filthy, nude men.

"Lash him to that pole," Cash directed Jones, pointing to the central column that held the roof up. Jones grabbed a length of rope up from the floor and jostled the bewildered man into position. He secured him and the fugitives began to rifle through the cupboards and chests. They quickly discovered that the convicts assigned to the hut kept an extra suit of prison greys, so began to grab whatever pieces fitted best. Cash grabbed a pair of hobnail boots and planted the sole of one against the underside of his foot to see if they would fit his large feet.

Now clothed, they rummaged through the commissariat for supplies, coming away with flour, bread, beef, tea, sugar, and a flint steel and tinder box. The supplies were shoved hastily into a sack, and Kavanagh grabbed a billy can from near the door. As they went to leave, Cash turned to the terrified overseer, still lashed to the support column.

"Now, my hearty, I suspect that the party will be back soon. I shouldn't fear you being left alone for long. There's plenty of men about, looking for us, who would shoot us as soon as look at us, who will come along and turn you loose. Though we are desperate men, we are not animals. Good day to you."

With that the men swept out of the hut as abruptly as they had entered.

They ventured a short distance into the bush and sat. The adrenaline rush of their first robbery wore off quickly and all three became quiet and visibly tired.

"What now?" Jones asked.

"Well," Cash began, "you can bet that East Bay Neck will be crawling with soldiers by now. News of our sudden absence will have reached Hobart Town too. It would be best to avoid the towns and roads for the next few days."

"What about Doctor Imlay's place?" Jones said, "they've a boat there we could take up around the neck. There's just one constable there keeping watch, we should have no trouble."

Cash and Kavanagh agreed that it was a good plan. The trio searched for a comfortable place to set up camp and prepared themselves a hearty feast from the stolen goods.

***

Two days passed and the trio ventured forth, trekking around Mount Forestier until they got a good view of the doctor's station. They were dismayed to find the place surrounded by soldiers and constables.

"Buggery," Jones snapped, "what do we do now?"

"Why don't we head up to Blackman's Bay and try there?" Kavanagh asked.

"It could be the best chance we have," replied Jones.

They continued on foot but had been walking no more than a mile before they heard branches snapping underfoot behind them. Dashing into the scrub the fugitives saw a party of grey-suited constables coming towards them led by Cash's old acquaintance, John Evenden. The men continued without breaking their gait, completely unaware that their targets were less than a dozen yards away watching them pass.

It was not long before the three bolters were in view of East Bay Neck. Soldiers and constables patrolled up and down the bank of the bay, pausing now and then to look around. The water in Blackman's Bay rushed powerfully against the shoreline, but the distance from bank to bank was far less than what they had crossed back at Eaglehawk Neck.

"It shouldn't take us more than five minutes to cross here," said Cash cheerfully.

"With those mud-sloggers everywhere? We wouldn't make it half-way before they started shooting at us," said Kavanagh.

"Well, let's find somewhere to rest until it gets darker," Cash directed.

The men sat quietly in the bush waiting for darkness.

"There's no doubt we'll reach the mainland now, boys," said Cash.

Jones and Kavanagh averted their gazes.

"What's the matter?"

"I don't have so much faith in this, Cash," said Kavanagh. "The last time I tried getting across here I was washed out into the bay. I thought myself lost for sure. Those waves are more powerful than what we faced at Eaglehawk Neck."

"If yer can do it," said Jones to Cash, "we won't stop you, and we won't raise an alarm, but we can't go with yer."

Cash frowned.

"I certainly can do it, and I believe anyone who is capable of swimming could if they applied themselves," Cash replied, "but I will not leave you behind if you choose not to attempt it. I came with you this far. We're in this together, whatever may come."

***

That night, they attempted to test the waters, but found the water too strong to safely cross.

The following day, with no more fresh drinking water and soldiers everywhere, the men stayed low. As night fell they moved to the water, removing their shoes and crawling along on their hands and knees towards a paddock. Cash observed a lone sentry through a fence and summoned the others to come close behind him. As they watched the sentry, he turned straight towards them, stepping forward, gazing into the darkness and shifting his grip on his musket. He then turned and walked in the opposite direction.

The trio continued onwards towards a farmhouse, vaulted over a fence and crossed over a railroad. As they continued to creep through the dark, suddenly a small terrier came bounding up, yapping furiously.

"Git! Git!" Cash snapped at the dog.

Kavanagh attempted to shoo the animal away with a stick whereupon it launched at him and bit at his legs. A sharp kick sent the dog flying and they scrambled away as fast as they could before the yapping could raise attention. They paused on an embankment.

"There's no way we'll get across now," said Jones.

"There's got to be a whole army coming up now," said Kavanagh.

"Come on, the pair-o-yers! I've never seen men give up so quickly with just a little hardship," said Cash with a spiteful laugh. Jones and Kavanagh refused to look at Cash and suddenly he erupted.

"You call yourselves men? Look at you. I brought you this far and this is my reward? If they catch me now, I'm like to hang! So, get off your arses and *keep moving!*"

Thalt was enough motivation for the men and they took off. They continued until they spied a sentry box beyond a tall thicket where two guards stood in conversation. When it was clear, they jumped a fence and crawled through the wheat field on the other side, emerging where they could see the lights from the nearby military barracks. After another mile, they burst into the bush where they were concealed from view.

They continued deeper into the dense forest until they reached a clearing and paused to catch their breath. Jones clamped a hand on Cash's shoulder.

"Martin Cash, if I'd a crown of gold I'd give it to yer right now!"

"I'd rather have some of the yellow stuff in my pocket at present," Cash replied. "We may have escaped the sharks of sea and land, but we must keep a sharp lookout still."

Further they ventured until they crumpled, exhausted, and fell asleep. It was late morning when they finally awoke.

Over breakfast, Kavanagh put forward the question of what they planned to do from then on.

"Well, I can't imagine we'll be welcome in town anytime soon," said Jones, "so I intend to take up arms and stand no repairs. What say, both of yers?"

Cash nodded, "Might as well. I'm through trying to make an honest go of it and getting nabbed as soon as I'm recognised. The bush is as good as anywhere to make it for me."

"I suppose there's no two ways about it now," said Kavenagh, "it's bushranging for us."

And so it was that the key to the gate of Port Arthur was purloined from O'Hara Booth's pocket, and Cash and Company was formed.

Martin Cash

> "...Although being perfectly aware of the fate that awaited us, and that our lives now were virtually forfeited, we nevertheless resolved that in our future peregrinations we would never resort to unnecessary violence, or offer insult to the other sex. We also firmly resolved to fight for our liberty, all being of opinion that it was better to get shot than to be taken alive..."
>
> — MARTIN CASH

Martin Cash was a native of Wexford in Ireland, and had been transported to Australia as a teenager in 1827 for — by his own account — shooting a love rival, though the official charge was house breaking. Once in Australia he was assigned as a servant to a farm in New South Wales, where he became a stockman. It was during this time that he met Bessie Clifford, who left her husband to run away with Cash. He managed to keep a low profile until he helped some young men brand stolen cattle. Cash claimed that he had no idea the cattle he was branding were stolen. Knowing he was bound for gaol unless he kept two steps ahead of the law, he and Bessie moved to Van Diemen's Land with the intention of starting fresh.

The couple eventually settled in Campbell Town, where Martin worked as a labourer and Bessie began referring to herself as Eliza Cash, but the law eventually caught up with him and he found himself arrested. This started a series of gaol escapes, which always resulted in Martin being assaulted, arrested, and locked up again, after attempting to make his way back to Bessie in Campbell Town.

Eventually, Cash was sent to Port Arthur, the so-called "Hell on Earth" on the

Tasman Peninsula. Not being a fan of his new lodgings, Cash managed to escape Port Arthur on his own. He got past the isthmus at Eaglehawk Neck, guarded as it was by the infamous dog line, an array of half-starved hounds chained to kennels along its width, and the sentries beyond them. Cash's new-found freedom wasn't long-lived however and after being lost for several days and starving, he was nabbed and sent back to Port Arthur.

It was during this second internment at Port Arthur that Cash befriended Lawrence Kavanagh and George Jones. The trio hastily devised a plan to escape Port Arthur. On Boxing Day of 1842, Cash, Kavanagh and Jones managed to peel away from their work party and make a break for freedom. When their absence was noticed, soldiers were sent to find them. Cash had anticipated this and the gang waited in the bush for several days before heading to Eaglehawk Neck, where they crossed through the water. Having successfully made it across, but losing all of their clothing in the water, they robbed a hut for clothes and supplies. Continuing their journey, they made it past East Bay Neck and took to bushranging.

They started out by robbing farmhouses around Pittwater and Jerusalem (modern day Colebrook) to acquire clothing, food and weapons. A reward of fifty sovereigns was offered for their capture, but there was no stopping them. They continued with robberies at Bagdad and Broadmarsh before they reached Mount Dromedary, where they constructed a log fort to use as their hideout.

The fort was well placed as it offered a wide view of the terrain to see who was coming and going, while also being very close to their sympathisers, Jack Bryan and his wife Nelly. Through Nelly Bryan, Cash got word to Bessie that he was alive and at large and organised to meet her. She then accompanied Martin back to the mountain hideaway where she lived with the boys and enjoyed the fruits of their nefarious labours.

The gang established themselves quickly as a menace to society, and the military presence throughout Van Diemen's Land was reinforced in an effort to suppress them.

On 31 January, 1843, the gang stuck up the Woolpack Inn at New Norfolk, but were unaware that they had been spotted and troopers were descending upon them. Cash opened fire at the troopers who promptly returned in kind. In the shootout, Kavanagh and Jones peeled away into the darkness but Cash continued to fight. Two constables were injured in the battle before Cash also took his leave.

The dramatic Woolpack Inn shootout was followed by more daring raids and robberies. On 22 February, they raided the property of Thomas Shone. The bush-rangers bailed up Shone, his wife, a friend, their seven farmhands, and their neighbour and three of his men, who were all guarded in Shone's drawing room by Jones. Cash and Kavanagh then ransacked the house before Shone's daughter arrived with guests. Despite the prisoners greatly outnumbering the bushrangers, none made any attempts to apprehend them.

Not long after this Bessie Clifford took her leave of the gang and moved to Hobart. She took with her many of the goods stolen for her by Martin. Meanwhile, George Jones had begun a secret affair with Nelly Bryan. Both of these women would cause the downfall of their lovers.

On 11 March, Cash and company raided James Triffitt's farm on the Ouse River. Triffitt had a history with Tasmania's bushrangers having been robbed by Michael Howe's gang as well as Musquito's and Matthew Brady's in previous decades. As at Shone's homestead, the occupants were bailed up and the house ransacked.

As the gang continued business as usual the authorities had been monitoring Bessie. She was charged on 13 March 1843 with possession of stolen goods and arrested. She remained in remand, appearing before the courts, until she was discharged on 28 April. Caught up in it all was James Pratt, her landlord, who was considered an accessory until he was found not guilty.

On 18 March, the gang robbed Dunrobin near Hamilton. During the robbery, Martin Cash decided to pen a letter to the governor of Van Diemen's Land. While he dictated, George Jones transcribed, and Cash warned that if Eliza was not released promptly then the gang would be forced to enact revenge. He also had Jones pen a seperate letter to Thomas Shone threatening him not to prosecute Eliza.

The remainder of the month saw more robberies near Hamilton, as well as the gang finding a new hideout in Hollow Tree Bottom. As the military presence around Dromedary had increased, the bushrangers had deemed it unwise to remain at the fort. Unfortunately they were now low on supplies and the next robberies they committed were in an effort to procure basics like food.

After robbing Thompson's farm at Green Ponds, Cash went into town and at Ellis' Tavern he purchased three cases of gin, passing the local constabulary on the way out without being recognised. He returned with his companions to their bush hideaway without confrontation.

The gang committed robberies around Lake Echo, Dee River and Bridgewater, planting red herrings by telling their victims that they were going to the Western Tiers. This meant that the military's attention was drawn away from Dromedary and the fort. The result was that the gang returned to their hideout and had a big party with the Bryans, complete with musicians in attendance.

By June, there were 500 men actively pursuing Cash and company, and the bushrangers were on the move again, heading through the Midlands. Robberies around Ross were followed by another shootout at Salt Pan Plains, then more robberies as they headed to Cressy, where they camped for several days.

On 3 July, the gang robbed the Launceston to Hobart mail coach as it passed through Epping Forest. The next day they robbed a shepherd's hut at the Western Tiers. Unfortunately for the gang, when travelling through Bothwell, Kavanagh tripped on a boulder and accidentally shot himself in the arm. His wound was very serious and he turned himself in on 9 July 1843, fearing he would perish if not given medical treatment. However, when he told the police how he had been injured, he lied, stating he was shot in a fight in which he killed Cash and Jones.

Cash and Jones, meanwhile, continued their depredations, but news soon reached Martin via Nelly Bryan that Bessie had found a new love in the form of James Pratt. It seemed she had grown tired of the bush and waiting for the rare opportunities to see Martin, and had settled for something more stable. Naturally, Cash responded with his typical Irish temper, resolving to murder both his unfaithful partner and her lover. Cash induced George Jones to join him in Hobart Town.

Things were moving fairly smoothly until they were recognised by a pair of constables and a running gunfight took place. Jones managed to escape but Cash was not so lucky. Cash's famous fleetness of foot did him wonders until he took a wrong turn and ended up in a *cul de sac*, ironically formed by the boundary wall of the penitentiary. A constable named Winstanley was roused, and as he approached Cash he was shot through the torso. As Winstanley lay dying, a shopkeeper grabbed Cash and attempted to disarm him. The pistol went off again, the ball passing through the shopkeeper's fingers and hitting another man in the face. Cash struggled as others piled on. One man kicked Cash in the head and another clubbed him with a revolver until he was unconscious and barely recognisable from his injuries.

Cash and Kavanagh were put on trial in Hobart, Kavanagh charged with armed robbery and Cash with wilful murder. Both were found guilty and sentenced to death, though this was commuted to life imprisonment on Norfolk Island.

Meanwhile, George Jones had teamed up with some other bushrangers named Platt and Moore, possibly at the encouragement of Nelly Bryan. These bushrangers were far more rough and ill-mannered than Jones' previous companions. In one house robbery at Black Brush, unconvinced at protestations that there was no money on the premises, a woman named Harriet Devereaux was tied to a table and a hot shovel was pressed to her legs, allegedly by Jones. It was believed that Nelly had convinced the bushrangers that Devereaux had a big cache of money hidden in the house.

In the end, Nelly Bryan dobbed Jones in to the authorities, and during a raid near Richmond in March 1844 the gang were besieged. The troopers set fire to the building and as the bushrangers evacuated, Moore was shot and mortally wounded, and Jones was shot in the face with a shotgun. The shot didn't kill him, though it left him blind. With Moore dead, Jones and Platt were tried for assault, robbery, and shooting with intent to murder. They were found guilty and sentenced to death.

On 30 April, 1844, Jones and Platt were hanged. Prior to his execution, Jones had been visited by Martin Cash to comfort him.

On 1 July, 1846, Lawrence Kavanagh was one of the convicts who took up arms with William Westwood in the "Cooking Pot Riot" on Norfolk Island, in response to the overly harsh and regressive measures brought in by the new Commandant. During the uprising, four men were murdered by Westwood. Kavanagh was among twelve men hanged for their part in the affair on 13 October 1846. He too had been allowed a visit from Cash before his execution.

Through all of this, a heartbroken Cash kept a low profile and in the following years earned himself a reputation as a well-behaved inmate, becoming a constable within the Norfolk Island prison. When he was eventually released he became commandant of the Government Gardens in Hobart Town and even remarried. He briefly lived in New Zealand, where he worked as a constable and allegedly ran a brothel, before returning to Tasmania in disgrace. When his young son died of Rheumatic Fever, Cash turned to alcohol and slowly drank himself to death at the age of 69.

Cash's memoirs, dictated to James Lester Burke and published in 1870, have been reprinted many times over the 100+ years since his death, and the many songs and tales about Cash remain as testament to his enduring folk hero status.

Launceston Examiner (Tas.: 1842 - 1899), Wednesday 25 January 1843, page 4

THE RUNAWAYS. — We regret to learn that three misguided men, who have escaped from Port Arthur, are at present at large, and levying contributions in the Richmond district. On Monday night they called at Blinkworth's, at Jerusalem and possessed themselves of a double-barrelled gun and some ammunition. All three are now armed; one with the double-barrelled gun, the others with single guns. Their names are, Martin Cash, Cavanagh, and Jones. We trust that we shall soon hear of their capture. They must cause some terror, groundless though it be, and may do some mischief, but can only protract, perhaps aggravate, their punishment. A reward of £50 has been offered for their apprehension. — *Ibid.*

Launceston Advertiser (Tas.: 1829 - 1846), Thursday 26 January 1843, page 4

REWARD!

Fifty Sovereigns, and a Conditional Pardon for the Apprehension of each of the Runaway Convicts hereunder named and described.

POLICE DEPARTMENT, HOBART, *January* 19.— Whereas the three Convicts (runaways from Port Arthur) Martin Cash, George Jones, and Lawrence Kavenagh, whose descriptions are as under, stand charged with having committed divers capital felonies, and are now illegally at large. This is to give notice, that I am authorised by his Excellency the Lieutenant Governor to offer a Reward of Fifty Sovereigns to any person or persons who shall apprehend or cause to be apprehended and lodged in safe custody either of the said felons; and should this service be performed by a Convict, then, in addition to such pecuniary reward, a Conditional Pardon.

M. FORSTER, *Chief Police Magistrate.*

Descriptions of the above-named Convicts.

Martin Cash, per *Francis Freeling*, tried at Launceston Q. S., 24th March, 1840, 7 years, labourer, 6 feet, age 33, native place Wexford, complexion very ruddy, head small and round, hair curly and carroty, whiskers red small, forehead low, eyebrows red, eyes blue small, nose small, mouth large, chin small. Remarks— remarkably long feet, a very swift runner.

Lawrence Kavenagh, per *Marian Watson*, tried at Sydney, 12th April, 1842, life, stone-mason, 5 feet 10 1/2, age 30, complexion pale, head long large, hair brown to grey, whiskers brown, visage long, forehead high, eyebrows brown, eyes light grey, nose long and sharp, mouth and chin medium size, native place Wicklow. Remarks— A. D. above elbow joint left arm, two scars on pain of left hand, lost little finger on right hand.

George Jones, per *Marian Watson*, tried at Sydney, 14th April, 1842, life, labourer, 5 feet 7, age 27, complexion ruddy fair, freckled, head long, hair brown, whiskers brown visage long, forehead perpendicular, eyebrows brown, eyes blue, nose medium, mouth medium, chin pointed, native place Westminster. Remarks— H. W. anchor on right arm, breast hairy.

IV

〜❦〜

Blood and Gin at Round Hill Station

About 40 miles from Albury, on the Billabong Creek, lay Round Hill Station, owned by Mr. Thomas Henty. Henty had purchased the station in 1860, along with 700 head of dairy cattle, for a whopping £10,000. The superintendent was Sam Watson, and the station was also attended by Mr. McNeil, overseer, and John McLean, cattle overseer. It was a bustling environment where men and women went about their jobs day after day, in blistering heat or sheets of rain, in flood or drought, just like so many pioneers of the New South Wales Riverina. Lately, Henty was enjoying some success. Indeed, it had attracted attention from the world of horticulture in 1863, when Watson and Henty's experiments with grafting resulted in blue-gums that could bear peaches. Henty was some-thing of a social climber, coming from an influential Melbourne family. He was also an enthusiast of horse racing and breeding race horses, with a prized racehorse named Huntsman he had raised. Naturally, the allure of a moderately successful farm with good thoroughbreds to ride was too good for Dan Morgan to pass up, and thus he set his sights on Round Hill Station.

On Sunday, 19 June 1864, Morgan set out from his camp at a large rock formation at Walla Walla and headed towards Round Hill Station. Along the way he crossed paths with Sergeant Carroll of the Wagga Wagga police, who recognised Morgan and immediately drew a revolver.

"Surrender in the name of the Queen," Carroll barked. Morgan had no intention to follow such an order and took off for the shelter of the bush. Carroll rode in hot pursuit, firing three times at Morgan but each shot missed its target. Morgan's thoroughbred picked up speed and Carroll's nag struggled to keep up. The nag struck a tree root as it galloped and took a tumble, throwing its rider off in the process. By the time Carroll regained his mount Morgan was gone and the animal was in no state to follow.

That day, Round Hill Station was visited by John Heriot, the nineteen year-old son of a neighbouring squatter, Elliot Heriot-Watt. Heriot, Watson and McLean were relaxing in the homestead when Mrs. Watson noticed someone looking in the front door. It was one o'clock in the afternoon, and, being a Sunday, nobody was working and no visitors were expected except young Heriot. Mrs. Watson immediately suspected that the visitor was none other than the notorious Morgan, whose growing notoriety in the area was well known about the station.

The visitor cut a striking figure with his flowing black beard and hair in long, raven-black ringlets tumbling over his shoulders under a rumpled felt hat. He stood a touch under six feet and his dark blue eyes looked like London sapphires. His aquiline nose combined with his steely gaze seemed to give him the appearance of some kind of bird of prey.

He looked to Mrs. Watson and spoke with his deep, drawling Australian voice, "Where's your husband?"

Mrs. Watson nervously gestured to the sitting room. Morgan presented a revolver from his belt, where five more were tucked away, ready for action.

"I'm Morgan. Perhaps you've heard of me?"
Mrs. Watson gasped.
"Can you tell me where you keep the grog?"
"My husband can take you, please don't hurt us," Mrs. Watson replied.

Morgan walked past the trembling woman into the sitting room. With a wave of his pistol, Morgan bailed up Watson, Heriot and McLean and began to march them outside

"Is there any grog about the place?" Morgan asked.
"I'll take you, follow me," said Watson.
They both walked a short distance to the storeroom where the supplies were kept, and entered.

"How many bottles is there?" Morgan asked.
Mr. Watson replied, "Six bottles of gin and one that's been broached."
This appeared to be all Morgan needed to hear and he gestured for Watson to fetch the booze.
Watson grabbed the bottles and placed them on a bench. He poured a glass of gin from the already broached bottle for himself and one for Morgan. Before taking a drink Morgan gave a wry smile behind the voluminous beard and curly moustache, "You must drink that yourself, as you may have had it ready for me."

Watson obliged and the pair proceeded to dig into the supplies. With arms full of bottles, they returned to the homestead.

They placed the bottles on the dining table and Morgan took a seat at the head of the table, taking two pistols from his belt and laying them on the table.

He called for one of the female servants, who hesitantly approached him.

"Yes, sir?"

"I want you to bring me some dinner. I've been riding hard and I'm famished."

The servant curtseyed and moved to leave when Morgan continued to talk.

"Also, can you see to it that one of the men has my horse fed and stabled?"

The servant nodded and left.

Morgan turned to Watson, his dark eyes making contact with the superintendent's.

"What rations do you give your men?"

"We give them full rations," replied Watson, "and if any say they have not enough we give them more."

Morgan looked at him with scepticism for a moment then relaxed. He gestured for the prisoners to get back into the corner.

"All good people can go together," Morgan mumbled as he pulled his chair in closer to the table.

In a short while, a plate of ham, bread and eggs was placed on the table in front of Morgan. He wasted no time before tucking in. With pistols either side of the plate, he scooped gloopy egg into his mouth with my a fork. The yolk dribbled into his beard somewhat, and he forced a piece of ham past his moustache, washing it down with neat gin.

His prisoners, still seated in the corner of the room, watched him eat. When his plate was cleared away he turned to his captives, with a revolver in each hand.

"You mustn't be afraid. I've not come here to hurt anyone," said Morgan.

"In that case, won't you please put those pistols away?" Mrs. Watson asked.

Morgan thought about the request and complied, tucking the pistols back into his belt.

"That was some good tucker. I've not eaten so well of late. I may pay for it later," said Morgan, "are there many here on the farm today?"

"About a dozen," replied Sam Watson.

"I shall need to round them all up."

After a brief and surprisingly comfortable conversation with his prisoners, Morgan took the initial four and rounded up the station staff, bringing the number of prisoners to eleven.

He directed them to the stable and ordered them to wait at the door while he checked in on his horse. It was a fine bay horse with a white star and snip, two white hind fetlocks and one white front fetlock. Morgan did not speak as he greeted the animal, focused entirely on the beast. He seemed to have a natural affinity with it and displayed much tenderness as he stroked its face.

Once satisfied that his horse had been looked after, he directed the crowd to a cattle shed no more than eight feet by six in size and sat everyone down on a bench. Once everyone was seated and counted, Morgan sent Watson to fetch more gin.

Once Watson returned with the drink, Morgan ordered the gin be passed amongst the staff and himself. Everyone was to drink, no matter their objections.

"You'll drink if I tell you to," Morgan said, waggling a revolver. He directed the prisoners to begin drinking, and every time the bottle reached the end of the line, Morgan would swig from it himself.

The prisoners began to feel the effects as they managed to empty four bottles. Watson began to sway in his seat and giggle. Morgan also began to loosen up, speaking freely, but with little coherence.

Now intoxicated and looking for amusement, Morgan went back to the stable and stashed a gin bottle in his saddle bag for later. The horse began to shy away from Morgan, sensing that he was not in a good way to be riding, but Morgan chastised the horse and climbed into the saddle. With some effort he guided it back to the shed where the inebriated captives remained seated and calm.

When Morgan reappeared, he brandished a revolver, waving it above his head. With a tug on the reins and a shift in his seat, Morgan made his elegant mount rear up with a loud snort. Many of the crowd applauded the impressive display, though not with much enthusiasm.

As Morgan dismounted and paraded the horse proudly, Sam Watson thought he recognised the stirrup irons. He stood, wobbling, having partaken in more of the drink than others, and called out, "Oi, those are Mr. Johnston's stirrups!"

Morgan made no reply to the comment, except by slowly mounting again with a smirk and kicking his legs out to show off the stirrup irons. He swayed somewhat as he sat erect in the saddle.

"You're a bloody thief, Morgan," Watson continued, slurring and gesturing with loose limbs.

Morgan grew annoyed and pulled a small pistol out from his belt. The piece was a tired old revolver from the goldfields with a hair trigger. As Morgan held the pistol out it went off. The glanced across the forehead of the station's carpenter but caused no serious injury. Morgan immediately ducked and looked around, furious.

"Who shot at me? Somebody shot at me!"

Morgan pointed the pistol at the prisoners, and in his drunken haze, fired again. The unfortunate Mr. Watson was directly in the line of fire and as he put his hand up reflexively the bullet pushed through it, cutting across his head as it came out the other side.

Watson clasped his punctured hand to his chest then ran and hid behind the barn, slipping in the dust as he went.

"You shot me, you bastard," Watson growled from afar.

John McLean emerged from the group and sternly addressed Morgan. "No, Morgan, nobody shot. It was your own revolver that went off!"
"Liar!"
Now in a blind rage, Morgan fired into the air shouting, "Now, you bastards, clear out of this!"

When the prisoners refused to move out of terror, he fired again into the crowd. This time the projectile struck young Heriot in the leg, fracturing his shin bone and cutting through the calf muscles before grazing the leg of another worker.

Everyone scattered in a panic. Heriot tried to escape, groaning in agony as he dragged his shattered leg around for thirty yards before collapsing. Mrs. Watson began running around the yard screaming hysterically. Morgan mounted and chased some of the men around the yard before he rode up to Heriot and glared down at the wounded man with the intensity of a thunder storm.

Morgan leapt down from his mount and held his pistol to Heriot's head.

"Don't kill me Morgan. You've broken my leg," gasped Heriot, reeling from pain and exhaustion.

Watson, seeing Morgan with a pistol to the young man's head, emerged from hiding shouting, "For God's sake Morgan, don't kill anyone!"

Morgan looked intently at his victim, the pathetic way he writhed in pain in the sepia-coloured dust, and it seemed as if a veil had been lifted from his eyes. At that instant he became aware of himself and what he was doing, but seemed deeply confused. He withdrew the firearm and clutched at his head. Trembling, he searched furiously around hollering, "where are all the damned wretches gone to?"

He sought help in the only way he knew how, screaming, "I'll blow the brains out of every man in this station if they don't come and help!"

None came.

Morgan took a knife from his boot and loomed over Heriot, who raised his hands in an attempt to hold him back. Morgan stooped and cut the boot from Heriot's wounded leg. He scooped up the injured young man and carried him to the homestead, where he directed McLean, and another man named Rushton, to take him inside.

Heriot was guided to a bed and laid on it. Morgan cut the other boot off and, overwhelmed with remorse, left him there to be treated by Rushton and McLean. The wound was serious and the men knew they were incapable of treating it properly with what was available at the station — a surgeon was required.

Outside, Morgan held his head in his hands as he tried to regain some sense of control over himself. He saw Watson in the shed, cradling his hand. Morgan approached him and, without a word, grabbed the man's arm and tied a handkerchief around the wound.

"I'm sorry I shot you, old man. I never meant to hurt anyone."
The chaos of the situation had cowed Morgan into repentance.

Amongst the mayhem two men, who were unknown to the staff, appeared. One was a half-Aboriginal man, who spoke at length with Morgan, the other a white man who was dressed like a farm hand. As Morgan spoke with the newcomers, John McLean approached him and suggested he could ride to fetch the doctor from a neighbouring station. Morgan, desperate to make amends for the injuries he had caused, allowed McLean to go. McLean told Heriot he was leaving to fetch Dr. Stitt and Heriot told him to take his horse for the task. McLean mounted Heriot's horse and galloped off at top speed.

However, Morgan's mates cautioned the bushranger and suggested that if nobody was keeping an eye on McLean he would head for the police. Morgan mounted his own steed and rode off, intending to overtake McLean and prevent any mischief.

Catching up to the farm hand, he called on McLean to stop but, having apparently not heard the command, McLean rode on. Morgan screamed, "you bloody wretch, you're going to give information!" He drew a revolver and fired at McLean's as he rode away. The bullet struck him in the back and tore out of McLean's body three inches above his navel. McLean lurched forward and tumbled from his mount as it recoiled, but he was still alive.

Morgan rode up and after assessing the situation took some of the alcohol from his saddle and gave McLean some to drink. He then slung the fallen man over his own saddle and rode back to the station with him.

When Morgan arrived back at Round Hill, just under two hours after McLean had left, he dismounted and carried McLean in his arms as he proceeded to the homestead. Rushton emerged to see who the arrival was and upon seeing Morgan was told, "Come here, young fellow, come and assist me." McLean was taken indoors by Morgan's half-Aboriginal mate and Rushton and laid on a bed.

Morgan sat by Heriot's bedside for two hours and intermittently checked on McLean.

After a while the bushranger went off and raided the grog supply with his friends. The three men withdrew to a more secluded spot on the station and drank and caroused well into the night in spite of the chaos and carnage that Morgan had just caused. It seemed that while the other men were drinking to get jolly, Morgan was drinking to forget the pain he had caused. The staff of the station were rather more concerned with the injuries to Watson and Heriot and the precarious state of McLean, and kept their distance from the unwelcome visitors.

In the early hours of the following morning, Morgan and his friends rode away from the station. Five minutes later a police party arrived at the station led by Superintendent McLerie. The men dressed in their blue jackets and kepi hats, white jodhpurs, and tall black boots looked smart as a lick of paint, but their late arrival was not greeted with the fanfare they had expected. Watson informed McLerie of what had transpired, and that Morgan and his mates had only just ridden away. He pointed in the direction the bushrangers went, the police superintendent thanked the man for the tip and the troopers immediately took off.

McLerie would continue the hunt relentlessly until exposure to the elements would diminish his health, causing his untimely death in November that same year.

A medical man, Hugh Scott, was summoned and attended to McLean who was in severe pain and vomiting convulsively. Scott came back to McLean several times, noting peritonitis had set in from the wound and made a request that McLean send for anyone he especially needed to see or speak to before leaving again.

While Scott was absent McLean was attended to by Dr. Stitt, the man McLean had been going to when he was shot, who had previously been a victim of Morgan himself.

Heriot was taken to Albury where he was looked after by his father in Botterill's Imperial Hotel. He made a full recovery.

When Scott returned to Round Hill two days after the Morgan affair he was informed that McLean had died. An autopsy was promptly conducted by Joseph Knight Barnett who noted that as the bullet had entered the body it has smashed a rib and that the projectile, as well as splinters from the rib, had perforated McLean's pancreas. The projectile had moved between the stomach and intestines and perforated the peritoneum and caused considerable inflammation, which was in the end the cause of death. The charge now levelled at Morgan for the first time was murder.

The newspapers were quick to express outrage and a sense of dread if the scourge of bushranging was not brought to heel promptly. The Age opined:

Can any man after this ride a mile from Albury without expecting a bullet through his head? No remarks of ours can fire the train, if this simple but hideous narrative does not. The whole country should be up in arms, and swear as one man, that they would never rest until this demon is brought to justice.

Already Albury has been moved to action, and volunteers, men who will not throw away a chance, are at work. Perhaps something may be done, and if the one life which has as yet been sacrificed will be the means of ridding the world of such a scoundrel, it is providential, but the country itself has this life to answer for.

In the wake of Round Hill, Morgan found himself becoming increasingly paranoid and quick to violence. It would not be long before this would result in another tragic loss.

Daniel Morgan

> *"Publish what you like but don't make the devil blacker than he really is."*
> — DANIEL MORGAN

There are multiple origin stories for the bushranger that would be known as Daniel Morgan. The most widely accepted one is that he was born in 1830 in New South Wales as John Fuller, the son of Mary "The Gypsy" Owen, a promiscuous Irish lass, and George Fuller, a greengrocer. Fuller, so the story goes, had an unstable childhood and was eventually fostered by a man named Jack the Welshman. At seventeen he became a stock-rider in Murrumbidgee where it is likely he developed his love for thoroughbreds.

However, one alternative is the origin uncovered by author Margaret Carnegie. In her research she came to believe that Morgan was really William Moran junior, the son of two convicts who was born in New South Wales in 1833 and raised around Campbelltown. This ties in with Morgan's own recollections of having grown up there and may also account for one of his many aliases: Sam Moran. Unfortunately, there is no way currently to prove either of these stories correct, and there remains the possibility neither of them is.

His first conviction came in 1854 when he was sentenced, as John Smith, to 12 years hard labour for highway robbery by Sir Redmond Barry at Castlemaine. He spent his sentence on the prison hulks *President* and *Success*, where he would have likely witnessed the murder of the notorious inspector of prisons, John Giles Price, by convicts on the beach at Point Gellibrand, and by some accounts he also did a portion of his sentence at Pentridge stockade.

When granted his Ticket-of-Leave in 1860, which allowed him to work in the Ovens district, he promptly bolted. He assumed many different identities including "Sydney Native", "Down-the-River Jack", and Sam Moran and occasionally picked up work on stations when he wasn't "on the hump"— an old expression for travelling on foot with a swag — but in the end the lure of bushranging proved too tempting.

During an early exploit, Morgan stole a valuable horse from Evan Evans named Grey Bobby. Evans and a neighbour tracked Morgan to his camp and confronted him. Morgan demanded to know who they were and was answered with a blast from a shotgun. The blast hit Morgan's arm and he escaped into the bush. He swore he would get revenge.

It wasn't long before Daniel Morgan, as he now identified himself, was committing robberies, the first of which was when he stole two racehorses and saddles from a pair of young men who were on their way to the races. Morgan was not alone, however, having a mate who was known either as Fancy Clarke or German Bill at his side. Morgan's love for race horses was a repeated factor in his crimes and he stole yet another, allegedly in order to ride to Bathurst for his mother's wedding, though this is very doubtful.

A short time later, the pair tried to rob a magistrate named Henry Bayliss. When they realised he was a magistrate they let him go, hoping he would be lenient on them if they ever came before him in court, but Baylis quickly formed a posse and went in search of the bushrangers. After days of scouring the bush, they found the bushrangers' camp. In the ensuing shoot-out Bayliss was injured by a bullet from the bushrangers and German Bill was mortally wounded. It was suggested that Morgan was the one that shot German Bill as a distraction, however Morgan escaped from the conflict taking his mate with him alive, making the distraction story unlikely. German Bill was found a considerable time later in the bush in a state of advanced decomposition where he had been slumped against a tree near a farm where Morgan had assaulted a farm hand who he believed had told the police where to find them.

Now with a reward of £200 on his head, Morgan continued to escalate his depredations, robbing stations from Henty to Tumbarumba. When he stuck up Burrumbuttock station he made the manager sign £400 worth of cheques for the staff, who he had been told were being underpaid.

Morgan began to gain a reputation as "the traveller's friend" because his criminal acts seemed to target unfair employers or people that mistreated swaggies, leading many such people to rethink their hostility lest the traveller send word to Morgan or turn out to be the bushranger himself. He often used Aboriginal boys as bush telegraphs to keep track of police movements, but had sympathisers throughout the New South Wales Riverina and north east Victoria that provided shelter and supplies. Unfortunately it was only a matter of time until things turned deadly.

When Morgan bailed up Round Hill Station, he raided the gin supply then later as he got onto his horse his gun went off. He assumed he was being shot at, and in the resulting chaos the station manager, Sam Watson, was shot in the hand, a neighbour named James Heriot was shot in the leg and this led to a stockman named John McLean being fatally shot through the midsection by Morgan while riding to fetch a doctor, as Morgan suspected him of going to the police instead. Accounts written posthumously have frequently spun fabrications and inaccuracies about this specific incident, including one version that has Watson's wife stepping between her husband and Morgan to beg for his life, after which Morgan opts to shoot him in the hand instead of killing him. Some reports are conflicted as to whether Morgan's shot had left a hole in Watson's hand or blown off one of his fingers. Most retellings leave Morgan's mates out completely to reinforce the lone wolf persona that makes him seem more dangerous.

A short time later, Morgan killed mounted trooper Sergeant David Maginnity. Maginnity and Constable Churchley were en route from Tumbarumba to Coppabella when they spotted Morgan, who they recognised from descriptions they were furnished with. Maginnity rode up to Morgan while Churchley stayed back about twenty yards (eighteen metres). There was a short exchange between Morgan and Maginnity before Morgan pulled his pistol and shot the trooper, having recognised him as a policeman. Churchley rode away, leaving Maginnity to his fate. Maginnity was believed to have been dragged into the bush a short distance by his spooked horse. Morgan laid the man out and took his weapons before leaving Maginnity's hat on the road as a marker for whoever came to find the body. Morgan would ever after carry Maginnity's revolver in his belt and show it off to people he encountered or bailed up.

Senior Sergeant Thomas Smyth was mortally wounded in September 1864 when shots were fired into his party's camp while they were on an expedition looking for Morgan. The troopers were turning in for the night when shots were fired from the bush, one of which hit Smyth in the chest. The assailants, of which there were likely two, were not identified at the time as the area around the camp was in pitch darkness, although James and Michael Corcoran were later arrested on suspicion of aiding Morgan in the shooting after tracks of unshod horses were found leading from the camp to the Corcoran farm a short distance away. The brothers had long been suspected of being sympathisers of Morgan. When Smyth died from his wounds Morgan was, naturally, blamed for his murder.

In April, 1865, Morgan crossed the border from New South Wales into Victoria and began operating near Glenrowan. His bush telegraph had gotten word to him that the Victorian police were bragging that Morgan would not last more than forty eight hours in Victoria so Morgan decided to take the flashness out of them. He decided it was also an opportunity to exact revenge on Evan Evans.

In the middle of the night Morgan set fire to the haystacks at the Evans' farm, *Whitfield*, in order to get their attention. All at the station came out to see what was happening and Morgan bailed them all up and demanded Evan Evans. Evans, as it transpired was out for the evening and Morgan proceeded to lecture the captives about his grudge with him, even showing the scars on his arm from where he had been shot. Eventually he had Evans' brother John escort him a short distance into the bush where a horse he had stolen was tethered to a tree. He asked Evans to see the animal got back to its owner before he left.

On 8 April he stuck up Peechelba Station and held the McPherson family and their staff captive while he got drunk. He forced one of the girls to play the piano for him as he had heard her playing when he arrived and liked the sound. One of the maids, Alice Keenan, escaped when Morgan allowed her to tend to a sick baby, raising the alarm that Morgan was in the homestead. Soon a posse had surrounded the house and when Morgan emerged in the morning to prepare a horse so he could return to New South Wales, he was shot in the back by one of McPherson's stockmen named John Windlaw (although there remains some level of confusion as to whether that was his actual name as it was also written as Wendlan and Quinlan in the press).

Morgan died slowly choking on his own blood, finally passing away that afternoon. His corpse was removed to Wangaratta where a post-mortem was conducted, after which people posed with it for photographs. The body was mutilated, with the attending doctor, Dr. Dobbyn, being instructed by a police Superintendent to skin the jaw so that the beard could be dried like a possum skin as a trophy. The onlookers took locks of hair either by cutting it with knives or pulling it out from the root, and it was alleged privately that Morgan's scrotum was removed to be used as a tobacco pouch. Morgan's head was hacked off then wrapped in brine-soaked rags and sent to

Melbourne in a wooden box where a cast was made for study. His headless remains were put in a wooden box and buried in Wangaratta cemetery where it remains to this day.

In the wake of Morgan's death there was some level of unrest as his sympathisers threatened an uprising, and one was arrested for attempting to hunt down and murder John Windlaw. Two anonymous women were also seen leaving flowers on Morgan's grave.

Morgan was around thirty-five when he was gunned down, though without knowing his true birth date it is impossible to know for a fact. Within a few weeks his contemporary Benjamin Hall would meet a similarly gruesome end. While Morgan's burning hatred of the authorities earned him many admirers, to many more Morgan was no more than a villainous thug and a lunatic. However, it would seem, upon a deeper examination, that many preconceived ideas about Morgan are derived from false and inaccurate accounts of his life and deeds.

Argus (Melbourne, Vic.: 1848 - 1957), Saturday 25 June 1864, page 5

MORGAN AT ROUND HILL STATION.

We are indebted to the *Border Post* for some further details of Morgan's exploit at the Round-hill Station, belonging to Mr. Henty, and which is about forty miles from Albury:– "On Sunday last, about half-past one o'clock, Mr. Watson, the superintendent; Mr. McNeil, the overseer; Mr. M'Lean, the cattle overseer and Mr. John Heriot, a young gentleman, son of a neighbouring squatter, who had come over with a message, were quietly sitting in a room. Mrs. Watson was in her bedroom, when a man, whom she immediately recognised as Morgan, looked in at the door, and asked where was Mr. Watson. She pointed out the room. He opened the door, presented a revolver, and introduced himself formally, and then asked where the grog was. He, with a revolver in each hand, cocked and capped, mustered the four to the apartment indicated, and demanded to know how many bottles there were Mr. Watson replied, six bottles of gin, and that one was broached. Out of the latter bottle Mr. Watson poured a glass, and offered it to the villain, who smiled, and said 'You must drink that yourself, as you may have had it ready for me.' He then drank himself, called the female servant, ordered dinner, and told her to tell one of the men to put his horse in the stable, and give him a feed, which was done. He ordered the four prisoners into a corner while he had his dinner: and chatted sociable, with a cocked revolver on either hand, and four more are ostentatiously displayed in his belt. After dinner he marched them all out, and mustered all the men, making a total of eleven, at and around the stable door, while he went to examine his horse.

He then drove them down to a little cattle shed, and made them sit on a bench there, sending Mr. Watson himself back to the house for a bottle of gin. One of the men served round the bottle, at the robber's desire, and after that another and another, until four were consumed, Morgan making every one drink it raw, he himself taking a small 'nip' each time. After this little amusement he thought he would try something else, and ordered his horse to be brought. Before mounting, without any provocation whatever, he fired one shot amongst them, which grazed the carpenter's head, and a second in another direction. Putting away a gin bottle for himself, he turned to and rode away, but when only about fifteen yards off, Mr. Watson rather rashly said, 'These are the irons (stirrup irons) you stole from so and so.' The ruffian coolly turned round in his saddle, took deliberate aim at Mr. Watson's head, and fired.

Seeing the deadly aim, Mr. Watson involuntarily put up his hand, through which the ball passed, turning it probably aside, as it only touched his scalp. The wounded man ran behind the shed and hid himself, but Morgan returned to the door of the shed, fired right and left amongst the inmates. The first shot went through young Mr. Heriot's leg, between the knee and ankle, shattering the bone in pieces, and then hit another man's leg behind, but not, luckily, breaking the skin as its force had been spent. The second ball hit no one. The men then all ran away in different directions, the poor wounded young man among them dragging his broken leg after him for about thirty yards, when he fell from pain and exhaustion.

In the meantime, Morgan galloped after another man across the yard, with pistol cocked; but the fugitive escaped through the kitchen. The horse stood fire well. Morgan then galloped back to young Heriot, dismounted, and put the revolver to his head. Mrs. Watson, in the meantime, was running screaming and terrified about the yard. Young Heriot said 'Don't kill me, Morgan, you have broken my leg;' and Mr. Watson, who had also. seeing Morgan with the pistol to the boy's head, came out of his hiding-place, cried out, 'For God's sake, Morgan, don't kill anyone!' The villain, who seemed to act with the inconsistency of drunkenness or of a murderer gone mad, then cried out, 'Where are all the d— wretches gone to?' and swore a fearful oath that he would blow the brains out of every man on the station if they did not come to Heriot's assistance. He himself knelt down, cut the boot off the wounded leg, and himself carried the unfortunate youth to the gate next the house. Two men then, frightened by his threats, came forward, and he swore he would shoot them dead if they did not carry him in which they did, and laid him on a bed.

At this time, also, two men — one a half-caste aboriginal — who had not yet appeared on the scene, but evidently Morgan's men, came up, and remained on the ground while Young Heriot was carried to a bed, where Morgan cut off the other boot and set a man to attend him. He then returned to Mr. Watson, and bound a hand-kerchief round his wounded hand, saying he was sorry he did that. Seeing Morgan apparently returning, as if satiated with bloodshed, Mr. M'Lean asked him if he might go for a doctor. Morgan answered 'Yes,' and then for a short time regaled himself and his mates; but apparently mistrusting M'Lean, he followed him upon the road, over-took him five or six miles from the station, and, without 'yea' or 'nay,' coming close behind him, fired at him. The ball entered the unfortunate man's back above the hip and came out close to the navel, and he of course fell mortally wounded. Morgan dismounted, lifted the wounded man on his horse, and led him back to the station, where he now lies with no hope of his recovery. Morgan and his men then remained carousing until two o'clock the next morning, when they departed as they came, and the police, under Mr. M'Lerie, at lived exactly five minutes after. A great many reports are circulated as to their conduct when they did come, but, until we can vouch for the truth, we decline to publish them.

"Already, Albury has been moved to action, and volunteers — men who will not throw away a chance — are at work. Perhaps something may be done, and if the one life which has as yet been sacrificed will be the means of ridding the world of such a scoundrel, it is providential, but the country itself has this life to answer for."

V

⚜

Black Day at Black Springs

Between Gundagai and Jugiong in New South Wales lies Black Springs, an area with rolling hills and girt by dense scrub. It was here that Johnny Gilbert, the flash Canadian bushranger, would cement his reputation as not only a violent criminal, but a murderer. The bushranging gang, consisting of Gilbert, Ben Hall, and John Dunn, were at the peak of their notoriety at the end of 1864. Always game to push the limits with more and more daring robberies, they had refined their operation to a fine art. They would find a decent stretch of road between towns on the mail route, bail up any travellers and keep them prisoner out of sight to prevent anyone raising an alarm, then bail up their main target – the mail coach. This had proven to be an effective way of collecting cash and valuables, although the prevalence of such highway robbery had meant fewer and fewer people were sending money via the mail.

On 15 November they had performed this exact routine at Deep Creek, and were lucky enough to find the mail coach without a police escort and therefore easily overpowered. It had been a productive day, though they were again frustrated by the lack of cash to be found in the mail bags. The following day, the decided, they would choose a spot on the western side of Jugiong and see how that compared.

**

On 16 November the gang went to work near Black Springs, bailing up travellers as they came along the mail route. Within a couple of hours of starting they had already bailed up five carts carrying parties of Chinese men, twelve teamsters and their wagons, a squatter named Hayes and his wife, and a horseman named Johnston. As it was mid-week it seemed there were a lot of people on the road to go about their business and this was just dandy for Gilbert, Dunn and Hall. The gang's takings were already over £100, and the chance of an even bigger taking from the mail coach kept the bushrangers excited. While the prisoners were kept under watch behind a hill, Ben Hall began to interrogate the squatter, Mr. Hayes.

"Do you know the whereabouts of the Bishop of Goulburn?" Hall asked.

"I don't know. I believe he may be in Deniliquin," said Hayes.

"Do you know if the Attorney-General has gone up to Tumut for his re-election?" Hall continued.

"I couldn't say," Hayes replied.

"We intend to bail them up. We want to take them hostage and offer them as ransom in exchange for the government granting us pardons. We would do no harm to a hair on their heads, of course, unless our demands were not met."

Hayes felt his stomach churning as he listened to the matter-of-fact way that Hall casually described holding a politician and a man of the cloth ransom.

"Please don't interfere with the bishop. He is a man of peace!"

"My mind is made up already, sir," Hall replied, "Gilbert and I are living day to day, never knowing when one of us will be shot or betrayed. The young fellow still has a chance, but we are marked men. For us it is a matter of hanging or liberty, and if it means capturing some nob' to use for bartering, then so be it. It might even do Mr. Martin, the esteemed Attorney-General, some good to see what the laws he upholds do to fellows like us."

Around 12:30pm a trooper was spotted by Gilbert, riding along the road with a packhorse. Immediately the bushranger mounted and headed down the hill at full tilt towards the constable calling on him to, "Stand! Bail up!" The trooper in question was Constable James McLaughlin, who had set out ahead of the mail coach from Gundagai to ensure the road was clear. He spotted the rider charging at him with pistols drawn — now joined by the other two who fired off three shots — and responded by drawing his own revolver.

The bushrangers hollered at McLaughlin to bail up, but he was no pushover and immediately let go of the pack horse and went for his colt revolver. He tried to hold his own – one against three – and began to fire at them. The trooper and the bushrangers weaved around each other on horseback letting fly with all the firepower they could. When Hall's horse stumbled, Dunn rode in front to fire at the trooper. It was not a long-lasting battle, however, as McLaughlin quickly ran out of bullets in his police issue Colt Navy revolver. Dunn closed in on the constable as he retreated, with Hall and Gilbert coming close behind to cut off any escape. Reluctantly, McLaughlin submitted to his foes and was added to the group of prisoners. He had fought valiantly but had been outgunned from the start. Luckily, he had avoided being hurt but his mount had been slightly wounded by one of the outlaws.

As they joined the others, Gilbert loudly proclaimed, "This man is the finest man in the shape of a constable I've ever encountered." The praise was hardly comfort to the trooper, who would now face the ridicule of his peers and reprimand from his superiors.

As the morning rolled on Ben Hall kept watch over his growing collection of captives, pacing slowly and lordly with his horse, with Gilbert and Dunn keeping the group covered with their revolvers. In the afternoon heat came the soft clomping of hooves in the dry earth and the rattle of coach wheels. The mail coach on its way from Gundagai to Yass rattled along with two police, Sergeant Edmund Parry and Sub-Inspector William O'Neill, a safe distance behind as escorts. Inside the coach, police magistrate Alfred Rose sweltered in the heat and up top Constable William Roche rode on the box seat beside the driver, William Geoghan. Suspicions were immediately aroused by the number of wagons and carts on the side of the road.

Hearing the arrival, Hall and Gilbert spurred into action, mounting and riding up to the crest of a hill overlooking the track. Gilbert flashed his impish grin as he clapped predatory eyes on their quarry. The bandits cocked their revolvers and pounded down the hill to the coach, leaving Dunn with the prisoners. Blocking the road, Hall bellowed, "Bail up," while training his weapon on the coach driver. Constable Roche moved to raise his rifle but was immediately discouraged by Gilbert who presented to his person six chambers of instant death and a promise to share their contents if Roche did not obey him. P. M. Rose wasn't quite so ready to let the coach be plundered and with a cry of, "Bushrangers," he signalled to Parry and O'Neill by waving his hat out the window of the coach. Digging their spurs into their mounts the escorts thundered towards the coach, drawing their revolvers as they went.

"There's a bloody lot of traps," said Hall as he spotted the incoming troopers and the pair quickly turned tail and galloped back up the hill as if retreating. As the outlaws paused at the top of the hill, where Dunn met them on horseback, Gilbert looked back to reassess their position.

"There are only two of them; Come on, let's rush the bastards!"

Any relief the lawmen and the coach driver must have felt at the apparent retreat was short lived as the entire gang charged like cavalry at the mounted policemen, with revolvers in each hand and their supreme horsemanship on show as they steered their mounts with their bodies like fearsome centaurs, screaming, "Fight us like men!"

The police were game and began to reel off shots at their opponents and called on them to surrender. Constable Roche began to panic as bullets zipped past him and raised his rifle. Geoghan grabbed Roche's tunic and threatened to throw him off the coach if he fired. Roche then leapt from his perch and scurried into the scrub with his rifle. The police escorts were separated with Dunn aiming for O'Neill, who fought like the devil, firing a shot at Ben Hall who effortlessly dodged the bullet. O'Neill's horse, spooked by the gunfire careened into a tree, the branch striking O'Neill and injuring his hip. Reeling in pain two shots struck him, one punching a hole in the right shoulder of his tunic, the other tearing through the left flap, yet miraculously neither left a mark on the man himself. In pain and panic, an impotent click from his revolver informed him that he was out of bullets. O'Neill drew his Calisher and Terry carbine and fired it at the approaching bushrangers. Hall unwisely came in close to O'Neill and received a bash on the skull with the butt of the carbine, briefly stunning him and almost pushing him out of the saddle. Dunn then came in close and attempted to wrestle the carbine away from O'Neill.

Meanwhile, Gilbert had drawn Sergeant Parry away from the others and the two duelled on horseback, spitting curses at each other until a blast from Gilbert found its mark. The shot struck Parry across the back of the head but was not enough to subdue him. Bleeding profusely from the head, Parry came at Gilbert to entreated him to surrender. Parry discarded his now empty revolver and screamed, "I'll never surrender to a bushranger. Not while I have a shot left!"

Gilbert was impressed by the recklessness and bravado of this trooper, which is why, in his own mind, it was so unfortunate that he had to shoot him. Gilbert raised his pistol and fired as the trooper was wheeling around, attempting to unsling his carbine. The bullet struck Parry in the left shoulder and perforated his body straight through, exiting his breast. He slumped in the saddle, causing his horse to jolt forward, and he tumbled lifelessly to the ground. Gilbert dismounted and walked over to his fallen foe. He turned the body over and examined his handy work. "He's got it in the cobra..." he said to nobody in particular.

Upon seeing his colleague hit the ground, O'Neill allowed himself to be captured. He could not tell from such a distance if Parry was alive or dead, but Gilbert's reaction was enough to convey the situation.

Dunn and Hall took Sub-Inspector O'Neill back downhill to the coach. As they walked, Hall asked O'Neill, "Where's the other bloke?"

"He's bolted," O'Neill replied with more than a hint of anger in his voice.

"You should dismiss the fellow at once, he is a coward and a wretch to leave you and your mate to fight," said Hall, "But I will say this for you both, you are two brave men."

Hall and Dunn demanded O'Neill turn over his valuables, taking a ring and his watch and chain.

"I really must demand the watch back," said O'Neill.

"You're not exactly in a position to make demands," said Hall.

"That watch was my father's. It is no mere trinket. Surely you can understand that?"

Hall paused and thought before gesturing for Dunn to hand over the timepiece. "I am not an unreasonable man. You can have the watch back."

Dunn unclipped the chain before handing over the watch. O'Neill nodded his thanks for the small gesture.

Upon reaching the coach, the bushrangers demanded the mailbags from the driver. Not in a position to argue, the driver complied. Tearing the bags open, Dunn and Gilbert rifled through the letters and took all they desired. Ben Hall wrenched open the door to the coach and dragged magistrate Rose out.

"I ought to blow your brains out for signalling the troopers," Hall growled, "who are you?"

"I'm the police magistrate of Gundagai," Rose replied.

"You're as bad as the bloody traps!"

"I am what I am."

Having plundered the mail, the bandits directed Rose, O'Neill and the coach driver uphill and promptly added them to the gang's collection of captives. O'Neill noticed that Hall carried five revolvers in his belt and felt compelled to draw attention to them.

"Five revolvers? We only have the one. Doesn't make for much of a fair fight, old chum."

Dunn replied, "We have plenty of spare cylinders about us to reload with too."

Gilbert sauntered up to Constable McLaughlin and scowled, "How would you like a cove like me after you?" McLaughlin was unimpressed. Gilbert pressed the point, "See what that bloody fool has got for not standing? He's the first man I ever shot; I don't like to shoot a man, but I can't help the unfortunate man now." McLaughlin asked if he could attend to Parry and see if anything was to be done and Gilbert allowed him to go, fully aware that it was pointless.

Constable Roche was soon uncovered by the gang, cowering in the undergrowth nearby. His carbine was confiscated, and he was forced to walk back to Yass. Before the gang left, Hall proclaimed that the police would need a bigger troop than what they'd mustered that day, for the gang planned to stick up another escort the next day. The gang shot off into the expanse leaving behind their bewildered captives and the body of the late Sergeant Edmund Parry.

***

The following day, following an inquest, Parry was buried in the Gundagai cemetery before a large crowd of mourners. It was determined that Gilbert had murdered Parry and that Hall and Dunn were accessories to the murder. In due time the reward for their capture would be raised.

Another measure employed to stymie the highwaymen was taking portions of the mail under cover of darkness on packhorses instead of in coaches. This proved as ineffectual as any of the other measures put in place because word inevitably reached the bushrangers of what was happening, and they began to work at night as well as during the day. Despite now being branded as murderers the Hall Gang showed no signs of stepping back from their depredations. It would only be a matter of time until yet another trooper would fall as a result of their crimes.

Johnny Gilbert

> "Now, my lads, I'm going to shout; but I wish to say a few words to you:—
> Generally when we go to a public-house we are in the habit of making ourselves
> agreeable; but those we meet with, after they get liquor in, get Dutch courage, and
> talk about mobbing us. Now, if we hear anything of that kind, somebody is apt to
> get hurt, and I don't think it will be us; and another thing, I will not allow any
> swearing, blackguard language, or obscene songs, before the females; and now, as
> we understand each other, let us liquor."
>
> — JOHN GILBERT

During his life Gilbert's origins were a mystery to most. Journalists would scramble
for the merest hint of a clue in the hope of uncovering the story behind the most
notorious highwayman in Australia. Gilbert was born in Hamilton, Ontario, Canada,
in 1842, the youngest child of English emigrants William and Eleanor Gilbert, whose
other children were Ellen, William jnr, Francis, James and Charles. When John was
still an infant his mother died, but soon afterwards William remarried to a Canadian
woman named Eliza. After this union John's half-brothers Thomas and Nicholson
were born.

As a ten-year-old he journeyed with his family from the beautiful waterside vistas
of Ontario into the United States, departing from New York on the *Revenue* to the
dry, sweltering goldfields of Victoria.

In 1854, twelve-year-old Johnny Gilbert took his leave of his family and obtained
employment as a stable boy for a pub in Kilmore. While this work provided pocket
money and good experience with horses, one of his greatest loves, his exposure to
the larrikins, louts and rogues travelling to and from the gold fields seems to have

fostered a fascination for lawlessness in the boy. When he was about eighteen, Gilbert headed to the gold fields of New South Wales to seek his fortune.

Gilbert worked around the boom town of Kiandra, one of the most bustling gold rush locations. The gold fields in this time were a cesspool of debauchery, lawlessness and other forms of villainy. Murders, riots, lynchings and robberies were everyday occurrences and put enormous strain on the understaffed and overextended colonial police, many of whom were poorly equipped and lacked training. A law passed in Britain had prevented the various regional police forces to unite as one entity, forcing the existing regional forces to remain fractured and overworked. This, combined with the rise in lawless behaviour and the huge influx of immigrants seeking riches on the goldfields, resulted in absolute mayhem.

No doubt this was a perfect environment for Johnny Gilbert who had a thirst for adventure and thrill-seeking. At this time bushranging in New South Wales had blossomed from sporadic cases of stock theft, home invasions, murder and highway robbery by criminals hiding in the untouched wilds into something almost industrial in its scale. The easy pickings from the mail coaches and less cautious miners meant that anyone that was unprepared for the backbreaking labour of mining for gold was very likely to "go bush".

It was around this that Gilbert crossed paths with Frank Gardiner. Gardiner was on the run, having violated his Ticket-of-Leave conditions, and had established himself in Lambing Flat — later renamed Young — with his mate William Fogg, running a dodgy butcher's shop that dealt in meat from stock that had been procured illegally. Gilbert adopted the Murringo region as his new home and picked up work as a stockman. Likely it was through Gardiner and Fogg that Gilbert became associated with men that were not known at that time but would soon become household names, such as John O'Meally, Fred Lowry and John Peisley.

By 1862 Gilbert was fully entrenched in the lawless lifestyle of Gardiner and his cohort and on 10 March that year he was involved in his first documented act as a bushranger. Along with Gardiner, O'Meally and Tom McGuinness he robbed two storekeepers of almost £2000 in gold and banknotes. Such a score was no doubt absolutely thrilling for the bandits but devastating for the victims. Gilbert took to adopting a very flash dress sense as his new outlaw lifestyle began to bring in spoils he could hardly have imagined on a stockman's wage. He was fond of ostentatious clothing such as bright red sashes and tassles, as well as jewellery and accessories, particularly fob chains and rings. He worked with Gardiner committing highway robberies including at least one involving a young squatter named Benjamin Hall. Gilbert seems to have worked his way up to being Frank Gardiner's closest bushranging associate as the only known photograph of Gilbert is a *carte de visite* of him and Gardiner together — though the figure in the photograph was never officially identified and may actually be of someone else entirely.

At the beginning of June 1862 Gilbert began to work without Gardiner. On the first of the month he and two others allegedly robbed Herbert's Store at Little Creek, taking monkey jackets and boots. They then went to Chard's store and attempted to rob the store owner of £30. The commotion roused some local miners who armed themselves and attempted to capture the bandits, but they managed to escape.

On 15 June, 1862, Gilbert accompanied Gardiner and his gang to Eugowra Rocks where they robbed a gold escort in one of the biggest gold heists in Australian history. The bushrangers had blocked off the road with drays from a waylaid bullock team in order to halt the Orange gold escort. When the escort arrived, Gardiner emerged from behind the boulders that rested uphill alongside the road and the gang promptly opened fire, injuring some of the policemen and spooking the horses, who bolted and caused the coach to crash.
The gang looted the vehicle as the police escaped, lifting around £14,000 in gold and cash (close to $4000,000 in modern Australian currency).

The police responded swiftly and Sub-Inspector Pottinger led a party of police that, almost by accident, managed to find the bushrangers' camp and recover a portion of the loot.
Just after this, Johnny Gilbert was joined by Henry Manns, one of Gardiner's gang, and his brother Charlie Gilbert as he attempted to leave the district to avoid the increased police activity. Gilbert converted his stolen gold into cash at a bank and carried the spoils – £2500 – in a valise on his saddle.

On 7 July, the trio were stopped by Sub-Inspector Pottinger who was accompanied by Detective Lyons and a volunteer named Richard Mitchell. When they asked Johnny Gilbert for documents proving his ownership of the horse he was riding, he duped and fled. Henry Manns and Charlie Gilbert were arrested but "Happy Jack" had a plan. He rode towards the Weddin Mountains and alerted members of Gardiner's gang and Gardiner himself. The police and their prisoners stayed overnight at a nearby station.
The following day, as the police and their prisoners continued on their way, the

bushrangers positioned themselves for ambush at Burrangong.

The bushrangers emerged from the bush and bailed up the escort and opened fire. Detective Lyons was thrown from his horse when it was clipped by gunfire and he chased it into the bush. Pottinger and Mitchell returned fire at the bushrangers without effect on both sides.

As Pottinger and Mitchell doubled back for reinforcements. Charlie Gilbert and Henry Manns were freed and the bushrangers escaped. Once clear the men split up, Manns heading to Murrumburrah where he would soon be arrested again, the Gilbert brothers heading to Victoria where they collected their brother James and left for the nearest port to make their way out of the colony.

The brothers managed to gain passage to New Zealand where they headed for the goldfields. They were determined to go straight and leave bushranging behind them. Johnny, however, became paranoid that he would be recognised and began cross-dressing in public to counter this. His disguise was unconvincing however and ended up drawing more attention to him than it diverted. Johnny told his brother that he had to return to Australia and Johnny soon made his way to Queensland.

Gilbert's time in Queensland was short lived as his sudden appearance and distinct features immediately put him on the radar and he returned to New South Wales at the beginning of 1863, where Ben Hall was making a name for himself as a bushranger.

As this was occurring, Frank Gardiner began to grow tired of the bushranging life and escaped out of New South Wales with his mistress Kitty Brown.

Initially teaming up with Fred Lowry, a tall and brash former stockman and prison escapee, Gilbert was involved in several robberies around the Yass gold fields. Gilbert decided to utilise his contacts from his time with Gardiner, teaming up with John O'Meally, Ben Hall, Patsy Daley and others. This new gang, known popularly as the Gilbert Gang, wasted no time in making a splash.

On 2 February, 1863, the gang robbed Dickenson's Store at Spring Creek, stealing £60 worth of goods. As they made their escape they bailed up a policeman and stole his horse. While positive identification of the culprits was impossible, it is more than likely that the Gilbert Gang was responsible.

On 15 February, Vincent Cirkell, a publican in Stoney Creek, was shot dead. It was believed the gang suspected him of being an informant and that O'Meally had been the trigger man. This version of events was merely a fabrication as the poor man was shot during a robbery that had escalated out of control and the assailants did not match the descriptions of any of the gang members. Such misidentification was commonplace as the hysteria surrounding the gang intensified and minor bush-rangers were happy to let the more prominent bandits take the blame.

The gang struck again on 28 February, robbing Solomon's store on the Wombat Diggings. The bushrangers fired at Meyers Solomon, the storekeeper, beat a young man named George Johnstone and threatened to kill Solomon's wife before leaving with £250 worth of loot.

The first gang member to be captured was Patsy Daley. Daley's aggression had made him particularly wanted by police and they got their man on 11 March when he was found hiding in a mine shaft. After this, the gang's numbers would fluctuate wildly.

On 1 April, Gilbert hit the road with Lowry and a recruit named Gibson. They were spotted by a party of police and engaged in a horseback shoot-out, ending in Gibson's capture and Gilbert and Lowry escaping into the bush. One of the officers had mocked Gilbert's shooting, yelling that he couldn't hit a haystack.

The Gilbert Gang continued their depredations unabated. Along with various robberies, the bushrangers made a point of partaking in less villainous activities. Gilbert and O'Meally at one point crashed a wedding and only left after being given some booze and cake. Despite such jovial incidents, the gang's robberies were becoming more frequent and less discerning. Nobody was exempt from their attention regardless of age, sex or social class. Gilbert had even taken to using fire as a tool to distract people from pursuing him after a robbery.

On 7 June the gang were particularly busy, robbing Henry's store near Possum Flat of half a chest of tea and dress prints; O'Brien's store was robbed of £37 cash; McCarthy's store was stuck up and the widow McCarthy liberated of her rings and 15 shillings, as well as taking four ounces of gold from one of her customers; finally they tried to bail up McConnell and Co. but when the staff refused to let them in they peppered the place with shot, broke in and looted the place, taking goods and £15 from the till. Having had their fill of robbing stores they robbed Heffernan's pub of booze, watches and firearms before moving on to Regan's Hotel while singing *O'er the Hills and Far Away*.

On 21 June, Gilbert and Lowry attempted to rob John McBride but were met with resistance. McBride drew a Colt revolver and started firing, blowing Lowry's hat off. In the battle McBride was hit in the thigh and the bushrangers bolted. McBride would die soon after from his wound. This appears to have been the last straw for

Lowry, who was not sighted with any of Gilbert's gang afterwards. He would go on to form his own gang and operate near Fish Creek.

After a series of brushes with police, Gilbert and O'Meally set their sights on bigger fish. On 30 July they rode into Carcoar and attempted to rob the Commercial Banking Company of Sydney. This was the first time of note that anyone had attempted to rob a bank in New South Wales.

Gilbert attempted to lure the clerk with a dodgy cheque while O'Meally watched the door. When O'Meally attempted to bail up the bank manager at the door, Gilbert was distracted and the clerk pulled a pistol on the bushrangers and fired a shot. At that moment the manager ran for help and scores of gawkers filed out into the street. The bushrangers cut their losses and mounted, riding out of town as fast as they could. Unwilling to call it a day, the pair robbed a store on the way back to their camp, leaving with around £300 worth of goods and cash.

The gang, now merely a duo comprising of Gilbert and O'Meally, had recruited a juvenile delinquent named John Vane as a telegraph and supplier of horses. Since the failed bank robbery the pair had decided they needed more manpower and adopted Vane and his mate Mickey Burke as junior gang members. Vane was tall, lanky and somewhat clumsy whereas Burke was younger-looking, energetic and enthusiastic.

The new look Gilbert Gang's first operation was on 2 August. At dusk they arrived at Coombing Park and stalked the grounds. Their intention was to steal a prized racehorse named Comus II, owned by Icely, the station owner. Vane and Burke took Comus II from the stable along with a grey gelding belonging to Sub-Inspector Davidson but were spotted by Icely's groom. The groom took aim but was shot in the mouth by Burke, allowing the bushrangers to escape.

Now the gang reconnected with Ben Hall and became a formidable force unlike anything yet seen in New South Wales in this period. On 24 August the gang bailed up nine diggers and held them captive while they waited for four storekeepers they had been informed were due to pass through. The gang robbed these storekeepers of whatever they had on them that was somewhat valuable, disappointed that these seemingly well-to-do men were not as flush as had been expected. The gang also stole the horses and gear from the men to replace the knocked up mounts they had been on and rode towards Junee.

In the meantime the alarm had been raised and a police party led by Sub-Inspector Pottinger rode out to catch the bushrangers. The groups crossed paths and there was a shoot-out, but the bandits escaped much to Pottinger's chagrin.

In Junee on 27 August, the gang got to work. Gilbert raided Hammond's Store with Vane and Hall while O'Meally and Burke struck Williams' pub. Gilbert left a good impression on the Hammonds and their servants with his fine clothing, well groomed appearance and pleasant demeanour during conversation. He even took the time to flirt with the ladies. When the gang left town they took two of Hammond's horses, five packhorses and goods and cash to the value of £250.

The gang continued to wreak havoc, robbing stores and distributing the stolen goods amongst their sympathiser and selling the surplus to traders.

At the end of August, O'Meally reputedly killed a storekeeper named Barnes who they had previously robbed. When they encountered Barnes they attempted to rob him but he turned to ride away. As he fled O'Meally shot him under the shoulder and he fell to the ground, smashing his head, dying instantly.

On 19 September the gang set up a mile out of Blayney and stuck up travellers. Nine people were captured and robbed and kept captive under some trees nearby. A mounted trooper was bailed up and robbed and made to join the others. This was followed by the mail coach from Carcoar, which was also bailed up. When one of the occupants refused to follow Gilbert's orders he threatened to blow the man's brains out. The unperturbed traveller, named Garland, called Gilbert's bluff but Ben Hall intervened and convinced Garland to do as instructed or receive a beating.

The mail was sifted through while Vane and Burke bailed up more travellers, taking possession of a racehorse named Retriever. Now with no less than a dozen prisoners the decision was made to head for Blayney.

As they went Gilbert bailed up a man named Beardmore who offered to write a cheque for £20 if Gilbert would loan him a revolver and duel at twelve paces. Gilbert refused, but Beardmore's jibe that he knew Gilbert wouldn't be game infuriated the bushranger and prompted him to accept the challenge. Hall again intervened. Gilbert relieved Beardmore of a gold ring, but when the man asked to have it back because it was a gift from his mother, Gilbert accepted because he admired Beardmore's pluck.

A few days later, the gang bailed up three constables. They stripped them naked and tied them to a tree. O'Meally threatened to shoot the men but Hall cooled him off. The gang took possession of the uniforms and with the one taken from the trooper near Blayney, they now had four complete troopers' uniforms, which they began using as disguises while riding. The gang was about to seal their place in history.

In September, the gang raided Grubbenbong Station, the property of John Loudon. They ransacked the place, taking any valuables they could find before demanding supper. When Mickey Burke went to smoke his pipe Gilbert ordered him outside as it was impolite to smoke near women. After the meal, Gilbert was so taken by the Loudons that he returned all they had taken. The gang then rode to William Rothery's Cliefden Station, where they again bailed up the household and demanded refreshments. Hall and Vane checked out Rothery's horses before the gang indulged in food and champagne. They rode off with two of the horses and headed for Canowindra.

Here they arrived at dusk the following day, bailing up Robinson's Hotel and shouted the patrons drinks and cigars. Gradually the townsfolk were all taken prisoner in the hotel and what began as a raid became a big party with dancing and piano. While the townsfolk were occupied with the dance the local store was raided, the loot put on packhorses. The local constable had been handcuffed and was brought in and placed on a chair to watch the amusements. The festivities continued into the early hours. The gang left at sunrise, but there was more to come.

On 3 October the gang raided Bathurst. Whereas Canowindra had a tiny population of a few dozen, Bathurst was a thriving city with more than 6000 residents. They arrived in the evening and made their way through the crowds of Saturday night shoppers. Their first stop was the gunsmith but none of the pieces on offer were to their taste. They moved on to the jewellers but when the jeweller's daughter saw what was happening she screamed and tried to raise the alarm. The bushrangers mounted and began riding wildly through the streets. They then bailed up the Sportsman's Arms Hotel with the intent of stealing a racehorse named Pasha, but the horse was not there so the gang departed.

With the gang's activities becoming ever more brazen, a reward of £2,500 was offered for the apprehension of the gang or information leading to it. This did not bother the bushrangers, however, and they continued business as usual. On 12 October, they once again struck Canowindra. As before, Robinson's Hotel was bailed up and the townsfolk herded inside for another night of festivities. The gang held the town for three days, covering the cost of meals and drinks. All who entered the town were detained but not once were they bothered by police.

Of course, the good fortune of the gang could not last and the first major blow to the gang was about to be landed. On 24 October, the gang descended upon Dunn's Plains near Bathurst. Here was the residence of Henry Keightley, a police magistrate who had been assisting police and openly bragging about what he would do if he encountered the gang. The gang ordered Keightley to surrender but instead he retreated inside and opened fire on the bushrangers. A heated battle ensued during which Burke was shot in the stomach. In incredible agony he tried to commit suicide by shooting himself in the head but still took half an hour to die. Keightley and the other occupants of the house surrendered when they ran out of ammunition. Vane, beside himself at Burke's death, beat Keightley and his friend Dr. Pechey. Keightley was then held to ransom. His wife was ordered into town to fetch £500, which would then be given to the bushrangers in exchange for Keightley's life. The demands were met and the gang took off, true to their word.

It was now held that Ben Hall had taken control of the gang. His generally calm demeanour during robberies proving to be more suited to leadership then Gilbert's impulsive and whimsical style, and Gilbert's short temper proved to be a recurring issue during their operations. The reward was raised to £4000 for the gang or £100 for their accomplices. The death of Burke had hit Vane hard and tensions arose between him and Gilbert who struck him during an argument and gave Vane a black eye. Vane promptly turned himself in, no longer seeing any appeal in the lifestyle he had adopted.
The gang was once again reduced to the trio of Gilbert, Hall and O'Meally. They passed through Canowindra again but only stayed for a drink. The police were soon hot on their heels and interrupted a robbery. The gang got away but the police were becoming an ever more problematic occurrence. Brushes with the police became more and more frequent with the gang having to drop everything and run on multiple occasions, rarely even having time to get their boots on. In this atmosphere of frustration and increased tension the gang decided to attack Goimbla Station.

Goimbla Station was the home of David Campbell, a squatter who had been assisting police. As with the Keightleys, the gang intended to intimidate him into no longer helping their enemies. Campbell refused to surrender to the bushrangers and took cover in the house and opened fire. Another battle took place, during which the gang burned a barn and a stable, roasting Campbell's horses alive. Mrs. Campbell joined in the fracas, fetching guns and ammunition while being fired at, and the squatter's brother William was wounded. David Campbell refused to give in and seeing O'Meally stand up from behind cover, he fired and hit him in the neck. He died instantaneously. Gilbert and Hall knew they stood no chance and ran away, leaving the blood-drenched corpse of their longest standing confederate behind after picking it clean of valuables.

For the remainder of 1863 and into 1864, the pair continued to rob travellers and raid stores. They recruited James Dunleavy and Jim "Old Man" Gordon to help out. The gang were involved in several shoot-outs with the police including one at the appropriately named Bang Bang Hotel.

These increasingly violent brushes with the law seemed to be bringing out the worst in Hall and Gilbert. When they bailed up a man named Barnes, who they suspected of being involved with the disaster at Goimbla, they threatened to burn his cart and hang him, even going so far as to procure a rope. Hall suggested that instead of a hanging they should flog him, so Barnes was tied to a tree and given 25 lashes with the rope.

Perhaps realising what the bushranging life was doing to him and those around him, Gilbert took his leave of the gang around August. While Ben Hall continued to commit crimes with Dunleavy and the Old Man, Gilbert returned to Victoria where his family lived.

In October 1864 Gilbert returned from his sojourn to rejoin Ben Hall who had been abandoned by the other two in the intervening months. They recruited John Dunn, a seventeen-year-old ex-jockey who had previously telegraphed for Gilbert and O'Meally but was now wanted for skipping bail. Straight away the gang launched into their old tricks with new blood.

Dunn was a natural, immediately keeping pace with the other two as they bailed up a buggy at Breadalbane Plains on 24 October, establishing the new outfit. Many more small-scale robberies followed but Hall was not satisfied with this and wanted another taste of the glory days.

16 November 1864 saw the Hall Gang strike at Black Springs, just outside Jugiong. Dozens of travellers were bailed up, including diggers, teamsters, squatters and Chinese workmen, who were robbed then kept prisoner on the opposite side of a hill to shield them from the road. The gang intended to rob the mail coach that was due that afternoon. A trooper named McLaughlin was bailed up and added to the collective and when the coach arrived shortly after, the gang were surprised by the police escort riding behind. A horseback gunfight ensued. During the gunfight Gilbert shot Sergeant Edmund Parry in the back, killing him instantly. This was the point of no return for Gilbert.

The gang continued a spate of smaller robberies, stealing valuables and horses from the Binalong region. The mail started sending the deliveries by horseback during the night in an effort to foil the robbers but the bush telegraph informed the gang and they adjusted operation accordingly. When they had taken all they desired from the mailbags, they burned the rest of the letters and papers. While Hall and Gilbert always rode together, Dunn was not always present for the gang's nefarious activities.

On Boxing Day, 1864, the gang bailed up Edward Morriss at his store in Binda. They raided the cashbox and took over £100. The gang then escorted Morriss and his wife to a ball at the Flag Hotel. With the bushrangers were their girlfriends Christina McKinnon and the Monks sisters Peggy and Ellen. At the ball the gang sang, danced and shouted drinks all the while acting in a lewd fashion with their female companions. When Morriss escaped to release the gang's horses, the bushrangers fired on him and then turned their ire on his store. The bushrangers set fire to the building causing £1000 in damages and destroying the records of Morriss' debtors.

26 January 1865, after a day of highway robbery, the gang rode to Kimberley's Inn, Collector, and held it up. While Hall and Gilbert raided the inside, Dunn tried to keep guard outside. When Constable Samuel Nelson arrived to arrest the bushrangers, Dunn shot him dead. When Gilbert examined the body, he took the murdered trooper's pistol belt to replace his own.

On 6 February 1865, the gang went to work near Springfield Station. After they had robbed several travellers and a bullock team, a buggy arrived carrying the four Faithfull boys, sons of the squatter who owned *Springfield*. When the gang attempted to bail them up, two of the boys, Percy and George, presented firearms. A gunfight broke out during which Gilbert's horse, spooked by the noise, reared just as he was aiming his revolver. The sudden movement blocked the aim and the horse was killed as the shot hit it in the head. Gilbert took cover behind a fence as bullets struck close. Hall chased the youths, intent on gunning them down as they retreated to their house. The gang ransacked the boys' things and retreated before they could return.

In response to the murders perpetrated by the gang as well as the depredations of Daniel Morgan who had been operating along the Murrumbidgee at the time, the New South Wales government passed the Felons Apprehension Act that would make the three Hall Gang members outlaws by act of parliament. They had thirty days to surrender before the act was passed.

The trio were unfazed, continuing to add to their long list of crimes by stealing horses and firearms, robbing travellers and mail coaches. They brought in a fourth member to the group, long rumoured to have been Braidwood bushranger Tommy Clarke, but more likely Dunn's mate Daniel Ryan. The quartet attempted to rob a gold escort on 13 March near Araluen. The gang opened fire and a battle erupted during which two troopers named Kelly and Byrne were injured while defending the gold. The bushrangers were outmaneuvered and forced to retreat without the loot.

The four bushrangers continued to operate in the wake of the failed heist. Moving their operations closer to Binalong, they stole horses to replace the ones they had been riding on in order to keep ahead of the police. By 17 March the gang was back down to three. They continued to rely on harbourers for food and shelter, the police becoming more dogged in their pursuit.

In May the gang split, Hall seemingly taking leave of Dunn and Gilbert. He set up camp at Billabong Creek but was sold out by one of his harbourers, Mick Coneley. On 5 May Hall was ambushed and shot to death, around 30 bullets being pumped into his body. He never fired a shot and was still days away from being declared an outlaw. Gilbert and Dunn must have sensed the net was closing in. They no longer knew who they could trust, but Dunn was sure his family would provide them shelter.

On 12 May, 1865, Gilbert and Dunn sought refuge with Dunn's grandfather near Binalong. Overnight, the police were informed, and they surrounded the house. The following day the police made their move and as the bushrangers tried to escape, a running gunfight took place. Gilbert was shot through the heart by Constable John Bright and killed instantly, but Dunn escaped. Gilbert was 23 years old. Dunn's grandfather, it would later emerge, was a police informant.

Gilbert's corpse was taken back to Binalong and autopsied. An inquest was held and Gilbert was buried in the paddock of the police station, the grave was unmarked. Dunn was captured nine months later and, after a trial, was hanged in Darlinghurst Gaol for the murder of Constable Nelson.

It has been claimed that in his short life Gilbert had committed more than 600 crimes. His flashy dress sense, jovial personality, chivalry around women, expert horsemanship and flair for drama made him instantly popular among the class of people that admired rogues. Yet, his short fuse, willingness to use lethal force and his lack of distinction between who he victimised are qualities that have painted him as one of the most villainous bushrangers to his detractors. Like many bushrangers he was both as noble and as ignoble as he is described by his supporters and detractors.

Hamilton Spectator and Grange District Advertiser (Vic.: 1860 - 1870),
Saturday 26 November 1864, page 3

THE MURDER OF SERGEANT PARRY

The *Albury Banner* give following particulars of the encounter between the police and Ben Hall's bushranging gang, which resulted in the death of Sergeant Parry — "Bushranging is still rampant. Scarcely had the excitement lulled which arose upon receiving the intelligence of the shooting of Sergeant McGinnerty — scarcely had the police time to remove the outward signs of their month's mourning 'in crepe' for poor Sergeant Smyth, when a third murder is to hand, with the news of another sergeant having had his life sacrificed to the monster crime which is at present disgracing our colony. No less than six times within fifteen days have the up and down mails between Albury and Sydney been stopped and robbed. The latest sticking up was of Monday's mail, near Jugiong. Last week two mails were robbed; the week before there were three; and up to this time, we have news of another robbery with a murder attached to its account.

It appears that the down mail, with an escort of police, was met by the notorious Ben Hall, Johnny Gilbert and Young Dunn. The rascals had previously bailed up no less than 60 persons when the mail arrived. Seeing the state of affairs, sub-inspector O'Neill and Sergeant Parry charged the rascals, but a third man of the force, Roach, ran away into a field and hid himself. The result was that the police ammunition, as usual, running short, each man having we presume one revolver to the bushranger's half-dozen. Parry was killed and sub-inspector O'Neill, after throwing his rifle at Ben Hall's head, was caught but after released. The following account, per telegram from sub-Inspector O'Neill, will give the best history of the encounter. He and Parry, who with his sub inspector, only a few days ago, left Albury, appear to have acted with courage; but in what terms is the despicable conduct of Roach to be regarded, who could run into a paddock and hide himself? What, also, where the sixty or seventy people about, including Constable McLoughlin, whilst this murderous affair was going on? Thus says sub-inspector O'Neill:—

"Gundagai, 17th November, 1864 — Just returned from Jugiong with the remains of Sergeant Parry. Yesterday morning early I started with Constable McLoughlin to Jugiong, with instructions to the police stationed there to be in readiness to relieve Sergeant Parry and myself, who would escort the down mail to Jugiong. At eleven o'clock a.m., Sergeant Parry and I left here riding behind the coach, Constable Roach, from Yass, was with the driver on the box seat. When we go within four and a half miles of Jugiong, we there found sixty or seventy people, including Constable McLoughlin, some carriers, a lot of Chinese, and others, stuck up by Ben Hall, Gilbert, and John Dunn. Sergeant Parry and myself charged the bushrangers, when a deadly encounter ensued. Ben Hall and Dunn opened fire on me, and Gilbert on Parry. We all fired simultaneously several times. I had one ball pass through the upper part of my right arm sleeve, and one in left side of coat, neither injuring me. Sergeant Parry was less fortunate. He received two mortal wounds, one in his left side, and another in the back of his head, and he died immediately. Constable Roach, on witnessing the engagement, took his carbine, revolver, and two old pistols with him, and bolted into a paddock of Pring's, where he took shelter. Had he stood by us Parry's life would have been spared, and Gilbert shot. After emptying my revolver and rifle, I let the latter fly at Hall, striking him severely on the left side of the head. He and Dunn then laid hold of my horse, and all was over — Parry shot, I a prisoner, and Roach an absconder. The party having rifled the mail bags left. Parry's body was brought into Jugiong, and an inquest held, ending with a verdict of wilful murder against Hall, Gilbert and Dunn. Sergeant Parry will be interred tomorrow."

VI

Harry Power at Buckland Gap

While Victoria was home to plenty of bushrangers of various ilks, there was one highwayman that stood (proverbially) head and shoulders above the rest – Harry Power. A former stock thief, horse dealer and prisoner on the *Success* hulk at Hobson's Bay, Power – *alias* Henry Johnstone – had recently escaped from Her Majesty's prison, Pentridge. Since then, the curmudgeonly criminal had taken to highway robberies as a means of survival, though he never had much luck in bailing up *wealthy* people. He'd stuck mostly to bailing up the odd traveller, but now he was determined to hit larger targets.

It was 27 August 1869, towards the end of winter, when Power built a small camp at the Buckland Gap, around a hundred yards from the road. He was situated right in the middle of the road that coaches and travellers would take when travelling between Bright, Beechworth, Bowman's Forest, Buckland and Whorouly among other surrounding towns – perfect positioning for an enterprising highwayman. On Saturdays the farmers would frequently pass through the intersection *en route* to market, and the nearest homestead was a quarter of a mile away from Power's camp, allowing him the freedom of relative isolation. Power built himself a fire and tried to keep warm in the bone-chilling winter cold. The bowel stricture and bunions that plagued him caused no end of discomfort in the winter wilderness, but he did manage to snare a few hours of disrupted sleep.

When morning came, he went about building his trap in the time-tested way that had been utilised by many bushrangers before him: laying logs in the road to create an obstacle for travellers. An oncoming coach would have no option but to halt at the blockade, then Power could make his move. It was a simple plan, but effective.

***

Edward Coady was an experienced coach driver, but even the most seasoned veteran might have gone their entire career without ever encountering a bushranger. In May he had been bailed up by Harry Power when he was taking a coach from Bright to Beechworth. Power had interrupted the journey near Porepunkah and demanded gold, but there was none to be had. The passengers were subjected to demands for payment, a Chinese man receiving particular scrutiny from Power who had an aversion to his people. In the end, Power stole a horse from a passing squatter and took his leave, allowing the coach to continue on.

On Saturday, 28 August, Coady was to drive the Buckland Mail to Myrtleford via Bowman's Forest. The journey began routinely at 6:00am. The coach trundled along its usual route with its cargo of passengers – a servant girl named Ellen Hart, employed by Mrs. Hay of Myrtleford; Mrs. Le Goo the wife of a Chinese storekeeper in Buckland; and William Hazelton, the Bright storekeeper who took position on the box seat.

Part way through the journey the coach stopped at the Gap Hotel. Here the passengers were joined by the young son of Mr. Holloway, the hotel's proprietor. The coach soon took off again, mailbags jostling and jumping with every curve and bump along the way. Riding close behind the coach was Mr. Holloway's daughter, Mrs. Boyd, who had joined the group at her father's pub.

As the horses pulled the coach down the Buckland Gap towards the forest, about 4 miles from Beechworth, suddenly the path was impassable. Coady planted his foot on the brake and peered down where he saw three large logs laying across the road. His gaze drifted up to the bank of the road and he noticed a squat figure waddling from the scrub with a double-barrelled shotgun. He had scarcely any time to think before a voice with a slight Lancashire accent, heavily inflected with an Irish brogue, boomed across the road, "Bail up!"

Harry Power stood six yards away, brandishing his shotgun, with two pistols tucked into his belt. He stood at slightly less than average height, at 5' 6¼" tall, and was covered in scars. Beneath his crumpled felt hat his hair flicked out in greasy silver shocks. His face was mostly beard, but when he spoke one could glimpse his mangled and missing teeth, stained yellow, with blackened gums from excessive pipe smoking. His bright blue eyes peered out from behind crow's feet and a heavy brow as he levelled the shotgun at Coady.

"I seen ye 'afore, ain't I?" Power asked. Coady merely sat agape as Power walked closer.

"Aye, Coady, ain't it? I know ye. I'm sure ye recognise old Harry Power when ye see him. Is there any constables aboard?"

"N-no. None," Coady replied.

"Ye got any firearms?"

Coady shook his head.

Power approached the coach, keeping Coady covered. He jerked the gun up at the driver and William Hazleton, who raised his hands in submission.

"How many passengers?" Power asked.

"Three, besides the boy," Coady replied.

Power ordered Hazleton to get down, which he promptly did. Coady remained seated with his foot on the brake.

"Turn out yer pockets, boy," Power directed Hazleton.

Hazleton took his gold pocket watch and coinage to the value of 4s 6d out of his pockets and extended them to the bushranger.

"On the ground."

Hazleton placed the money and the watch on the ground and stepped back. Power tucked his gun into his elbow and used both hands to take the spoils.

He turned to Coady, "Got any money? Up with it!"

Coady produced a pocketbook and a purse and passed them down. From these Power plucked out £2 13s 6d and a separate threepence. In the pocketbook he found nothing of use, only papers, then handed the purse and pocketbook back. He placed his loot in the pocket of his coat, then approached the side of the coach and peered inside.

He brusquely ordered Ms. Hart, Mrs. Le Goo, and young Holloway to step down from the coach. The women were instructed to hand over their valuables.

Power moved on to the Chinese storekeeper's wife, Mrs. Le Goo, who handed over her purse and Power immediately rifled through it and took the money from inside — a grand total of thirteen shillings.

"Is this all?" Power enquired, gruffly.

"That's all the money I have," Mrs. Le Goo replied.

Power looked the woman over. She was almost as tall as him and outfitted splendidly in a printed dress and a Gainsborough hat. Her ears were pierced but she had no jewellery about her, and she looked far from malnourished, with round cheeks and full bust. He hardened his expression.

"I know yer've got more. Yer've got money or jewellery hidden in there someplace, and I'll strip ye naked as a newborn to find yer hidden treasures!"

Power stepped forward and reached for the woman's chest, dirt-ingrained fingers fixing upon a pearl button. Mrs. Le Goo gasped and tried to back away.

"Give it over," Power barked.

The others attempted to push Power away as he popped open the buttons on the terrified woman's dress with remarkable skill. Hazelton squeezed himself in between the two and shoved Power away.

"That's enough! She has nothing more!"

Power stood back and Coady shrunk away. The bushranger glowered at the woman, whose cheeks were flushed. Mrs. Le Goo still had some pluck in her, and met the highwayman's gaze.

"If it isn't too discourteous, may I have just one shilling so that I may purchase a serve of coffee on the journey?"

Power smirked. He took a shilling from his haul and placed it in the woman's palm. She held his gaze as she opened up her shirt just enough to place the coin in her cleavage before buttoning herself up again. Power shook his head and moved on.

The servant girl, Ellen Hart, stood staring at her feet as Power advanced towards her.

"I have nothing of value, sir," she said, unprompted.

"No money at all? No jewellery?" Power asked.

"None, sir."

"Alright then, as you were," Power grumbled, "Never let it be said that Harry Power was a tyrant to women."

At that moment there was the sound of hoof-beats on the road and Mrs. Boyd finally caught up to the coach. As she came into view she was met by the halted coach and Harry Power aiming a gun at her.

"Bail up!"

The young woman pulled at the reins and her horse came reluctantly to a stop. She dropped down and held her hands up. Her eyes flicked nervously around as she tried to assess the situation.

"Money, girl! Now!"

"I haven't any," Mrs. Boyd replied.

"Hogwash! Up with it now."

"I swear, I have nothing," the trembling woman answered.

Power lowered his gun in frustration.

"A young woman riding a fine horse like that, with such a sidesaddle and saddlebags? That gear must be worth upwards of fourteen pounds! Ye can't tell me that yer've no money."

Power drew close to the woman and stared her down. She could smell the foulness of his breath.

"If yer've no money for me, I'll have to make do with the mount."

Mrs. Boyd's eyes began to well with tears and she clasped her hands together.

"Please, please, mister, let me keep my horse and saddle. They're all I have. Please!"

Power was unmoved and began to walk to the horse.

"Sir, please," Mrs. Boyd continued, "let me ride back to my father's hotel; it's just up the Gap. I'll get you anything you like; anything! Just let me keep my belongings."

"Ye'll be riding nowhere," said Power, "but for £5 I'll give yer horse back."

Mrs. Boyd began to sob.

"I have no money, I already told you that!"

Power paused and looked back at the woman.

"If ye really are strapped, as ye say, then ye can borrow the money from one of the other women."

"But you've just robbed them," Coady called out from his perch on the coach.

"Aye, so I have, but I know the tall one's got some money about her still. Ask her. I don't care where the damned money comes from."

As Power took the reins of the horse, Mrs. Boyd began to sob into her hands. The bushranger was unaffected by the sorrow of the woman and simply directed everyone into the bush where he had a fire waiting.

"It's a cold morning. I wouldn't want yers to freeze to death. Get warmed up and then come back."

As the group walked into the bush, Coady remained on the coach with the Holloway boy. Power glared up at Coady.

"I've a good mind to shoot ye," Power said.

"What for?"

"I've eyes and ears everywhere. I know yer been talking disrespectfully of me in Fisher's pub."

Coady's mind began to race.

"No, no, nothing of the sort, Harry. All I said was that if I ever saw you at a shanty or a public house I'd shout for you."

Power grunted then turned his attention to the child.

Holloway had a comforter around his shoulders to keep himself warm, and he was clasping a penknife. As the bushranger approached he showed no sign of fear.

"Got a penknife there, lad?" Power asked. Holloway nodded. "I'll give ye a shilling fer it."

Holloway offered up no protest and passed the knife to Power, who pressed a shilling into the boy's hand.

"Mr. Power," Holloway began, "I'll give you the shilling back if you give my sister back her horse."

Power smiled and chuckled, but did not oblige.

"Fer a sixpence I'll take that quilt, " said Power. Holloway hesitated, but upon seeing Power tighten his grip on his weapon he relented. Power pressed a sixpence into the boy's hand while maintaining eye contact.

"Good boy."

As the group stood around the fire, which was a welcome warmth in the biting cold morning, none spoke. Ellen Hart plated a hand reassuringly on Mrs. Boyd's back, but it was little comfort.

"It's not fair," Mrs. Boyd bemoaned, "I won that saddle in a raffle. It's the only thing of value I have and I couldn't possibly afford to replace it or my dear horse."

When the group returned to the road, Power was waiting, cradling the shotgun in his arms.

"Alright, now, I want them mailbags out."

Coady grabbed the bags of mail from the coach and threw them at Power's feet.

Hazelton had, by this point, had a gutful and approached Power.

"Power, I should inform you that Mrs. Boyd is indeed a poor woman, and the gear on her horse was won at a raffle, not purchased outright. It's a blackguard that would take the only things of worth from a woman who has so little to her name."

Power cocked an eyebrow.

"Is that so, is it?"

"Indeed it is."

"Any other words of wisdom for me, boy?"

Hazelton spluttered slightly, but regained his composure. He pointed to the mailbags that Power had begun to empty.

"Yes. You won't get any money out of those."

"Won't I, now?" Power said without looking up.

"They're of no use to you. Any letters containing money only travel by escort."

Power dropped the mail in his hands into the bag and rose to his full height.

"Well," he said menacingly to Hazelton, "yer just a wealth of knowledge, ain't ye?"

The heated exchange was suddenly interrupted by the arrival of a new traveller, to which Hazelton snidely remarked, "Here's a haul for you."

The traveller, a dairyman named John Hughes, was on his way up to Beechworth. As he approached the stalled coach, he was promptly bailed up and ordered to turn out his pockets.

When the man reached for his inside coat pocket, Power cocked his gun.

"It is not there where people are in the habit of keeping their money."

Hesitantly, the man withdrew money from his coat and handed it over.

"Alright, turn out the pockets in them trousers," Power said, waving his gun.

The man pulled out the lining of the trousers and showed the bushranger that they were empty. Power grunted and pointed for him to join the others.

At this juncture Coady leaned over and called to Power. The bushranger waddled over, putting the stolen money away as he went.

"Could I move the coach a little way off the road? The incline is putting strain on the brakes."

"Stay where I can see ye," Power said, gesturing to the scrub. Coady moved the coach off the road and climbed down.

Soon a Chinese man came along the road and was halted and ordered to give up his money, but managed to keep the two ounces of gold hidden in his coat a secret. He then was added to the throng. In quick succession there followed two carts; both were bailed up and the drivers relieved of their valuables.

Then came a spring-cart, driven by a man named McGuffie who was on his way from Buffalo to O'Brien's Station. Power brandished his shotgun to urge the driver to come to a halt.

"Bail up!"

The cart came to a stop and Power approached.

"I'll be taking any money ye have on ye," said Power.

"I'm afraid I don't have much. I'm a poor man myself."

Power was unmoved. "Be that as it may, hop down and hand it over."

The man did as he was told, placing his money on the ground. Power took the spoils

"Please, I'm very poor and I work hard for my money..."

"And I am sorry to hear it," said Power, "but I want money, and I am obliged to take it."

With the enforced cooperation of his victims, Harry Power had taken £1 16s from Hughes and 17s 6d from a Bowman's Forest local named Rath to add to his booty.

For the next three hours, Power kept eleven prisoners under his command by the fire, occupying their attention by spinning yarns. He also mentioned that he had been intending on bailing up James Emptage, a colleague of Coady's, but as Emptage had been driving much too fast, he had not had a chance to stop him. Despite the number of people at his mercy, none attempted to overpower him.

Power fished a saddle and bridle from McGuffie's spring-cart and approached Coady's coach. Having decided to return Mrs. Boyd's horse, and needing a good mount to carry him away, Power attempted to take the snip horse from the Buckland coach, (that is the horse on the offhand side closest to the wheel). The horse bucked and refused to allow the bushranger to prepare him to ride, to which Power replied by striking the animal repeatedly with the butt of his shotgun. Power then took the lead horse, named Little Johnny, from the coach, equipped it with the stolen saddle and bridle, and disappeared into the bush. Harry Power would next be spotted near Stanley at 4:00pm.

Dazed and confused by the bizarre turn of events they had just experienced, the victims slowly began to return to their conveyances, counting their blessings that things had not escalated.

When news of the bail ups reached Beechworth, Sgt. Baber launched a search party to head to Bowman's Forest to find Power's trail. Alas, as was an all too common problem, there were not enough men to get a reasonable sweep of the area and thus Power got away without further incident.

It was not long before the government, frustrated by Power's ability to avoid capture, offered a £200 reward for his capture. Power was now officially in the big league but he would soon discover he needed an accomplice, and it would signal his downfall.

Harry Power

When we picture bushrangers we think of wild young men on horseback dodging police and sticking up coaches but Harry Power certainly did not fit that image. Power — *alias* Henry Johnstone — is forever remembered as the tutor in crime of Ned Kelly but there was a time when he could capture the imagination on his own terms.

Power was born in Waterford, Ireland, in 1819 before emigrating with his family to England during the Great Famine. Settling in the north of England, Harry worked in a spinning mill in Manchester. It was not long before his rebellious nature manifested.

Power received three months imprisonment for vagrancy and later did time for drunkenness. His first major offence, however, was stealing shoes, which got him transported for seven years, arriving in Van Dieman's Land in May, 1842. It's probable that Power reunited with his mother upon gaining his freedom as she had been transported to Van Dieman's Land for stealing chickens in 1841. Receiving his Ticket-of-Leave in November 1847, Harry soon travelled to the mainland. He worked as a stockman in New South Wales before going south and becoming a horse dealer in Geelong.

In 1855 he was accosted by two mounted troopers who questioned him on where he got his horse. They refused to believe that he had legitimate ownership of the animal and when he refused to go with them to the station one trooper drew his sabre and threatened him. In a panic, Power shot the trooper in the arm and fled for the newly formed border between New South Wales and what had become Victoria. Here he was arrested. He was tried for horse stealing as Henry Johnstone and on 26 September 1855 was sentenced to thirteen years hard labour, despite having paperwork to prove the legitimacy of his ownership of the horse. He was sent to Williamstown where he was imprisoned on the hulk *Success*.

While doing time on *Success*, Power was involved in a mutiny. The bush-ranger Captain Melville led a small group of inmates to steal the tow boat that took the launch boat from *Success* to shore on 22 October 1856. During the ensuing scuffle a man named John Turner was drowned and a constable named Owen Owens was killed by a blow to the head with a rock breaking hammer or metal hook. The convicts were soon recaptured. Harry, still as Henry Johnstone, was charged with the other seven men with two counts of murder. Only Melville was sentenced.

Power gained his new Ticket-of-Leave in 1862 and headed back to Geelong where he immediately broke the conditions of his ticket and took to the diggings. He was soon back in court and in 1863 he was convicted of horse stealing in Beechworth. While in prison on that offence more charges were raised and Harry was dragged out of prison and tried again. He was found guilty of these charges, keeping him in prison for seven years. He was sent to Pentridge Prison but it would not hold him long.

In Pentridge Harry was prone to visits to the prison hospital due to a bowel stricture that could cause bouts of extreme discomfort and render him useless for labour for two to three weeks at a time.

On 16 February 1869 Power escaped from Pentridge. Having been assigned to a party clearing land by Merri Creek in preparation for construction on the perimeter wall, Harry had made sure that he was on light duties due to his health. Entrusted with taking the plant waste to the mullock heap, Power hid in a divot under the heap and when muster was called he slipped out through a gap in the wall before his absence was noticed. He acquired clothing from a nearby farm and armed himself with a crude handmade spear before stealing a horse and riding to freedom.

After a great deal of travel, he set up a camp on a mountain overlooking the King River Valley now known as Power's Lookout. From here he sought support from the Lloyds and their relatives the Quinns, gradually expanding his network of sympathisers all the way out to Whitfield. Power knew that he would have to keep his sympathisers on his side and began a career of highway robbery in order to fund his supporters.

Power worked solo robbing shanties and farms, and was unafraid to use violence if necessary. However this proved to be too much work for too little reward. Power now turned to highway robbery. Far from a charming highwayman in the mold of his New South Wales contemporaries like Gilbert, Hall and Thunderbolt, Power's demeanour was coarse and belligerent and won him no sympathy from his victims.
This sudden spate of robberies led to a big manhunt and much consternation around the fledgling colony. Power was believed to be cohabiting with a woman near Benalla at the time but nobody could find him.

In July he was spotted eyeing off horses at Mount Battery station and fired upon. With him was a young man who was probably fifteen year old Ned Kelly, a nephew of his harbourers the Lloyds and Quinns. The owner of the station sneaked up behind the pair and fired at them causing young Kelly to momentarily freeze in terror before they mounted and escaped. Power seems to have discarded Kelly from his service after that for a time, courting others as assistants before opting to simply get on with bushranging on his own.

One of Power's most infamous robberies was near Beechworth when he stopped a mail coach by placing logs in the road. He proceeded to take what little money he could from the travellers, including taking a quilt from a young boy, and attempted to deprive a young woman of her horse and saddle before sticking up a dairy cart and robbing that too. Power took one of the horses from the cart and used it to get away leaving the small group of his victims standing around a little bonfire he had made.

Power had quickly become a big problem for the Victoria Police and a £200 reward was offered for his capture. Power ventured into New South Wales at this time and committed a series of robberies around the Riverina. It seemed for all intents and purposes that this cranky, grey bandit was untouchable and by the end of 1869 Power had seemingly vanished with no reported sightings or leads, rendering police pursuits ineffective.

Unfortunately, Power was not invincible and his health made for a difficult time in the bush. His bowel stricture and bunions resulted in frequent clandestine visits to doctors. To alleviate the pain in his feet he would wear oversized boots. The fact that he was well into middle age, with all of the physical difficulties that brings with it, would not have been much help either.

February 1870 saw Power re-emerge with a vengeance robbing everyone from stockmen to police officers. After the initial string of robberies Harry Power and Ned Kelly reunited briefly. Likely Ned, in a bid to get some money for his mother who was behind in her rent, had begged Power for another chance. Together they robbed Robert McBean, a well respected magistrate, of his watch, horse and riding gear on his own property. The duo travelled as far as Geelong where Power reputedly checked out his old haunts with Ned by his side. They eventually returned to Power's hideout, where he had a pet peacock that acted as a guard dog. Power's shelter was a mia-mia, or lean-to, that had a shotgun hanging up inside so that Power had a weapon to hand in case anybody tried to sneak up on him in his sleep.

When teenage Ned was found trying to open the gates at the Moyhu pound to release impounded stock, the poundkeeper threw him out of the saddle and thrashed him. This resulted in Harry and Ned later bailing the poundkeeper up. Ned threatened to shoot the poundkeeper on the spot but instead Power gave him three months to get his affairs in order before he would be shot. Shortly afterwards Ned was arrested for assisting Power. During interrogation, Kelly described Harry as irascible and with a violent temper. He also described a hollow tree Power used as a lookout point — his "watchbox" — and his habit of seeing a doctor about his stricture. Ned was bounced around the courts but the various charges never stuck and he was soon released, but he was viewed afterwards with great suspicion.

At this time Jack Lloyd was detained on suspicion of highway robbery. It was believed that he had committed several of the crimes attributed to Power, which he denied. Robert McBean, still furious about his encounter with the bushranger, had remembered a statement Power had made that he could buy his watch back from Jack Lloyd for £15. McBean suggested this to the police and soon Lloyd negotiated a deal with superintendents Nicolson and Hare to turn Power in; the temptation of the reward — now £500 — proving irresistible.

Lloyd took a police party, consisting of Nicolson, Hare, Sergeant Montford and an Aboriginal tracker named Donald most of the way but got spooked and left the police to find their own way up during torrential rain. Fortunately, after days without food or sleep, Donald was able to find the camp due to smoke from a campfire. They approached Power's mia-mia as he slept and Nicolson pounced on him. Dragged out by his feet, Power was unable to resist and was promptly arrested, complaining about not having a fair chance of escape while the starving police ate his food rations. It turned out that the rain had forced Power's peacock to find shelter where it did not detect the arrival of the police, and as he had no warning Power was unable to prepare himself with the hanging shotgun.

Power was put on trial in Beechworth and promptly imprisoned in Pentridge for fifteen years. While in the gaol he became somewhat of a celebrity, being interviewed for a newspaper feature called the Vagabond Papers where he opened up about his life of roguery. He did not live quietly, frequently getting into trouble for smoking, being where he wasn't meant to be and generally getting into mischief.

In 1885 Power was released into a world that had left him behind. The Kelly Gang and the Moonliters had come and gone. The towns were becoming rapidly urbanised with trains and other modern conveniences. The prison hulks at Williamstown were decommissioned and scrapped save for one – *Success*. Power now found himself in his twilight years acting as a tour guide on a craft that was once the source of much misery to him. Meanwhile, he was living with his half-sister and her daughter in law. When *Success* went on tour in 1891 Power stayed behind to do a victory lap of the places he had known when his notoriety was fresh.

Shortly after he departed, an unidentified body was found drowned in the Murray River, partly eaten by aquatic creatures. Due to items found on the body, it was identified as that of Harry Power. It was believed that he had drowned in the river.

Leader (Melbourne, Vic. : 1862 - 1918, 1935), Saturday 18 June 1870, page 19

COMMITTAL OF POWER, THE BUSHRANGER.
[FROM THE *OVENS AND MURRAY ADVERTISER.*]

Henry Power, alias Johnston, was brought up charged with highway robbery under arms, near Hooper's Crossing on the Ovens, on the 7th May, 1869. Arthur Woodside, a squatter, detailed the occurrence. He deposed that he was on the road when the Bright coach was approaching the crossing. He saw the prisoner walk out of the bush with a double-barrelled gun in his hand and stop the coach. Witness rode up, but Power presented the gun at him and ordered him to dismount. Prisoner then told the driver to throw out the parcels, which was done. (Prisoner here told witness to speak up, and said he could speak loud enough when they had met on a previous occasion.) Prisoner, after making a Chinaman in the coach show his money, some few shillings, took witness's horse, bridle, saddle, and spurs. Prisoner promised to return the horse, and did so about five weeks afterwards. The prisoner's gun was cocked and capped. Witness offered no resistance. Edward Coady, coachdriver, stated that on 7th May he was returning from Bright to Beechworth. When about two miles on the Beechworth side of Hooper's, the prisoner came across the bush, and, presenting a gun at witness, told him to "pull up." He then told witness to turn out the swag of gold he had on the. coach. Told him there was no gold. Prisoner said. "Here's another coming; don't you stir." When Woodside came close, prisoner told him to pull up and dismount. Witness then pulled out some of the mail bags. Prisoner took one or two of them in his hand and threw them back, saying there was nothing he wanted in them. He did not open them. Witness then threw a paper parcel put. Prisoner broke the paper and threw it back, saying it was of no use to him. The Chinaman's carpet bag was then thrown out by the owner. Prisoner opened the bag, looked at some of the things which were in it, but took nothing from it. Prisoner wanted to take the leading horse. He (witness) told the prisoner that the horse would be of no use to him, as it had not been broken in to saddle. Prisoner said that he wanted nothing from witness on that occasion, as whatever he (witness) had he worked hard for. Woodside got on the coach with witness, and prisoner told them that they could start. Prisoner rode off on Mr. Woodside's horse towards the Ovens River. The prisoner informed the magistrate that the gun was cocked, and entered into an explanation as to his having wished to purchase an oilskin coat and pair of leggings from the driver, which the latter refused to sell. He further stated that he told the driver that he would not take any money from him, as he (Power) knew that drivers earned their money hardly, as he did himself. Power was next charged with highway robbery under arms from Thomas Thomas, at the Buckland road, on the 7th May, 1869.

Thomas Oliver Thomas, storekeeper, residing at Wangaratta, stated that on 7th May, 1869, he was on the Buckland road travelling on horseback to Hooper's Crossing. He was riding one horse and leading another, and when within about seven yards of him observed that the prisoner had him covered with a double-barrelled gun. Prisoner called out to witness to stop. Witness was on the point of going when prisoner called out "If you go, I'll fire." He (witness) then came towards prisoner, who told him not to come too near, and said that his gun could kill at 300 yards. Prisoner then asked witness what money he had. Told him first that he had none. Told him afterwards that he had a couple of notes. Prisoner said to hand them to him, which witness did. Prisoner then asked him what had become of the other fellow who was with him (witness). Told prisoner that he did not know. Witness then asked prisoner to give him one of the pounds back, as he had taken all his money. Prisoner said he would not, as he had just stuck up the coach and got nothing. He further told witness to consider himself lucky that he did not take his hat and coat from him. In answer to the prisoner, witness said that he did not remember his asking whether he was a policeman or detective, or inquiring what he was doing off the road. Power then entered into an explanation of the circumstances that occurred, stating it was a matter of indifference to him what charges were brought, only he wanted to hear the truth spoken.

Henry Power was then charged with highway robbery under arms at the Buckland Gap, on 28th August, 1869. Edward Coady stated he was driving the Buckland coach from Beechworth to Bright on the 28th August, 1869. When going down the Gap, witness observed some logs on the road. Put his foot on the break to stop the coach, and pulled up, when he saw prisoner standing on the bank about five or six yards distant with a gun presented. Prisoner said that he thought he had seen witness before, and asked whether there were any constables on board, whether he had any firearms, and how many passengers there were. Told him that there were no constables or firearms, and that there were three passengers besides the boy. Mr. Hazleton, a passenger, turned out his pockets and produced some silver and a watch at prisoner's direction. Prisoner told Mr. Hazleton to put his money and watch on the ground, and he did so. Prisoner told Hazleton to stand back, and came forward and took up the money and watch. Prisoner then told witness to turn out whatever money he had. Gave him a pocket-book and purse, in which were £2 13s. 6d. and a threepenny piece; the latter coin prisoner gave to the little boy in the coach. After emptying the purse, prisoner returned the pocket-book, containing some papers, to witness. Prisoner told the ladies to turn out. Both came out of the coach, and one of them, Mrs. Le Goo, handed her purse to prisoner. He opened it and took out the money, which amounted to 13s. She told prisoner that was all the money she had, and asked him for a shilling back to get a cup of coffee on the road. Prisoner returned her a shilling. Miss Hart told prisoner she had no money, and he took no further notice of her. At this time, another young, lady— Mrs. Boyd he believed was her name — came down the Gap on horseback. Prisoner also told her to bail up, and asked whether she had any money; she replied that she had not. Prisoner said he did not know how it was that young ladies could ride round the country with horses and side-saddles and yet had no money in their pockets. Prisoner then said he would take the horse and saddle from her. Mrs. Boyd asked him if he would allow her to go back to her father's on top of the Gap, and she would give him anything he wanted. Prisoner told her he would not, but that if she gave him £5 he would give her the horse. Mrs. Boyd replied she had no money. Prisoner said if she chose to borrow the money from the other ladies in the coach — he knew that the tall one had money — he would not ask where she got it, but would give her back the horse. Prisoner then said as it was a cold morning he had got a fire ready for them close by, at his camp. Prisoner then said he had a good mind to shoot him (witness). He inquired what for. Prisoner replied for speaking disrespectfully of him in Fisher's bar. Witness replied that he had said nothing further than that if he met Power at a shanty or public house he would shout for him. The other persons then went to the fire, about a hundred yards distant, close to the road side, leaving witness on the coach. Prisoner stopped close to the coach and purchased a knife from a little boy, who also remained. He gave the boy a shilling for the knife, and the little boy offered him back the shilling if prisoner would give his sister (Mrs. Boyd) her horse. The prisoner smiled at this. The passengers then came back from the fire, and prisoner told him (witness) to turn out some of the mail bags, which was done. Mr. Hazleton told him that the bags would be of no use to him, as no money went that way, that all went by escort. Prisoner returned the bags. A man on foot was at that time coming up the Gap, and on his approach prisoner told him to bail up and deliver up his money.

The man put his hand into his coat pocket, when prisoner told him to take it out, saying, "It was not there people were in the habit of carrying their money." Prisoner then told the man to turn out his trousers' pockets, which was done, but there was no money in them. Witness had his foot on the break all this time, and asked prisoner to allow him to take the coach further down the Gap. Prisoner gave him permission to do so. A Chinaman coming along was then stopped; then two drays were noticed proceeding towards where they were standing. Power told all who were standing round to keep still, or he would shoot them. When the drays, with which were two men, came near, prisoner ordered them to stop and deliver up their money. A man, with a spring cart then came forward, and he was likewise stopped by prisoner, and told to give up his money. This man said that he was a very poor man, and had not much money. Prisoner told him to get out of the cart, put his money on the ground, and then stand back. This was done. Prisoner then came forward and took up the money. Prisoner then said to witness that he must have one of his horses. He took a saddle and bridle from one of the drays that came down the Gap. Prisoner said that he must have the snip horse — the off-side wheeler from the coach — and told some of the men who were standing about to unharness the horse and saddle it for him. One of them led the horse to the prisoner after it was saddled. Prisoner led the horse about forty yards further off. He tried to get on the horse with the gun in his hand, but the horse would not allow him to get near it. Witness thought that prisoner then laid down the gun, and tried to mount the horse, but could not. Prisoner then said he would take the brown horse, one of the leaders. The horse was unharnessed and saddled, and led away by prisoner. He got on this horse, and rode back to where the coach was, and told those assembled there they could start. Before starting prisoner gave Mrs. Boyd her horse, saddle, and bridle. Prisoner said that he would ride on ahead, and stick up in front of the coach. He rode down as far as Rowe's, and then turned back. When he met the coach on his return, he said to witness and the others that he had changed his mind. That was the last witness saw of the prisoner. The coach was stopped about three hours.

Prisoner, on being asked whether he had any questions to ask witness, said no, that all the driver had said was correct. Wm. S. Hazleton, storekeeper, residing at Bright, and Ellen Hart, residing at Wahgunyah, also gave corroborative testimony.

Prisoner, to last witness: I never asked you for money.

Witness: Yes; you asked me if I had any money, and when I replied "No," you replied, "I don't suppose you have."

This closed the evidence in the third charge. The prisoner was then charged with the highway robbery of John Hughes, on the 28th August.

John Hughes, dairyman, residing at Whorouley, deposed that on the 28th of last August he was travelling towards Beechworth. On coming near the Buckland Gap he saw the coach standing in the road and a number of persons crowding about. On driving up saw prisoner walking about with a gun in his hand. Prisoner ordered witness to drive on one side, and then told him (witness) that he was doing a little sticking-up business. He asked witness for money, and on being told that he had very little, prisoner cocked both barrels of the gun and ordered witness out of the cart, in order to see how much he had. Witness got down and drew £1 18s. from his pocket, which he handed to prisoner. This witness corroborated the evidence of Hazleton and Coady.

William B. Montford, sergeant of police stationed in Melbourne, deposed to the arrest of the prisoner in the Glenmore ranges as already reported in these columns.

In reply to the bench, prisoner said he had nothing to say to any of the charges. The prisoner was committed to take his trial on the first three charges at the General Sessions to be held in August, and on the fourth charge he was committed for trial at the Circuit Court in October.

* * *

The *Ovens Spectator* writes :— " It is not generally known, but it is nevertheless a fact, that about four years ago, when Power's former companion, M'Kay, was arrested and placed in Beechworth gaol, he stated to one of the police officers that Power and another man were the murderers of Somes Davis, who disappeared so mysteriously about six or seven years ago, and that Power took the most prominent part in the foul deed. The information given was not sufficient for the police to act upon, and so the matter dropped. Among those, however, who made inquiry into the matter, suspicion was generally directed against Power and the notorious Toke, of Mitta Mitta. It will be in the recollection of our readers that about six or seven years back, Somes Davis, a storekeeper and gold buyer, left Yackandandah in the direction of the Mitta Mitta, to buy gold, and he disappeared and was never seen again. From the marks of his spurs on the saddle, and from some other circumstances, it seemed as if he had been violently dragged from his horse, previously to his being killed. The rumor at first spread that Davis was still alive and was keeping out of the way of his creditors was soon disproved, as it turned out, on his affairs being wound up, that he could pay a good deal more than 20s. in the pound. His body never yet has been found, and the mystery has never been cleared up. If, however, M'Kay's statement was true, Power has something more to answer for than all his known crimes."

"It is alleged," says the *Kyneton Guardian*, "that the black tracker who led the police to Power's retreat was no other than the man Kelly, who was so soon discharged after his arrest, in consequence of no one being able to identify him. If it had been reflected that Kelly was standing in the dock of the Kyneton Police Court between 10 and 11 o'clock on Friday morning, it would have been seen that it was a physical impossibility for him to have assisted in any way in the capture of Power, which took place at half-past 7 on Sunday morning, at a place over 200 miles distant from Kyneton. Kelly has never left Kyneton since his discharge. He has been seen about the streets every day, and he is waiting for his friends either to come for him — they were expected last night — or to send him money with which to defray the expenses of his journey home."

The Bulletin (Sydney, N.S.W.), Vol. 13 No. 704 (12 Aug 1893), p.20

HARRY POWER: A PERSONAL REMINISCENCE.
(FOR THE BULLETIN.)

Hare's one-sided "Last of the Bushrangers" had started the talk, and yarns of the Kelly Gang led to stories of Harry Power, the daring bushranger, who, after spending some 20 years in prison, twice escaping therefrom at Williamstown and Pentridge, and being four times "east for death," yet lived long enough to meet an unromantic, "natural" death in the dull waters of the Murray. Let me here tell my story.

One day at the end of 1889 I had gone up to Melb. University on official business connected with the Australasian Association for the Advance of Science. While I was there, a little grey man in black trousers, blue coat and soft felt hat, entered and asked for the Association secretary. The Professor being absent, however, the quiet-looking, little grey man was directed to me as a possible source of information on Association subjects.

"My name is Power," said he. Noting my uninformed look, the visitor, with a peculiar quick, furtive, sidelong glance from the corner of his eye, observed, "I'm Harry Power!"

Something in the glance and the tone told me that he was none other than the ex-bushranger, and apparently my understanding was recorded on my face, for the little grey man, with "I see you know me, sir," showed his appreciation of the fact. Power was desirous of being engaged as guide to a party of A.A.A.S. members who purposed an excursion into Gippsland. "There ain't many people who know the ranges like I do," said the little grey man.

"I had to know them once, you see, so I learned near every rock and stump, and every wallaby-track on them. I believe I'm the only man alive who knows where the crows nest in those parts. It's a long time now since I was there, but I could take you to it still." Then he described to me a wondrous, great rocky cliff, whitened with the crow-slime of ages, which at a certain time of the year was rendered almost black by the thousands of nesting crows upon it. His style was graphic, especially when his yarn verged upon the Sinbadic in its steepness.

"Once," he went on, "when they were out after me, I was going through the ranges a little off the track, when I saw old Judge A'Beckett riding along the road on circuit. I followed him most of the afternoon waiting for a chance. I didn't want to kill him, for I'd never kill anyone except in self-defence. My notion was to lift his purse, and so on, and splice him to a fence, and so keep him late for the assizes."

So intent, however, was he on watching the Judge, that he neglected to keep an eye on his own safety. Then it came about that he himself was captured by a party of police and others who were following the Judge at some distance. That night, Judge A'Beckett, bearing that Power was in the gaol, and knowing the bushranger well, visited him in his cell. The Judge was much amused when the bushranger told him how near he had come to being the unwilling subject of a highway robbery.

"I knew I was safe in telling him, for I knew he was a good fellow and a straight, honest man, and wouldn't use it against me. Ah, but his eye twinkled when he came to sum up in my case. No one but himself and me knew what I was after when they got me, and no one knew why the Judge smiled at me from the Bench. But he only gave me my proper stretch for horse-stealing. Yes, Judge A'Beckett was a decent fellow."

I asked whether he had ever thought of writing his autobiography. "Yes, I've sometimes thought about it," said he, "but I've made up my mind never to do it. You see, I've a married sister, who's a decent, hard-working woman, and she has children. Now, it wouldn't be nice for those children if I wrote a book about myself, with piles of stuff in it that any dirty blackguard could throw up at them when they were grown up to decent men and women. No, sir, books live longer and reach farther than memories, and I think it just as well to let the memory of their bad old uncle, Harry Power, die out quietly, and not have his doings always stuck before them in print. 'The Vagabond' once offered me a few hundreds for the true history of my life, but I thought of those little children, and I refused."

In answer to an inquiry as to whether he didn't find life pretty slow now, he said, smiling, "Well, I'm an old man now, you see. Besides, living up there (here his thumb pointed Pentridge-wards over his shoulder) gets you used to living quietly."

Here he drifted on into reminiscences of Pentridge, and the time when he was chief cook there — and a good cook he was, so they say, thrifty as a Chinaman and cleanly as a Scotch housewife.

"Once," said Power, "I had a dirty devil for an assistant, who wouldn't keep his pots clean. He burned the skilly a couple of times, and I warned him, for that was bad for them all. A day or two afterwards I watched him again, and I saw the copper was dirty. It was bad luck for him. He put in the water, and when it was on the boil and he was going to put the meal in, I up with his heels and sent him in instead. Just so. He cried a bit after he got out, but it did him good. Of course, I got into a bit of a row, but I didn't get much for it. You see, he sort of deserved it."

Over another piece of his rough justice he escaped all punishment. He was in hospital, and very sick. A couple of larrikins were in, too, just well enough to make themselves a special and grievous nuisance. One of them had a concertina. How he contrived to get it into the gaol hospital was a mystery, but that he did manage it, the gaol records concerning Power's interference with it and its owner prove. After "lock-up" at night, the larrikin owner of the squeaking instrument used to play on it, much to his own delight, but more to the disgust of the others.

"I waited one night," said the little grey man, "till 'lock-up' was over, and the keys placed in guard. I knew then that, no matter how much row I made, no one could get into the ward inside a quarter of an hour. The blackguard began with his squeaking windbag, and a poor sick wretch asked him to stop. He wouldn't. So I slipped out of bed, and took the towel-rollers off the door. I made the concertina-man take one, and I took the other. 'Now, my boy,' says I, 'you and me's going to play a duet, and I hope you'll like it.' He made a devil of a row. When the warders got in, I was a bit tired myself, but he was in a bad mess, and his concertina was smashed to smithereens. He didn't play any more. They had me up, of course, over the business, but the visiting magistrate dismissed the case, saying my conduct deserved praise rather than punishment. He was right, too!"

"Since I've been out, though, I've got on pretty well. Big Clarke is very kind to me, and wants me to live on one of his stations for the rest of my life. But I prefer to knock about a bit. Sometimes I stay awhile at one of his places, and sometimes I go to see my sister. But I have an adventure now and again. Last time I went to see my sister, I found some surveyors at work on her place, and I asked her what they were doing there. She said they were surveying it, because someone had made a claim to it. You see she had no title, but had lived on it nearly long enough to get possessory title. My blood was up, and I wasn't going to see the sister and the children done out of their bit of land. So I took my gun and rode out after those surveyors. I came on them, and ordered them to clear out. They said they didn't take orders from old swagmen. 'Then, by God,' says I, 'you'll take orders from me. I'm Harry Power, the bushranger who always kept his word, and I give you my word now that if you ain't on your horses and away inside two minutes I'll shoot you in your tracks.' Lord, it was fun to see them. They dropped their fixings and ran for their horses. Just to frighten them thoroughly, I rode after them about 10 miles. Their fixings are at the sister's now. They never called for them, and I don't think they will so long as they know I'm alive!"

If my memory serves, the old man lived long enough to see his sister get the coveted title. The A.A.A.S. excursion to Gippsland was, however, only to be a pleasure-trip, so Harry Power's services as a guide were not required, I never met him again.

VII

꧁❧꧂

Thunderbolt's Last Ride

Wednesday, 25 May 1870, began as any usual day would for Frederick Wordsworth Ward, *alias* Captain Thunderbolt. He arose early and left his camp at the Big Rock on horseback. The rock was a bizarre natural structure, like a huge marble defying physics to teeter on a cliff, split down the middle providing ample space to hide for a bushranger. As he set about packing up his camp, a deep ache in his knee reminded him of the time he was shot while evading capture with his old partner Fred Britten at this very location, back in the infancy of his bushranging career. That was over half a decade ago by now. For nearly a year Ward had stayed fairly dormant, avoiding his usual occupation and instead relying on harbourers for his supplies and shelter most of the time. Bushranging had lost its lustre and Ward was now seen by many as the last of that dying breed. The most notorious of the lot had collected the wages of their sins already: Morgan, shot by a bounty hunter; Hall, shot thirty times by a police party; Gilbert, shot during a chase by police; Pat Connell, shot and trampled by mounted troopers; Tommy Clarke, hanged in Darlinghurst. Since his wife Mary Ann had left him, and his offsiders had done the same, Ward was now a lone wolf with a price on his head, so he had withdrawn except when he was desperate for cash. That hospitality he had relied on for the past ten months or so had begun to dry up now he no longer had significant income from his robberies to pay the harbourers off with, and now he was back at the robbery game.

As usual, Ward had only a vague idea of what he wanted to do for the day. Living as an outlaw meant that he had nobody to answer to except his own conscience, but it also meant that he was often rudderless. After some internal deliberation, he decided he felt like visiting John Blanch's Royal Oak Inn for a mix of business and pleasure. Two nights previously Ward had visited the inn to buy a quart of rum. When he attempted to pay with a £5 cash order from a local squatter named Wyndham, Blanch had become suspicious and refused to cash it. Ward had harboured the feeling of indignity and decided to take out some revenge on the publican. He bundled up his gear and went to where he had hobbled his two horses, both greys and finely built, packed the bundle onto one horse before mounting the other and heading down from his lair.

Blanch's Inn was situated at Church Gully between Bendemeer and Uralla, and it was on the stretch of road leading up to the inn that he began work for the day. It was a simple, weatherboard building that was a little more upmarket than the normal bush pubs Ward had encountered. Naturally, the pub's placement meant that it attracted plenty of customers, and that made it an excellent place to sit in wait for a bushranger. Ward rode to the inn and hobbled his packhorse near the veranda. Now all he had to do was wait.

At 2:00pm, Ward saw a vehicle coming from the direction of Uralla carrying a man and woman. The occupants of the buggy were Blanch, the proprietor of the inn, and his wife, who were returning on a spring cart from an outing to Uralla. Ward moved his mount into the road, and upon the cart coming close he ordered the occupants to, "Bail up!"

Blanch and his wife were incredulous but did as they were instructed. Ward ordered Blanch to hand over his money, but when the man instead laughed Ward barked, "No humbugging, you would not give me the bottle of rum a few nights ago. I am a robber!" Ward presented a revolver and though Blanch was not certain who this man was, he knew better than to take the situation lightly. He feebly offered up coins to the value of four shillings and sixpence, to which Ward scoffed.

"I don't take silver. I'm laid onto you. I know the missus has money."

Ward jabbed the revolver in the direction of Mrs. Blanch, who took out a small leather purse and began to fish out some coinage. Ward grew impatient.

"None of your picking, give me the leather bag!"

Ward snatched the purse from the woman's hand and peered inside. There was nothing but coins within. He was disappointed and gave the purse back with a grunt. Ward allowed them to go the 200-odd yards to the inn, following them along the way. When they had almost reached the inn, Ward spotted some young men coming along the track from Carlisle Gully with a bunch of packhorses.

"Who are they?" Ward asked.

"How am I to know?" Blanch replied.

"Stay here," Ward said, then rode out to the men, robbed them and then ordered them into the pub. Soon after, an old man named Williamson was bailed up and robbed at the same spot. He was also instructed to head into the Royal Oak and wait.

Ward galloped back to Mr. and Mrs. Blanch and motioned for them to head to the inn.

"Do not be frightened, it's alright."

***

Around an hour had elapsed after his initial confrontation with Mr. and Mrs. Blanch, Ward now spotted a very promising target and made a bee line. Trundling along the road was Giovanni Cappasotti, a hawker, who was taking his cart back to Tamworth from the Uralla races where he had been plying his wares. Ward promptly ordered Cappasotti to stand and swiftly relieved him of £3.13s.6d, a watch and chain, and a gold nugget. He moved around to the back of the cart to look for anything useful or valuable and spotted a locked jewellery box. He demanded the key and, with great trepidation, Cappasotti unlocked the box and handed it over to the bushranger. Ward poked around inside the box with bony fingers. He fished out some pieces of jewellery – two brooches, two pairs of gold earrings, a finger ring and necklace – and pocketed them before returning the box. Searching the cart further, Ward snared himself an additional pocketknife and match box.

"Hand over your revolver," Ward ordered.

"I don't have one," Cappasotti replied.

"If I find one in the cart, or any money, I will burn everything in the dray. Understood?"

Cappasotti nodded. Ward gave the cart a once-over and, once satisfied he had gotten everything he desired from the indignant Italian, ordered him into the pub where his other captives were waiting.

As they entered, Ward asked his newest victim what he wanted to drink. "Port wine," was the response, so Ward ordered a glass of port for Cappasotti. He then proceeded to order drinks for the rest of the people in the bar but was at pains to point out that the first round was Williamson's "shout". For every subsequent round, Ward paid for all drinks using his takings, refusing to accept the change.

Ward gradually became very jolly and began to sing. He spontaneously broke out into a chorus of *Black Velvet Band* and began conducting his captives while dancing around the bar room in a pseudo-waltz. Though reluctant, several of the prisoners joined in the singing. Mrs. Blanch found herself starting to almost like this strange highwayman despite him having stuck them up a little over an hour previously.

It was at this time that the Italian hawker, Cappasotti, asked permission to leave. Ward nodded. "You can go, but you must not go towards Uralla, or you will receive a very unpleasant visit from me directly."

Cappasotti took his leave and then drove his wagon to Dorrington's farm two miles away. Having halted his horse, he headed to the homestead and informed Mrs. Dorrington of what had happened and explained that he was going to ride to the police in Uralla to raise the alarm, so he would be leaving his cart at the farm for a short while. With that, he took a saddle from the cart and unharnessed the animal from the cart. He saddled and bridled the horse and rode as fast as his mount could carry him to the Uralla police station, making sure to give the Royal Oak a wide berth.

Meanwhile, at the inn, Ward leaned against the bar and motioned for John Blanch to approach. He was now quite merry from rum.

"Do you know who I am?"

"I don't," replied Blanch.

"I am known as Ward, or Thunderbolt."

Naturally Blanch viewed this revelation with some level of scepticism but humoured the robber.

"I really was not appreciative of you turning down my payment the other night. Were I any other bushranger, I might have blown your brains out. But I am not that sort of fellow, as my reputation well demonstrates."

Ward pointed to an area visible through the window in the rough direction of the Big Rock.

"Do you recall some seven years ago a fellow was shot by police up there at the rock?"

Blanch nodded. He had not witnessed the event but had heard about it on the grapevine.

"I am the man, I was shot in the knee," said Ward. He proceeded to tug off his boot and roll up his left trouser leg to show off the scar on his knee. Blanch was unimpressed.

Ward turned to look out the window in the direction of the Big Rock, which was only a couple of hundred yards from the inn. He spotted a young man on the track with some horses. He put his boot back on and headed out telling the publican, "Do not leave this building – at the peril of your life!" He mounted his grey horse and rode to meet the drover – a nineteen-year-old named Michael A. Coughlan who was transporting the horses from Singleton for his employer Mr. Huxham in Armidale.

The bushranger bailed up Coughlan and led him back to the inn. Once there he began to look over the horses to see if there were any that might be a decent replacement for his. A grey took his fancy, and he began to remove his tack from his mount to put on the new one. Though Coughlan protested, the bushranger was far too jolly and eager for a good ride around on a fresh mount to listen.

Word reached the police in Uralla at 3:30pm when Cappasotti burst in and made a complaint that a bushranger had stuck him up at Blanch's Inn. In response to the news, Senior Constable John Mulhall and Constable Alexander Binney Walker set out in pursuit of the infamous Captain Thunderbolt. Walker had been off duty and was dressed in his regular bush clothes, but time was of the essence, and he wasted none of it getting changed into a uniform when the desperado was so close at hand. Mulhall had the faster mount and took off like lightning with Walker bringing up the rear.

Ward was putting his new steed to the test, much to Coughlan's dismay, when Senior Constable Mulhall came into view. The hapless victim was attempting to get his employer's horse back when they were interrupted by Mulhall's arrival. Spotting the trooper, Ward immediately rode towards them and fired twice at him, with Coughlan trying to catch up behind. Mulhall, thinking Coughlan was Thunderbolt's offsider, returned fire twice in their direction. Ward turned towards Kentucky Creek, and Coughlan attempted to intersect him and prevent his flight. As always, Ward's inclination had been to fly from the scene before he could be caught, rather than engage in a firefight like many of his contemporaries did – Coughlan was frustrating this.

Mulhall turned back as Walker caught up and pointed down the hill, "There is the wretch; I have exchanged shots with him. Shoot him!"

Walker immediately pursued Ward. Ward and Coughlan ran their horses along the fence line, as Walker drew his revolver. In the commotion, he accidentally discharged it into the ground. Ward, believing he was being shot at, returned fire at Walker but missed. The bushranger turned to Coughlan with a look of absolute fury.

"Get out of the way or I'll put a bullet through you!"

Coughlan allowed Ward to pass, and he took off as fast as the horse would take him, with the trooper following close behind.

In all the years past, Ward had been able to outride the police and escape capture at every opportunity, however this time he was missing the key ingredient for his success – his wife Mary Ann Bugg. In previous incidents, Mary Ann had often run interference for Ward, allowing herself to be captured in order to give her lover time to get away. Now that

Ward was operating alone, he was entirely reliant on his horsemanship and the speed and endurance of his horse to escape unscathed.

Ward was finding it hard to control the new mount, which was obviously spooked by the gunfire, and he took a moment to pause and taunt his pursuer while he tried to settle the animal.

"Come on!"

"Alright," said Constable Walker, who galloped after Ward, brandishing his revolver as he went. Ward took off, firing at the trooper with a pistol, which was returned in kind.

The hooves of the animals churned up the dust, which coiled in sandy coloured clouds behind them. The rhythmic pounding of the galloping passed through the bodies of the riders. Wind whipped at Ward's thin curls, and he jabbed his spurs into the horse's flanks to make it move faster. Walker stuck to him like glue, matching every dodge and weave as they bounded over creeks and through bush, uphill and down for nigh on seven miles. Every now and then Ward would peek over his shoulder to check where the trooper was. Walker remained cool and in control. Unlike some police, Walker was a native-born Australian and was used to the unpredictable bush around the area. He stuck to his horse like a louse and pushed it to its maximum capacity.

Ward commanded the new horse expertly, though he had not built up the connection he typically would have with a new beast before pushing it to such extremes. He attempted to fire again at his nemesis, but the weapon jammed. He tucked it into his belt and focused on evading capture.

Finally, Ward reached a junction of Chilcott's Waterhole and Kentucky Creek. His horse was huffing and foamy, and he dare not attempt to get it across the water in such an agitated state. He dismounted and began to wade out into the waterhole, expecting that Walker's horse would also baulk at the water, and perhaps give him the ability to escape on foot.

Walker rode towards the bank, shooting Ward's horse to make escape impossible should the bushranger double back. The shot was fatal. As Walker pushed his horse towards the water's edge, Ward climbed out of the waterhole and discarded his tweed coat. He ran 120 yards up Kentucky Creek and crossed to the opposite bank. By now Walker had caught up and was by the creek with his pistol drawn and only one bullet left. Ward also had his revolver drawn but knew that it would not fire. He hoped that fear would keep the horseman at bay.

As they faced off, Walker finally got a good look at the legendary Captain Thunderbolt. Far from being a handsome, dashing highwayman in stolen finery, Ward was skinny, ill-kempt and balding. His grey eyes were wild, and he panted in such a way that suggested his lungs were weak. His sinewy hand flexed as he steadied his revolver towards the trooper.

"Who are you?" Ward demanded of the stranger.

"Walker."

"Are you a trooper?"

"Yes, and a married man," Walker stated.

"In that case, think of your family and keep off," Ward barked, waving the harmless pistol threateningly.

"Will you surrender?" Walker asked. Ward threw his gaze towards the dead horse on the bank behind Walker and knew his lifeline had been cut.

"No! I will die first."

Walker tightened his grip on the reins of his horse. He could feel his heart in his throat.

"Well, then it is you or I for it," Walker said. With that he directed his mount into the water, but the beast lost its footing and crashed into the creek, becoming totally submerged.

Ward, rushed into the water attempted to drag Walker out of the saddle. He reasoned that if he could steal this horse, he had a chance to escape. Water splashed around them as they struggled, the horse whinnying as it became increasingly hard to control. Walker fired his last shot into Ward's left breast. The ball punctured both lungs as it made its way out under the right shoulder blade. Ward grunted and collapsed into the water but began to panic when he found he couldn't breathe. He rose again and lunged at Walker, trying to get some purchase to keep himself above water. The trooper responded by clubbing the bushranger in the head with the pistol until he let go. Blood gushed from Ward's mouth as he sank into the water, unconscious. Walker waited for a resurgence, but none came. From the moment the chase had begun to the death of Captain Thunderbolt, less than an hour had passed.

He rode back onto land and dismounted before wading into the water to recover the corpse. He dragged the drenched bushranger onto the bank but by now dusk was settling in. Walker rode back to Blanch's Inn hoping to get some kind of conveyance for the remains.

***

When Walker reached the inn, he saw Mulhall with Coughlan, who he had detained as an accomplice to Thunderbolt. Walker, still soaked through, approached the young drover.

"Ain't you Thunderbolt's mate?"

"No, he stole my horse, and I was after him for it," Coughlan replied, "Where is the horse?"

"The horse is dead. I shot it."

At once Coughlan clutched his head and tears began to stream down his cheeks.

"That was my master's horse! Do you understand how much trouble I'm going to be in now?"

Walker was unmoved, instead informing Coughlan that he was to join him in his mission to reclaim the bushranger's corpse from Kentucky Creek. Coughlan knew he could not refuse. Mounting up, he followed Walker into the bush but by the time they reached Kentucky Creek it was too dark to find the body and they turned back.

***

The following day at 3:00am, Walker and Senior Constable Scott returned to the junction of Kentucky Creek. The body was loaded into the cart and taken back to Blanch's Inn to be identified. When the corpse was inspected by the troopers they found a collection of jewellery taken from the Italian hawker, a silver stop watch, a small gold nugget, imitation gold jewellery and a well-used meerschaum pipe in a case. They also found an iron horseshoeing hammer that they suspected was Ward's own. Ward was dressed in strapped moleskin trousers, long boots, two Crimean shirts, and had been wearing an old cabbage tree hat.

After a postmortem examination was hastily completed, the incision was sewn up and the corpse was photographed so that it could be identified without the body having to be viewed in person, as there were not adequate facilities for the body to be preserved for a prolonged period.

J. Buchanan, esquire, the local police magistrate, helmed the magisterial inquiry into the remains at 2:00pm that day. For six hours evidence was taken from a range of witnesses including Walker, Mulhall, and Cappasotti the hawker. The body was compared to the official description put out by police in October 1863, when he had first escaped from Cockatoo Island:

5'8 1/4" tall; pale, fallow complexion; light brown, curly hair; hazel eyes; mole on right wrist and two warts on the back of the middle finger of the left hand.

In consequence of his meritorious conduct, Alexander Binning Walker was given a promotion to the rank of Senior Constable and placed in charge of a station in Glen Innes. He also received £32 from a subscription collected at the conclusion of the inquest, and The Sons and Daughters of Temperance awarded him with an inscribed watch and illuminated scroll. Celebrations were many for both Walker's heroism and the end to bushranging in New South Wales. There were rallies, parades and glowing appraisals in the press. They were not to know that Thunderbolt would not be the last bushranger.

Many were hopeful that now they could travel safely through the colony without fear of molestation, and they need not worry that their farms or stores would be raided. It was true that the worst years of bushranging ended with Thunderbolt's death, but it would be at least another fifty years before the scourge of bushranging had totally evaporated.

Captain Thunderbolt

> *"You talk of people being honest. I'm a robber, and at one time I lived with a gentleman whose name I'll not mention, and in one season helped to run in and brand seven hundred head of cattle that he and all of us knew were 'nuggets;' he is protected by law, but I'm an outlaw."*
> — **FREDERICK WORDSWORTH WARD**

Frederick Wordsworth Ward was born near Wilberforce in New South Wales in around 1834. Fred Ward was the youngest of the eleven children of ex-convict Michael Ward and free settler Sophia. When Fred was still young the family moved from Wilberforce to Maitland, and at age eleven he worked as a station hand at Aberbaldie Station in New England. From these early days, Fred had a passion for all things equine, and he had already developed bush skills that would serve him well in years to come. He spent the bulk of his adolescence working at various stations including the renowned horse stud Tocal Station.

Through early 1856 a huge theft of horses and cattle was made from Tocal and surrounding stations. Fred Ward was spotted helping his nephew John Garbutt, who had been using aliases to employ auctioneers to sell stolen horses and cattle. It was widely believed at the time that many of the Ward and Garbutt siblings were in on the crimes, engaged in wholesale and cattle theft. In fact, James' brother John Garbutt, who was considered the ringleader, was sentenced to ten years hard labour in June of that year over his involvement. Ward was nabbed and held in Maitland Gaol until his trial. When he finally went to court with James Garbutt on 13 August 1856, it was on a charge of having stolen sixty horses from William Zuill, fifteen horses from Charles Reynolds, and a second charge of knowingly receiving stolen goods. This got him his first and only conviction: ten years hard labour to be served on Cockatoo Island.

After four years in prison, in 1860 Ward earned himself a Ticket-of-Leave that allowed him to work within the Mudgee district. However he was required to attend a parole muster every three months as part of the conditions of his ticket. This was when he met the charming Mary Ann Bugg, a well-educated half-Aboriginal woman who was married to a squatter. The marriage didn't seem to bother the pair much as evidenced by the fact that soon Mary Ann was pregnant to Ward. He decided to take her back to her father near Dungog for the birth, which was an unfortunate decision as not only did this require him to leave his district, it resulted in him arriving late to his muster and thus violating the ticket of leave. Moreover, in his rush to get to the muster, Ward had pinched a horse to get him there. Needless to say this combination resulted in Ward back on Cockatoo Island, with an extra three years for the stolen horse to boot.

During his re-internment he was informed that he had to remain imprisoned for the entire duration of the sentence — a total of seven years — with no option to obtain a Ticket-of-Leave due to new regulations. Ward was subsequently involved in a prison riot. Unwilling to ride out his sentence in penal servitude, Ward conspired with a fellow inmate, highwayman Frederick Britten, to escape.

Absconding on 11 September 1863, Ward and Britten managed to breach the prison walls and swim to Woolwich. Some claimed that Mary Ann was there to help but she was accounted for elsewhere at the time. Ward would never again see the inside of a prison.

Taking to the bush, Ward and Britten began committing highway robberies around New England. With word of the crimes reaching authorities came a reward of £25 offered for their capture, and with it was an increase in search parties. Inevitably the bushrangers were spotted by a search party near the Big Rock — nowadays known as Thunderbolt's Rock — outside of Uralla and a conflict arose. Ward was shot in the back of the left knee as they escaped, but even with this injury the police could not keep up. They followed him into the rock but only managed to collect some of his supplies.

Soon the pair went their own ways and Ward began calling himself Captain Thunderbolt, possibly as a homage to a British highwayman who used the same moniker. One story goes that late one night Ward robbed a toll-keeper at Rutherford who responded that the bushranger's bashing on his door sounded like thunder. It is said Ward presented a pistol and introduced himself, "I am the thunder and this is my bolt."

He reunited with Mary Ann and, leaving her children with family, they kept a low profile throughout much of 1864 in the Bourke district of New South Wales. By the end of the year, however, Ward teamed up with three other desperadoes: Thomas "The Bull" Hogan, McIntosh (AKA "The Scotsman") and John Thompson. The gang committed robberies around Bourke, Walgett, Barraba and Narrabri but in April 1865 things fell apart. During a robbery at the Boggy Creek Inn in Millie, the gang, carousing and already slightly intoxicated from a previous raid, were interrupted by a party of police in bush clothes. A gunfight ensued during which Constable Dalton was shot and wounded through the body, and Thompson was shot through the jaw and captured. Both survived their injuries. As for the others, they fled to Queensland to avoid the increased police presence with McIntosh seemingly vanishing and Hogan getting himself arrested after a drunken spree.

Thunderbolt was on his own again and now more robberies were committed around Collarendabry and Liverpool Plains before a daring raid on the township of Quirindi on 8 December 1865. Thunderbolt was now accompanied by two men and they committed various robberies in town before rounding up the locals in the pub for singing and dancing. They evacuated just before a party of police arrived to chase them. The bushrangers returned the following day and did it all again.
Realising that he again faced operating alone, Ward had recruited Jemmy "the Whisperer" and Patrick Kelly. While undertaking a raid at the Carroll Inn a few days after the Quirindi caper, Jemmy shot and wounded Senior Constable Lang in yet another gunfight. This iteration of the gang did not last long and was disbanded in early 1866, whereupon Ward took Mary Ann to the Gloucester district where she was soon arrested for vagrancy and imprisoned, but was later liberated by the Governor after protests from the public.

With the new Felons Apprehension Act in place, and pressure from the public on the police force to put an end to bushranging, more search parties were sent out after Thunderbolt. Despite police and bounty hunters being hot on his tail, Ward continued his depredations.
On 25 May 1867 a Proclamation was made announcing a reward of £200 for the capture of Thunderbolt. At around the same time Ward recruited teenager Thomas Mason and they robbed coaches, inns and stations until Mason was nabbed after

a horseback chase in September of that year. He was subsequently convicted at Tamworth and given three years hard labour. Around this time Mary Ann was also nabbed for possession of stolen goods and imprisoned.

Desperate for company, Ward took up with a married, part-Aboriginal woman named Louisa Mason, also known as "Yellow Long", who accompanied him on his robberies but died of pneumonia at Denman on 24 November 1867.

After this turn of events Ward went back to Mary Ann who was now at liberty again. Soon Mary Ann was pregnant to Ward with their third child, and they both knew that a life on the road was not suited to her condition, so they separated for the last time. In August 1868 Mary Ann bore Ward a son whom she named Frederick Wordsworth Ward junior.

Ward continued his epic tally of crimes during 1868, this time with a young lad named William Monckton, who had joined Ward after running away from home. One of their most renowned adventures during this period was when they bailed up Wirth's band at Tenterfield on 19 March 1868. As the story goes, Thunderbolt and his sidekick stuck up the travelling German band and were displeased with the mere £16 takings from the robbery, so Thunderbolt ordered them to perform for him for several hours. When the musicians complained about how poor they were, Thunderbolt took down a postal address and promised to send them the money back when he had more, which he supposedly did some months later.

The reward for Ward's capture was raised to £400 just in time for Christmas 1868. While it was a fraction of what had been offered for his peers Dan Morgan, Ben Hall, Johnny Gilbert, John Dunn, and the Clarkes and Connells, it was still an enormous amount to the average settler of the 1860s.

Ward and Monckton split in December 1868 and Monckton found work at Wellingrove Station. He got himself into trouble over some minor offences after leaving Ward, and was eventually recognised as Ward's accomplice and tried in 1869. He was sentenced to serve six years hard labour, the first year in Darlinghurst Gaol, the rest in a reformatory.

After the split, Ward went quiet and would not make any notable appearances until he began to undertake intermittent mail robberies in New England. When he did appear he was alone. He would never take on any other accomplices ever again.

On 25 May 1870, Ward was spotted near Blanch's Inn near Uralla by two constables responding to a complaint about an Italian hawker having been robbed. Fleeing on horseback, Ward was pursued by Constable Alex Walker and engaged in a riding gunfight for almost an hour. Ward's horse was shot dead and he attempted to cross Kentucky Creek on foot. Walker rode into the stream, shot Ward in the chest and clubbed him with his revolver until he was unresponsive. Walker dragged Ward onto land and rode back to the inn. The next day he and his partner rode back to retrieve the body.

The corpse was taken to the courthouse, identified and autopsied. Photographs were taken post mortem to help establish the identity in the event that decomposition began to take hold before a positive identification could be recorded. One of the people that positively identified Ward was his former sidekick Monckton who had been released after serving the first year of his sentence. Ward was buried in the local cemetery.

Despite Ward's body being positively identified, rumours were started posthumously that it was not actually him, and moreover that there was a government conspiracy to cover up the fact that he had actually escaped. The stories of Ward's survival have been frequently debunked, but to the minority that choose to believe the folklore over the history the facts are not enough to prove them wrong.

While other bushrangers have been somewhat lionised for having never taken life, Thunderbolt conducted himself in such a way that his largely non-violent career is far more laudable. This is perhaps reflected in the way that despite his innumerable robberies, the reward for his capture was so comparably low when measured against other bushrangers. He seemed to be viewed more as a nuisance than a threat. This has helped considerably in fostering the image of Thunderbolt as a "gentleman bushranger".

Maitland Mercury and Hunter River General Advertiser (NSW: 1843 - 1893),
Saturday 4 June 1870, page 5

DEATH OF THUNDERBOLT.

Although we have already published a full account of the gallant conduct of constable Walker, in pursuing the bushranger Thunderbolt alone, and in attempting to capture him, and finally shooting him in defence of his own life while struggling in the water—we find so complete an account of the occurrence, from a special correspondent, published in the Sydney Morning Herald, accompanied by a full report of the evidence at the inquest on the body, that we copy the report in full, as follows:

STICKING UP.

Fred. Ward, alias Thunderbolt, is dead. The circumstance which led to the result, I will, as far as I can, briefly relate. On Wednesday, 25th May, about two o'clock, as Mr. Blanche and his wife were returning home from Uralla, and within about 200 yards from his own house, a man riding one horse and leading another rode up to him, and called out, "Bail up!" stating that he was a robber, and would have no hum-bugging. On some silver being tendered, he refused to have it, stating that he knew the mistress had money on her, as he was laid on to them. He also reminded Blanche that a few evenings before he (Blanche) had refused to accept a £5 order as payment for a quart of rum. Subsequently he told Blanche that he might go on to his house. On reaching there some other men came up from Carlisle Gully way, and Ward (as we shall call him) stuck them up also, and an old man named Williamson. A little after a dealer named Giovanni Cappisote came from towards Uralla in a spring cart. Ward bailed him up, taking from him £3 13s. 6d, a watch, some jewellery, and other articles.

After a little delay the dealer was permitted to proceed on towards Kentucky, Ward returning to Blanche's inn, when he called upon the old man Williamson to shout, and also shouted himself, and sang and danced. During this time he asked Blanche if he remembered an encounter the police had with Thunderbolt about seven years ago, and on his answering in the affirmative, stated that he was the man, that he had been wounded in the leg, and that the affair took place at the Rocks, about 300 yards from the house.

THE POLICE APPEAL.

Ward, it appears, also took one of the horses from a young man he had stuck up, and was trying its speed when Senior-constable Mulhall appeared in sight, galloping down the hill from Uralla. I may state that after the hawker (Cappisote) was permitted to proceed on his journey, he went about a mile and a-half to a selector named Dorrington, and there taking his horse out of the cart, he put the saddle on, and by taking a wide detour from the road through the bush, managed to pass Blanche's house unobserved, and galloped to Uralla.

Senior-constable Mulhall and Constable Walker, immediately on receiving information, started in pursuit. But Mulhall's horse being the fastest, he gained about half-a-mile on Walker. Mulhall then first arrived, and observed two men near the fence, the oldest of whom fired. Mulhall returned the shot, and, according to his own statement, his horse bolted at the discharge.

By this time Walker was galloping down the hill, when Mulhall met him, and said, "There they are - I have exchanged shots with them. Go on, and shoot the wretch." Walker kept right on, when the oldest of the two endeavoured to cut into the road, but the young man blocked him. The two then galloped down the line of fence from the road to the bush. In raising his pistol Walker happened to discharge it accidentally, and the shot went into the ground. Ward thereupon turned and fired, but missed his man. Ward then apparently spoke something to the young man, who turned away and left Ward alone, with Walker following him. Ward then beckoned to Walker, and cried out "Come on," to which Walker answered, "All right." For a little more than half an hour they raced through timber, over gully and creek, dry ground and boggy, up hill and down, Ward doubling like a hare, and Walker pursuing – it was a chase for life. Ward seemed to awaken to the fact now that the avenger was on his path and, bold rider though he was, he was at last matched. In one place they galloped over a piece of ground where the tussocks of earth and grass were standing like stumps, from one to two feet high, with a boggy waterhole about four feet deep, into which Ward floundered, and Walker followed; throughout, the pace must have been terrific, as the tracks next morning testified.

THE FINAL STRUGGLE.

At length Ward turned up a bit of a hill, and when on the highest part turned as if to face Walker, but if so he altered his mind, for off he went until he was pulled up by a water-hole directly in front of him, and about 350 yards long. At once Ward dismounted and took to the water, swimming over; Walker, seeing this, rode up to Ward's horse and shot it dead, and then galloped about two hundred yards down the creek to the end of the waterhole; here Walker crossed the creek, and then saw Ward, who had swum across, divest himself of his coat and run up the creek about one hundred and fifty yards to where there was a narrow channel about fifteen to eighteen feet wide; across this Ward dashed, and had got out on the other side when Walker arrived at the edge, and there they stood with about fifteen or eighteen feet of a creek between them. Walker told Ward to surrender; but Ward presenting his pistol asked him who he was, and his name; also whether he had a family. On Walker replying that he had a family, Ward told him he should think of them. " Oh," said Walker, "I thought about all that, will you surrender?" — to which Ward replied, "No, I will die first." "All right," said Walker, "You or I for it then," and immediately rushed his horse into the creek. Whether it was the sudden fall, or, as Walker supposes, his horse went on his knees, it so happened that his horse went right under head and shoulders, and whilst in that position Ward jumped towards Walker to receive his death wound, for Walker at once fired, the ball entering under the left collar bone near the arm-pit, and travelling direct downwards and backwards to about three inches below the right shoulder blade, where it came out. Both lungs were pierced. Ward fell, but immediately rose again and grappled at Walker, who then struck him over the forehead with his revolver, and again knocked him under water. Walker then turned his horse out of the creek, and dismounting went into the water and pulled the man out — apparently dead. Walker then, as it was getting dusk, rode back to Blanche's and procured a horse and cart, but though he searched for three hours in the dark, he could not find the body. The next morning he went out again in company with some others, and brought the body in. It was afterwards identified as that of Fred Ward, alias Thunderbolt. In the chase and final encounter constable Walker exhibited undaunted pluck, and good riding, combined with much prudence. Few men in the excitement of a chase such as Walker rode, would have had coolness enough to stop and shoot the busnranger's horse. It not only exhibits coolness, but also determination, for thus cutting off Ward's chance of escape, he rendered him desperate, and of course the more dangerous to encounter. Besides, when Walker shot the horse he had but one charge left, the others having been expended while chasing Ward.

It appears as if Ward, finding what a sticker was after him, thought to double Walker by swimming across, and then, if Walker galloped round, either entice him to follow him into the creek — or else by swimming back again mount his horse, and thus gain a start. If such was his idea it was frustrated by Walker's promptitude in shooting the horse. Ward's action at the last encounter also showed the desperate strait into which he was brought, and Walker's pluck in facing him. With Thunderbolt it was life or death. With Walker it was simply duty. Thunderbolt knew that if he started to run on dry ground Walker would soon overtake him; therefore he stood on the bank of the creek, ready to avail himself of any chance which might turn up to struggle with Walker in the water, where as much might depend on accident as strength. Besides Walker, though active, is but a slight made man. All these were chances in Ward's favour if a hand-to-hand struggle took place in the water. It was, indeed, as Walker said, "You or I for it." Ward's opportunity came when Walker's horse floundered, head under. The rush was made; but fortunately Walker had one shot left, and that, in taking Ward's life, very probably saved his own. From the direction the ball took, and also the distance it traversed, Walker must have been almost directly over Ward, and within a very short distance, when the shot was fired. Evidently Ward's motive was to pull him off his horse, and one moment later he would have had hold of Walker; but that moment sealed his doom — and Thunderbolt, the scourge of the Northern district, is no more.

The inhabitants of Uralla, especially those who have rode over the ground traversed in the chase, and viewed the water-hole where the final encounter took place, are loud in their approbation of Walker's pluck, and a testimonial has been started (Mr. George Weston heading it with £20) to testify in a substantial manner their appreciation of his cool bravery. Alexander Binney Walker is a young man, a native of the colony, and, like most really brave men, is a very quiet, unassuming person. The Sons of Temperance are proud of him, and say he shows that alcoholic stimulants are not required to give a man a dash and pluck. Walker belongs to the "Belmore Division," Uralla. On the intelligence reaching Armidale, Mr. Buchanan, police magistrate, immediately started off, accompanied by Mr. Mitchell, solicitor, arriving at the inn about half-past 1.

THE INQUEST.

After viewing the body, an inquiry was commenced by Mr. Buchanan, and conducted for over six hours, with much patience and skill, Mr. Mitchell writing down the depositions. Mr. Cleghorn and Mr. Western, justices of the peace, Uralla, were also present throughout the inquiry. Appended is the evidence.

Senior-constable Mulhall deposed that on Wednesday afternoon a hawker (Giovanni Cappisote) gave him information about a bushranger being at Blanche's; himself and Walker then started, but he gained on Walker; on coming towards Blanche's house, he observed two men riding up quick; one of these men, on meeting him (Mulhall), drew his revolver, and fired; I returned the shot; both men then rode round the fence; my horse shied; I turned, and over-took them just round the fence; I then fired at one of the men a second time; Walker then came up; I told him to go ahead and shoot that wretch, we have exchanged shots; both of us pursued the two men; after a few seconds, one of the men turned round — not the man who fired the shot; I followed after him, the man who turned round; he went towards the inn; constable Walker followed the man who fired; I searched several places for the other man, but without success; on retiring to Blanche's, I recognised the man whom I pursued; I shepherded him all night, and when the dead body was found in the morning, I apprehended him, and told him I did so as an accomplice of a man called Thunderbolt, or Ward; constable Walker followed the other man; I believe he never lost sight of him; I believe he shot him; the man I followed I lost sight of until I found him at the inn; I produce the *Police Gazette*, 21st October, 1863, No. 42, in which there is a description of Ward :— Native of Windsor; labourer; age 27; height, 5 feet 8¼ inches; pale sallow complexion; light brown curly hair; mole right wrist; two warts on the back middle finger of the left hand. I have seen the dead body in the room; I believe the man described in the *Gazette* is now lying dead in the other room; I believe it is the body of Frederick Ward.

Giovanni Cappisote deposed: I am a hawker; about three p.m., on Wednesday, a man riding a grey horse came to me, about one hundred and fifty yards from this house, and, with a revolver in hand, told me to stand and give up my money; I took my purse and gave him, with £3 13s. 6d., a small nugget of gold, watch, and chain; he took my jewellery-box from the dray, and asked for the key; I opened it for him; he took two brooches, two pairs gold ear-rings, purse, finger ring, pocket knife, match box, and necklace; he asked my name, and where I came from; I told him Uralla races, and was going to Tamworth; he asked me for a revolver; I had none; he said if he found one in the cart, or any money, he would then burn everything in the dray; after a bit I said can I go; I then went to the public-house — this house — and got a glass of port wine; the robber came in and asked me what I would have; he shouted for five; I then drove off to Dorrington's, near two miles, and told Mrs Dorrington what happened; I then put my saddle on my horse, and rode through the bush to Uralla; I reported the affair to the police; I have seen the dead body inside; that is the body of the man who stuck me up yesterday; I am sure it is him; I never saw Thunderbolt before; I have heard of him.

Constable Mulhall recalled: On arresting the young man, I found two swags on the horses he claimed (produced); there were three swags altogether — two on one saddle, and one on the other saddle.

Giovanni Cappisote, recalled: I recognise the oilcloth; it was on a horse feeding a little way from the robber when I was stuck up; I believe the horse was the property of the deceased; I do not recognise anything else; the man who stuck me up had two horses, one grey and one nearly black; each horse had a dark swag on; only one man stuck me up, I only saw one man.

Alexander Binney Walker, constable, stationed at Uralla, deposed: From information received, I started along with Senior-constable Mulhall yesterday about 4pm from Uralla; Mulhall's horse was faster than mine, and he went ahead of me; when I got to the hill descending to Blanche's, I met senior-constable Mulhall, who said, "Come on — I have exchanged shots with the bushrangers;" when I got half-way down the hill, I saw two men on grey horses galloping; when they saw me the oldest man took a turn towards the public-house, the young man blocked him (crossed him), and stopped him from coming to the road; both then raced along the fence; I was behind them, and my revolver accidentally went off; the old man then turned and fired at me; this I returned; he then said something to the young man, who at once turned right away; the old man then beckoned to me, calling out "Come on!"; I said "All right;" we both galloped; he turned round and fired at me again; I returned his fire; we then raced for a good bit, across a few creeks and up a bit of a hill; as soon as he got to the top he wheeled round and faced down to me; I was going np hill; I again fired at him; he then turned again up another hill, and we raced for about a quarter of an hour; my horse was gradually pulling him; he then faced over a spur and down to the creek, where he jumped off his horse into the water; whilst he was swimming across I shot his horse; I then had to gallop down a good bit, to cross the creek and turn up the other side; when I came to where he had crossed he was running up the creek; before I reached him he had crossed the creek again in a narrow place; he stood on the bank until I came up; I said, "You had better surrender before you do any harm;" he said, "Who are you?" I said, "Never mind who I am;" he asked my name; I told him; he said, "Are you a trooper?" I said "Yes;" he asked, "Are you a married man?" I answered "Yes;" he then stood on the bank with the revolver in his hand, and said, "Walker, keep back: you are a married man, remember your family;" I was then about twelve or fourteen feet from him — the creek was between us; I said, "Will you surrender;" he said "No, I'll die first;" I then said, "All right, you or I for it;" I then faced my horse into the water; my horse went head first under, right under; whilst my horse was under, the man made a rush at me with revolver in hand; as soon as I saw that I fired at him; he went under the water; when he rose he made a grapple at me, and I struck him over the head with my revolver; he again went down; as soon as he came up I saw blood oozing from his mouth; I then turned my horse and came out of the creek; I then dismounted, and went into the creek up to my waist, and pulled the man out; I drew him out on to the bank; I fancied he was dead; I then mounted, and came back to Blanche, where I borrowed a horse and cart, and went to look for the body, but could not find it in the dark; about three o'clock this morning I started again, and found the body where the encounter took place; I have seen the body now lying in the room; it is that of the man of whom I have given evidence — the man with whom I had the encounter last night and shot; it was the last shot, when he was closing with me, that killed him; never saw deceased before that I am aware of; I was entirely alone; I never saw any person from the time his companion left him until I pulled him out of the creek; I was alone all the time; it was Kentucky Creek where the encounter took place; senior-constable Scott searched the body at the creek in my presence; there was a cheque for £27, and two orders for £5 each, a watch, and other articles enumerated found upon the body; when I returned to Blanche's after the encounter I met the young man now in custody, deceased's companion; he was in front of Blanche's, at large; he said, "Oh, I am all right;" I said, "Ain't you that bushranger's mate?" he said, "No, he stole my horse, and I was after him for it;" he asked "Where is the horse!" when I told him it was shot he commenced to cry, and said, "It was his master's horse, and he would get into trouble over it;" Blanche told me the young man was stuck up as well as the rest; the young man then got a horse, and came with me to search for the dead body; it was dark, we did not find it; on searching a second time we found it, and on returning with it to the inn, I found the police had the young man in custody; before he went with me the young man said he had come from Singleton, and was hired by Mr. Huxham to bring up horses, and take cattle down; from where the young man left the old man until the final encounter I followed him six or seven miles; the young man left him about a quarter of a mile from the main road; I never saw any person from the time I commenced to follow deceased until I returned to Blanche's; I saw nobody following me; I never looked behind; the young man was in custody of senior-constable Mulhall when I returned with the dead body; the revolver the deceased used against me he dropped in the water at the final encounter; he had it in his hand when he rushed at me, and it was not in his hand when I drew him out; deceased had on moleskin pants, strapped; two crimean shirts, riding boots, cabbage-tree hat, and tweed coat; these clothes were on the body when I last saw it a few hours ago in the other room, excepting the coat, in another room in this house.

Geo. Walter Scott, senior-constable at Rocky River, deposed: Between 7 and 8 a.m. this day, from information received, I went down to Kentucky Creek, to the junction of the Creek and Chilcott's swamp, and there found the body of a man lying alongside a waterhole; I searched it in presence of constable Walker; found on it two orders for £5 each on Messrs. Wyndham, Dalwood, meerschaum pipe (in case), a stop watch and albert chain, looking glass, cheque (drawn by Mr. Lee, of Tenterfield, for £27 6s 3d., payable to Keep and Parsons), leather purse (containing 18s in silver, a locket, nugget of gold, and 2d. stamp), a cigar case (containing two watch chains, two brooches, and plain ring) match box, penknife, pair gloves, also a shoeing hammer, now produced;

the body inside is the body of the man I found at the creek, and from which I took the property; I never saw him before.

John Blanche, publican, Church Gully, four miles south of Uralla: Yesterday, myself and wife were coming from Uralla about two o'clock; I saw two grey horses hanging at my door; a person mounted one and led the other, and came up to us, calling out, "Bail up;" I laughed; he said, "No humbugging, you would not give me the bottle of rum a few nights ago;" I then recognised him as the same man I had drawn a quart of rum for, but refused to take payment out of a £5 order on Wyndhams, Dalwood: he said, " I am a robber," and presented a revolver; he wanted my money; I offered him 4s. 6d.; he would not take it, saying the missus had the money; while she was getting the silver, he said, "None of your picking, give me the leather bag;" he did not take the silver; there were then some other people coming up from Carlisle Gully way, with pack horses; the robber asked who they were; I did I not know; he then told me to remain where I was; he went up to the people, and then beckoned me to come up to my house, saying, "Do not be frightened, it is all right;" an old man, named Williamson, who had also been stuck-up, "shouted;" afterwards the robber "shouted," first time paying nothing, but the second time he paid me 5s., and would not take change; he "shouted" several times, and paid each time; after a little time he went outside and mounted his horse, at the same time telling me, in the presence of all in the bar, not to go out of doors at the peril of my life; the young man now in custody was one of the strangers I saw coming up from Carlisle Gully way, with pack-horses, when I was bailed up; the young man had had nothing to do with bailing me up, nor with any occurrence in the bar; I cannot tell which horse the young man had; the robber had two greys; he hitched one up, and let the other go with a halter on his head; the hawker was not stuck up until after I was; the man who bailed me up asked me, "Do you know who I am?" I answered, " No!" he said "I am called Ward, or Thunderbolt;" he remonstrated with me about not letting him have a quart of rum a few evenings before, he asked me if I remembered an occurrence some seven years ago with Thunderbolt, at the Rocks, and remarked, "I am the man, I got shot in the knee;" the Rocks are in sight from my house, about 200 or 300 yards distant; there was an encounter with Thunderbolt and the police at that place, I believe, about six or seven years ago; the man now lying dead in another room is the same as was singing and dancing in my house, and stuck me up, I never saw the man before the evening he called for the rum.

John Thomas Ward, assistant storekeeper, Armidale: I have seen the dead body of a man in this house, I identify the body as that of a man who bailed me up on the

19th April, between Inverell and Armidale, the bushranger at that time, said to me, "I robbed a mail several years ago at Weebong;" I lived there at that time, a mail was robbed, and, it was said, by Thunderbolt; I said, "Are you Thunderbolt?" he said, "You must find out;" I have no doubt that the man now lying dead in another room is the same man who stuck me up.

John George Balls, senior sergeant, Armidale: I have seen the dead body of a man lying in this house this day; I identify the body as that of Fred Ward, alias Thunderbolt; I produce *Police Gazette* of 21st October, 1863, wherein Ward is described; I have minutely examined the body, and it tallies exactly with that description; further I knew Ward as a prisoner when I was an official on Cockatoo Island, from that knowledge and the *Police Gazette* I positively identify the deceased as Fred Ward, or Thunderbolt.

George William Pearson, bushman now residing at Dorrington, within two miles of this house: I have seen the dead body lying in this house; I knew that man when alive, his name was Fred. Ward; I last saw him alive the day before yesterday, coming down from the mountain (Marsh's Mountain) towards this place; he said, "Am I going right for Blanche's?"; I am certain the man was Fred. Ward; the man now lying dead is the same man; I was horse breaking with him at Cooyal, near Mudgee, before he was lagged; I knew him well; I have no doubt he is Fred. Ward, or Thunderbolt; when I met him I asked him if he remembered George William Pearson, who was horse-breaking with him at Cooyal; he said "Yes;" I think it is nine or ten years since deceased was lagged from Mudgee; he told me when in Mudgee that he was holding a ticket-of-leave; I am certain he is the same man; I was living in Mudgee district when he bolted; when I met him the day before yesterday he told me had no time for talking — he must be off.

Samuel Peirce Spasshat, legally qualified medical practitioner, medical adviser to Government, Armidale district: I have to-day made a post-mortem examination on the body of a man lying in this house; it is that of a man apparently from thirty-five to forty years of age; the height by measurement is 5 feet 8¼; brown curly hair, top of head partially bald, light grey eyes, complexion of face discoloured from effusion of blood, that of body fair; there is a small mole on back of right arm, a little above the wrist; three warts on the left hand, one at back of first joint of thumb, and two others between first joint middle finger; there is a mark as of an old scar indistinctly visible on left knee; found tongue protruding from between lips, with mouth very bloody; mark of a gun-shot wound below left collar bone towards arm-pit; on examination, I found the aperture communicated with lungs, both of which, right and left, had been penetrated; there was an aperture as if the exit of a ball on the right side of chest, three inches below and two inches anterior to lower point right shoulder-blade; there was a large quantity of fluid blood in cavity of pleura; the wound was just such as might have been inflicted by a pistol bullet discharged in immediate proximity to and rather above the body; I am of opinion that the wound was the cause of death; the lungs and heart presented evidence of previous disease; I look at the *Police Gazette*, 21st October, 1863, No. 42; I see in it a description of a man named Ward, the description tallies exactly with the body of the man of whom I have just given evidence; the body is that of a spare man, but well-conditioned; the eyes are described in the *Gazette* as hazel grey, I should call them decidedly grey.

This closed the evidence. The investigation took over six hours, commencing at a quarter past two and closing at half-past eight.

At the close a unanimous opinion prevailed that constable Walker deserved the thanks of the community for his daring in thus singly grappling with a desperado who was determined to die rather than surrender, and not only the thanks but a substantial testimonial of their appreciation of his conduct. A list was at once opened, and £32 10s. subscribed in the room. The northern portion of the colony should make it £500. I trust they will. The body was left at Blanche's inn until Friday, when it was removed to the Court-house, Uralla, and will be interred this Saturday, 28th May. The body, as it lay at Blanche's public-house, might furnish a warning to any youthful aspirant after bushranging adventures. "The way of transgressors is hard, and the wicked shall not live out half their days," were both exemplified in the life and death of Fred Ward, alias Thunderbolt.

VIII

❧

Escape from Ballarat Gaol

In April 1872, Andrew George Scott was released from Parramatta Gaol. He had just finished a sentence for buying a yacht he called *Why-Not* with valueless cheques. Unfortunately for Scott, his liberty would be comically short lived. As soon as he was released he was re-arrested and extradited to Victoria to stand trial, accused of robbing the Second London Bank in Mount Egerton back in 1869.

Scott had long before declared his innocence of the crime, and in fact had been a witness in the original court case for the prosecution of the two leading suspects: Julius Bruun and John Simpson. After a committal hearing at Gordon police court, Scott was remanded in Ballarat, where he was due to be tried before Sir Redmond Barry. Barry was one of the most senior and respected judges in Victoria, known for his philanthropy as much as his lack of tolerance for criminals. He was a perfect foil for the verbose Scott, who was accruing quite a reputation as a man with the gift of the gab.

Ballarat Gaol was a sadly ill-prepared, facility when Scott was brought within its walls. The brick and mortar construction had been completed quickly and cheaply in an effort to deal with the ballooning lawlessness in the area due to the gold rush. This flimsiness would play a crucial role in what followed. Scott was a trained civil engineer and deviously clever. He was always analysing his surrounds in order to find any weaknesses that could be exploited. A prime example of this was that while in prison in New South Wales he had convinced prison authorities that he was insane in a bid to be transferred to the Parramatta Lunatic Asylum: a low security facility he thought he could easily escape. His plan fell apart when he was caught recruiting inmates to help him escape as well as attempting to craft a weighted rope he could toss over the perimeter wall for climbing.

Remanded in Ballarat for weeks to await his trial, the indignant Scott had plenty of time to scheme. He formed an alliance with four other prisoners: James Plunkett, *alias* Roach, up on three charges of burglary and larceny; John Harris, *alias* Dermoody, *alias* Williams, an American butcher doing three months for stealing a coat and about to stand trial on a charge of stealing a watch; James Stapleton, *alias* Fitzpatrick, an illiterate Irishman up on four charges of burglary and larceny; and William Taylor, a carpenter who was doing 12 months for stealing two silver cups. His plan was almost identical to the one he had devised in Parramatta before he was foiled — get a group together and climb over the wall. Scott had very quickly discovered major weaknesses in his cell; notably the extremely soft mortar around the bricks and the thin, soft, sheet tin covering the inside of the wooden door and the lock mechanism. Herein lay the crucial first steps of his plan for it allowed him access to the neighbouring cell and the mechanism that kept him incarcerated.

***

On Monday 10 June 1872, Scott put his plan into motion. The previous day the gang had ironed out the details of the plan before being returned to their cells at 1:00pm. After the final inspection at 10:00pm, using a piece of iron he had managed to procure from outside of the prison, Scott dug out the mortar around a set of bricks, two lengths wide and five rows tall, allowing a hole big enough for Plunkett, who was in the next cell, to squeeze through. The work was harder than he had expected and he had worn a shallow pit into his palm from the digging. The noise in the cell had alerted the warder, a man named Irwin. When asked what the noise was about, Scott said that he had been experiencing severe discomfort from his bowels and was only using the facility in his cell to relieve himself.

Once Scott had succeeded in creating the hole, Plunkett joined him. With the two men sharing Scott's cell, they peeled back the tin on the door, which was barely thicker than stiff paper, and using a knife Plunkett had stolen they chipped away at the wood to reveal the lock. Scott managed to unlock the door from inside, then tied a string to the bolt to allow them to yank it open at the right moment.

Scott rang a bell to alert the unarmed warder that he required assistance as warders were forbidden from going into cells after dark except in an emergency. As the warder reached the cell Scott and Plunkett burst open the door and the pair flew out like startled pigeons and tackled Irwin. Scott attempted to restrain Irwin while Plunkett roughed him up. The warder managed to bite Plunkett's thumb hard enough to draw blood and leave his teeth marks behind. Irwin screamed, "murder," in order to gain attention, but was gagged by Scott shoving a blanket into his mouth, then restrained. Irwin was secured to a dining table in the kitchen and the escapees took an iron bar to break their mates out as the keys were being kept by the Governor in an office at the front of the building.

Scott and Plunkett then proceeded to locate the others and release them, using the bar to break the locks. Scott asked the men if there was anyone else they wanted freed, which led to William Marshall, a London tailor doing time for stealing a cash box, being the last to be released upon Dermoody's request as the pair were mates.

Scott went up to Marshall's cell and told him to get ready, but Marshall refused as he only had one month of his sentence left. Scott replied, "Oh, Dermoody says you're to come, so come on." Marshall was then liberated in spite of himself.

Scott also tried to free another inmate named Jones, who also refused, but this time he was allowed to stay. Scott then made his way to where the others were and could see them bickering.

"What is all of this?" asked Scott.

"Plunkett wants the screw's watch, but I say no," said Dermoody.

"We don't need to take any watches, there's no time for such trivia. We need to get over the wall before someone notices what we've done."

They ran to the south yard where the cell block met the west wall. They had with them knives and benches stolen from the kitchen, a large rope used for raising the prisoners' dinners to the upper levels of the cell block, and a lock from the north-eastern yard. Scott stood against the bricks, the benches helping his height, while the other men climbed on his shoulders. Once Dermoody reached the top he hitched a rope to the bars on the window of a cell. By holding onto the rope and getting a purchase on the water spout, the others were able to scale the wall after him, Scott being the last to climb. Once they were on top of the wall, then came the riddle of how to get down, which Scott solved by reclaiming the rope and hitching it through a window on the guard tower. The men then abseiled down the wall.

They ran along Skipton Street, then down Sebastopol Road to the intersection of Smythesdale Road. It was here that the gang decided to catch their breath.

Plunkett took Scott aside with a look of fury on his face. "Why did you break so many out? You told me there was only going to be two or three with us!"

"If we only had two men, would we have made it over that wall?" Scott replied.

"That wasn't what we agreed to, Scott."

"It takes a leader to read the situation and improvise. I improvised. If you don't like the way I do things, perhaps you would like to go to the gate and ask the gaoler to let you back in?"

Plunkett balled his hand into a fist and raised it threateningly, but Scott did not flinch. He simply stared down the rogue with his intense blue eyes and Plunkett backed down.

"Have it your way," said Plunkett, "I'm going my own way."

Plunkett re-joined the group and announced his intention. "Who's with me?" he asked. There was hesitation in the other men, but the men eventually moved to Plunkett's side.

Scott stood stoically opposite Plunkett. "By all means, go with Plunkett, but remember who masterminded this escape. Would you rather stick to the man who got you out of that purgatory, or the man who almost certainly will see you back inside it?"

"What are you offering, Scott?" asked Taylor.

"Unlike that blunt instrument over there, I have a plan. We will stick up the Soldiers' Hill police station and procure firearms and ammunition. Thence we are to cut the telegraph wires, head for the coast at Geelong or Williamstown, steal a boat, then seize a larger craft for the purpose of heading for Fiji and freedom."

"What if it doesn't work?" asked Stapleton.

"Then we sail down the Murray in a canoe and make for South Australia, or head north into New South Wales," Scott replied. "Either way, once we are out of the colony they cannot pursue us."

The men looked at each other in silence, and after a few moments Dermoody and Marshall joined Scott, leaving Taylor and Stapleton with Plunkett.

"Why are you going with him?" Dermoody asked the others.

"We've made our choice," Stapleton replied bluntly without further explanation.

"You'd have to be mad to believe you could achieve even half of what Scott is saying," said Plunkett. "Best of luck to you. You'll be nabbed by week's end and probably hanged."

Scott, Dermoody and Marshall turned and headed down Smythesdale Road, while Plunkett led Taylor and Stapleton in the opposite direction towards Mount Misery. It was now up to fate to determine who would last the longest.

The escape was not discovered until 6:00am, by which time the enormous search that followed was fruitless. The inmates were gone and had now become bushrangers.

***

When Scott's gang reached Haddon the following day around 7:00pm, they spotted a boy named Alfred King walking with his younger brother and confronted him. William Marshall stood before the young man and blocked his path, holding a large stick.

"I'm a bushranger. Hand over your money," Marshall said. King looked around with fright. Marshall lashed out and struck Alfred across the head with the stick. "Money! Now!"

Alfred reached into his pocket and extracted 5 shillings and a box of matches. "This is all I have on me," he said with a quiver in his voice. Marshall snatched both up and sneered before walking back to the scrub where the others were waiting.

The brothers wasted no time in telling the local police what had happened and Constable Daly was quickly on the case.

After trekking a bit further, Marshall was sent to buy supplies in town. Here he was spotted by none other than the recent robbery victims. Alfred alerted some men that this was the bushranger that had robbed him and Marshall was quickly accosted by Constable Daly.

"What's your name?" Daly asked.

"Reginald Beaumont," Marshall replied with a sneer.

"Well, 'Reginald', you're coming back to the office with me."

With that, Marshall was the first of the escapees to get nicked. He was locked up in Smythesdale overnight before being sent back to Ballarat. When Marshall was later interrogated, he stated that Scott had decided to rob a bank at Linton. It certainly sounded like something the notorious Captain Moonlite would do.

Scott and Dermoody speculated that something had happened to their companion when he had not returned after an hour. They elected to cut their losses and managed to escape unseen.

They remained at large, doubling back to Ballarat and making their way into the rugged Dead Horse Ranges. The pair hid in the bush and gathering necessary items as they went, which included a shotgun and a Bowie knife. Though neither was a natural bushman, Scott recalled enough of his trading from the army in New Zealand to know how to survive. The nights were frigid, and the bush a tangle of roots and branches that felt like they were always snatching at them or trying to bowl them over. It was strange, it was difficult, but it was better than gaol.

The police in the district were on high alert, with troopers from Ballarat, Smythesdale, Rokewood and Piggoreet looking for the escapees. Bands of volunteers also kept a vigil for the bushrangers, but they somehow managed to avoid detection.

Unfortunately tensions were beginning to mount. Dermoody found himself becoming infuriated by Scott's arrogance, and Scott found himself considering Dermoody to be a dullard with a mean temper. They bickered often, Scott raising his voice like a preacher at the pulpit, while Dermoody hollered back in his American accent.

On 12 June, Plunkett was arrested near Sydney Gully, 8 miles from Rokewood. Senior Constables Harding and Hayes of Rokewood met up with a party of police from Ballarat at Kangaroo Jack's near Grassy Gully, then split up to scour the area. The two Senior Constables each took a division. Meanwhile, Stapleton and Taylor had directed Plunkett to a nearby shepherd's hut to procure firearms and food.

***

It was the division led by Hayes that located Plunkett cowering behind a tree shortly thereafter. The bushranger tried to make a break but realised he was trapped. Plunkett was visibly trembling and bemoaned that he'd have had no problem escaping if he had a firearm. The following day he was returned to Ballarat Gaol via train under the watchful eye of Senior Constable Harding.

After he was arrested, Plunkett was very forthcoming with telling his version of events. He described Taylor as the worst kind of coward and thief and went on to describe the plans they had. He claimed their intention was to bail up a taxidermist called Bungaree Jack, take firearms and two stores and rob the Rokewood bank. Ironically, while searching for Taylor and Stapleton, the police accidentally found a man named Collins who had a warrant out on him for stealing harnesses.

***

On 14 June, a reward of £50 each was offered for the remaining escapees. Descriptions of the men at large were supplied in the press to aid recapture:

1. *Andrew George Scott, native of Cos. Tyrone, Ireland, with a strong north of Ireland accent, aged 27 years, 5 feet 8 3/4 inches high, medium and well built, round face, long sharp pointed nose, dark eyes, with a keen and determined expression, dark whiskers and moustache, shaven chin, drags the left leg and foot slightly in walking; wore light tweed coat, black cloth cap with peak; and appearance of a sailor. Was under committal for trial to the next sittings of the Ballarat Circuit Court for the Egerton bank robbery.*

2. *William Taylor, a Londoner, a carpenter, aged 50 years, 5 feet 4 3/4 inches high, stout build, sallow complexion, brown hair and eyes.*

3. *James Stapleton alias Fitzpatrick. Irish, aged 61 years, 5 feet 4 inches high, sallow complexion, grey hair and beard, brown eyes, arms freckled, scar corner left eyebrow, and has lost upper front teeth.*

4. *John Dermoody alias Harris, an American, aged 21 years, 5 feet 8 1/4 inches high, stout build, fresh complexion, light brown hair, blue eyes, nose inclined to the left, three warts on knuckles of left hand, and anchor tatooed on left wrist.*

By this time Dermoody had reached the end of his tether and decided to go alone.

"I'm out of here," said Dermoody, "you act all high and mighty, but you haven't got a clue. You told me we would be getting out of this two bit colony, but here we are in the middle of nowhere going around in circles and eating charred cockatoo for dinner!"

Scott bristled but remained quiet as Dermoody ranted and gathered his things.

"You gonna say something, preacher?"

"I have nothing to say to you except good luck. I would say it has been a pleasure to have come this far with you, but it would be a lie."

Scott was glad to be rid of Dermoody, considering him cur. He didn't feel the need to have an accomplice. He could use the sun and stars to guide him in a northeast direction, and he knew to always travel along the upper ridges of the ranges to find his way without a map or compass.

He passed Creswick and went through Smeaton, coming close to Castlemaine. The journey was incredibly tough and his supplies ran out. Having been without food for two days he resorted to chewing gum leaves in an effort to procure some form of sustenance.

During a wet night he lit a fire in a hollow log but the heat attracted a snake that he quickly dispatched with his Bowie knife. He considered trying to cook it for the meat. Scott's desperation was temporarily relieved when he emerged from the ranges near Lockwood and was given food and shelter by a woman there. Bread had never tasted so good.

He continued on his way with renewed energy, but his prison clothes were becoming ragged. Along the way he noticed a small camp where it seemed a gold miner had hung up his clothes while he bathed in the creek. Scott stealthily approached and took the clothes, swapping them with his, before sneaking away. Using his knife and a reflection in the creek, Scott reshaped his facial hair. Thus with new clothes and a new beard he found it far easier to go unrecognised as he headed towards New South Wales.

***

It was a Tuesday evening, 18 June, when Scott appeared in the vicinity of Marong Road where he found a miner's hut tucked away in dense scrub in New Zealand Gully. The hut was occupied by a boy and as Scott made his way inside he demanded a bed. The boy permitted this but, feeling uncomfortable about the desperate looking stranger, quickly informed two nearby miners who came to the house to check out the new arrival. The miners were suspicious of this shabby, gentleman armed with a shotgun and a revolver and promptly went to the police.

Detectives Alexander and Brown, Sergeant Drought and Constable Bradley responded straight away, riding out in the dead of night with a horse and cart. The police arrived at Specimen Hill where they left the cart before heading for the hut. Crawling through the scrub, they found it locked from the inside. They retreated to a machine workshop nearby where they found the boy working the night shift.

"Are you the lad that raised the alarm?"

"Yes," came the reply.

"Is he still in there?" asked Detective Alexander.

"He is. He just forced his way in and took my bed. How was I to resist an armed man such as that?"

The police thought for a moment and consulted privately before continuing the conversation.

"We need you to go to the hut and lure him to the door. He's locked it from inside," said the sergeant.

The boy shook his head. "Not me, you can do that yourselves."

"We will be right behind you. We just need him to come to the door so that we can get in and tackle him. If it's you at the door he won't be suspicious."

After several minutes, the police convinced the boy to lure the bushranger out and he returned to the hut and knocked on the door.

Inside, Scott grumbled. The police waited by the door – Brown and Bradley on one side, Drought and Alexander on the other – and found a chink in the wall that allowed them to see the sleeping bandit. By his side were his shotgun and Bowie knife, the revolver was capped but unloaded.

The boy knocked again. "What is it?" Scott snapped.

"Mate, give me my billy." came the reply. Scott was unimpressed to have his slumber interrupted over such a triviality.

"What billy?" Scott asked.

"The black billy in the chimney," answered the boy.

"Why do you need it?"

"It's our tea time."

Scott was awake now and noticed the pitch blackness. "What time is it?"

"Twelve o'clock," the boy answered.

Scott was displeased but seeing no alternative to allow him a decent rest he got up and located the billy can. When he opened the door and passed out the can, Sergeant Drought grabbed his wrist. Scott yanked himself free and tried to make for his gun but the troopers pinned him to the ground. He struggled and continued to reach for his weapons, growling like a wounded bear all the time but with the weight of four men on him he inevitably gave up. They had finally nabbed the notorious Captain Moonlite after only eight days on the run.

Scott was still willing and able to shoot his mouth off despite being handcuffed in the police cart.

"I am Scott. It is all up a tree with me. I am glad there were no lives lost; my intention was not to be taken alive. No one man in the country could arrest me; numbers might have done so. If it were not that you took me so suddenly I would have shot the first man that entered, and if I saw a chance of escape every other would be done the same to. I have suffered much misery since I escaped. If it was in daylight when you came to arrest me, I would have cautioned you to come only a certain distance, and if you ventured to approach then I would have shot you and then destroyed myself."

Now securely in custody and *en route* back to prison, Scott was happy to talk about his exploits. He stated that it was actually Plunkett, Stapleton and Taylor that had intended on robbing a bank and they had split off for Rokewood for that purpose. Crowds flooded the train stations in the hope of catching a glimpse of Scott, which irked him greatly. The leering crowds prompted him to state, "It is enough to make one believe in the Darwinian theory to see such a lot of grinning monkeys."

***

On 19 July, Stapleton was captured while sleeping in a *mia-mia* on the summit of Mount Bolton. Constable Kennedy of Coghill's Creek had been searching the area on foot after a tip-off from two local boys who had spotted a fire there, as well as some sportsmen whose dog had found a sheep Stapleton had duffed. They scaled the summit backed up by a man named William Morrison, where they found Stapleton's resting place nestled between two rocks. Stapleton was rudely awakened by the arrest and armed himself with a tomahawk. There was a struggle wherein Kennedy's revolver was wrenched out of his hand but the cumulative effect of starvation, exposure and rheumatism made resistance impossible for Stapleton. When Kennedy inspected Stapleton's stronghold, he noted a bed comprising of an empty mattress, along with a myriad of supplies: half a bag of flour, potatoes, a straight knife and one with a jagged edge for sawing, three linen shirts with "James Fry" written inside, gimlets, stubby candles, matches and a black crepe face mask.

Before being sent to the Ballarat Gaol, Stapleton was given tea to warm him up and closely monitored due to his seemingly frail condition. The bushranger seemed almost grateful to be back in custody and was forthcoming with details of his adventures. He stated that within the first three days after the escape he had nothing to eat and took his leave of the others. He headed to Little Hard Hills, then on to Egerton and Bullarook. All of his food and supplies were stolen as he could find nobody that would help him. On one occasion he managed to pass by a policeman without being recognised, but soon after decided not to risk being so close to civilisation and took refuge on Mount Bolton.

***

Scott was returned to Ballarat and was tried, as planned, defending himself in court. In the end, despite performing admirably as an untrained lawyer, Scott was found guilty of the Egerton bank robbery and given ten years to be served at Pentridge Prison. This would be a major turning point for Scott as he wrestled with what he saw as the injustices and corruption of the prison system. This sense of moral outrage would define the remainder of his life.

***

The final escapee to be captured was Dermoody, the American butcher. After parting with Scott, he had stayed briefly at Sandhurst before crossing the New South Wales border and heading to Wagga Wagga. Here he found work as a butcher and lived quietly until, by chance, some former associates of his arrived in town. When they found him they asked for money, but fearing they would dob him in Dermoody bolted and hid in an abandoned hut on the outskirts of town where he was found by police and arrested in March 1873, over a year after the escape. He was extradited and returned to Ballarat where he was tried for larceny and sentenced to 2 years and given an additional year for absconding.

Like Scott, he was transferred to Pentridge Prison where he racked up an impressive list of infractions ranging from quarrelling and attacking a warder to having a hat band and throwing hominy at another prisoner. After his release he would wind up in and out of gaol for essentially the rest of his life. In his later years he would try to use his connection to the infamous Captain Moonlite to gain recognition and a little money while living as a tramp.

***

In the end, the only one that appeared to make good their escape was William Taylor. However, with reports of a William Taylor in and out of gaol in New South Wales then Queensland in the late 1870s, it seems he may not have been so successful after all.

Captain Moonlite

> *"We had no intention of being bushrangers [...] misery and hunger produced despair and in one wild hour we proved how much the wretched dare. It must be seen that Wantabadgery was the place where the voice of hunger drowned the voice of reason, and we became criminals."*
>
> **– ANDREW GEORGE SCOTT**

Andrew George Scott was born in 1842 and raised in Rathfriland, Ireland. He was the son of a minister, who encouraged him to take up a career in the church. Scott as a young man was more interested in earthly pursuits and studied to become a civil engineer. Scott showed early signs of promise but soon became rather distracted. One of the stories that later circulated about this time in his life — one of many falsehoods peddled by journalists looking for an exciting story to attach to Scott — reported that while he was studying in London he was courted by the most esteemed clubs in high society and allegedly had an affair with the wife of a well known society figure. When the cuckolded husband found out, he threatened to thrash Scott. Though Scott would later be prone to scandal, at this time in his life he had not yet begun to accumulate such notoriety.

Another report, later disproved, was that he had sent word to his father that he was going to Rome to study the aqueducts but instead fought as a Redshirt in Garibaldi's army during the Second Italian War of Independence. In fact, Scott had moved with his family to New Zealand, where he fought in the Maori Wars. He was injured in a skirmish, his ankles being badly broken, which left him permanently with a pronounced limp and his right foot turned in. He was eventually discharged from the army for malingering, though Scott would allege that it was because he refused to resume participating in the slaughter of women and children. It is believed it was during his recuperation that he gained the nickname "Captain Moonlite", but it is not known why.

Newspapers would later allege that following this discharge from the armed forces, Scott moved to California and joined the Union army in the American Civil War — another fanciful rumour easily disproven — before seeking gold in Australia. It was at this time he felt compelled to follow his father's example and became a lay reader for the Anglican Church. While stationed in Bacchus Marsh in 1869, Scott proved to be remarkably popular with the locals and his sermons were well attended. He was involved in a small controversy after giving a questionable alibi for the son of a prominent local squatter around the time he transferred to the goldfields at Mount Egerton. Unfortunately, the church withheld Scott's wages while he was at this new assignment, and after inevitably becoming destitute it would appear he turned to crime.

On 7 May 1869, the bank at Mount Egerton was robbed by a man calling himself "Captain Moonlite". There has been much conjecture about exactly what happened, but what is known is that the bank safe was cleared out and the bank clerk Ludwig Bruun was found restrained in the schoolhouse with a note exonerating him of cowardice or collusion signed by the aforementioned "Captain". Bruun accused Scott of the crime, claiming he had tried to disguise himself with a cloak and a black mask, but he had recognised Scott's voice. Scott denied anything to do with it and suggested that the handwriting on the note matched that of Simpson, the schoolmaster. Simpson in turn accused Bruun of forging his handwriting and both Simpson and Bruun ended up in trouble with the law with their reputations in tatters, while Scott, after giving evidence in their trial, headed north to New South Wales with an unexplained cake of gold in his luggage.

He was soon in trouble again, however, being arrested by the Sydney water police while preparing to sail to Fiji in a yacht he had bought using bad cheques. Scott had been living large — mostly on the money he got from cashing in the cake of gold — boozing and partying and living above his means. He had convinced others to join him in a plan to buy an island in Fiji in order to begin an agricultural business, but had become distracted with his life of excess upon returning to Sydney, using the money for that on his vices too. When he ran out of money he attempted to use valueless cheques to buy things, but the ploy was soon discovered and raised with the authorities.

Scott did most of his time in Maitland Gaol, and he spent four months in Parramatta Lunatic Asylum after feigning madness in an attempt to engineer his escape from the minimum security facility. He was soon deemed sane and returned to prison. After his eventual release in 1872, he was immediately extradited to Victoria and was kept in Ballarat Gaol on remand over the Egerton robbery, thanks to new evidence that had come to light since his imprisonment.

Unwilling to be held, even to await his trial, he induced five other prisoners to join him in an escape. After subduing the guard and climbing the perimeter wall with a stolen rope, the gang split up. Gradually the men were recaptured, and Scott managed to make it all the way to Bendigo on foot before he was caught. He acted as his own defence when tried before Sir Redmond Barry, but was found guilty of the bank robbery and sentenced to twelve years hard labour to be served in Pentridge Prison. Scott maintained that he had not robbed the bank even after his conviction, and would continue to profess the same for the remainder of his life.

In Pentridge he proved to be a very disruptive prisoner and was frequently in trouble with the guards. He was often found with contraband, frequently losing privileges or being put in solitary confinement. He was also involved with the trial of a fellow inmate named Weachurch for whom he gave evidence as a defence witness. He also met James Nesbitt, a young man from an abusive home in Richmond with a history of petty crimes. The pair became close almost immediately and Nesbitt was once punished for smuggling tea to Scott. As Nesbitt had been released first, he waited and was reunited with Scott on the outside upon his release.

Scott and Nesbitt lived together in Fitzroy, where Scott decided the best way to utilise his prison experience and oratory skills would be to tour Victoria giving lectures on prison reform. He obtained the services of an agent and hit the road. While on tour, Scott recruited a former confectionary maker named Frank Johns to be a stage assistant. Johns, who had a crippled hand from an industrial accident, adopted the pseudonym Thomas Williams.

During the tour Scott and Nesbitt found themselves being targeted by police, who would arrest them on any possible pretence to interrogate them over a myriad of crimes that they had no connection to, including an attempted breakout at the prisoner barracks at Point Gellibrand, and a bank robbery in Lancefield that had previously been pinned on the Kelly Gang.

Police also caused Scott's lectures to be shut down and interfered in his attempts to gain other employment, forcing Scott and his companions into desperation. Scott convinced Nesbitt and Williams to join him on a journey to New South Wales in search of a new start.

Other tagalongs that joined them as they trekked were teenager Augustus "Gus" Wernicke, who was the son of a publican, and Thomas Rogan, *aka* Baker, who also had a history of crime, having done time in Beechworth Gaol for horse stealing. However, the troupe's lack of bush survival skills began to create issues for them, and they were repeatedly rejected for work at stations to support themselves, which was due to a mix of police interference and the dire economic situation of the time. They became desperate for supplies, having sold everything they could in exchange for food, and decided to take up bushranging as a means of survival. It was alleged that they began sticking up stores and stations as they travelled by foot and were frequently mistaken for the Kelly Gang, which Scott then used to their advantage in gaining submission from victims. While plausible, there were many other amateur bushrangers at the time doing the same thing and none of Scott's gang ever gave a recorded confession to these incidents.

The gang travelled through the New South Wales Riverina, continuing their attempts to find legitimate work. They were joined by a swaggie named Graham Bennett near Gundagai, and proceeded to Wantabadgery Station. Scott enquired after the manager, but after being made to wait for hours in the heat were given marching orders.

Forced to sleep in the open without shelter overnight, they were soaked through in a downpour that left their sleeping gear unusable. Scott came to the conclusion that he needed to retaliate.

The next day, the gang stuck up Wantabadgery Station and took the staff prisoner inside the homestead while the gang took turns eating and sleeping. Over the course of the day more prisoners were captured and in one incident Scott killed a horse that he attempted to steal because it had resisted his attempts to mount it.

That night there was a party of sorts and Scott went to the nearby pub, the Australian Arms, for more drinks, but instead came back having robbed the place and kidnapped the publican's children. In the early hours of the morning word reached the police in Wagga Wagga that something was up at Wantabadgery and the station was subsequently besieged by four of the Wagga Wagga mounted police. A shoot out commenced between the outlaws, who were directed by Scott, and the overwhelmed police, who were soundly defeated and forced to retreat from the battle on foot as the bushrangers had stolen their horses.

In the morning Scott and the gang rode to the nearby McGlede's farm, though only Scott and Rogan had experience on horseback. On the way they crossed paths with a posse of volunteers who were out looking for them. Scott held a mock trial of the party and ordered one of the men to shoot his own horse as a punishment. The posse were then marched as prisoners alongside the gang as they headed towards McGlede's farm.

Soon the police from Wagga Wagga were reinforced by a party from Gundagai and rode back to pursue the bushrangers. They managed to catch up to them and another shoot out erupted. As the gang ran to the safety of the homestead, Gus Wernicke was mortally wounded by a shot from one of the police. The rest of the gang hunkered down in the kitchen, though Rogan ran into the house and hid under a bed.

In the heat of the battle Constable Webb-Bowen was mortally wounded by a shot to the neck, and James Nesbitt was shot through the head by a trooper while standing at a window. Scott was beside himself and held Nesbitt in his arms and kissed him as he died. Scott ran out to rescue Wernicke who subsequently also died in his arms. The demoralised bushrangers were then arrested following the police breaking into the kitchen. Rogan was located later and all were taken to Gundagai to await trial.

During the trial of the "Wantabadgery Bushrangers", Scott provided his own defence and pleaded for mercy for Rogan, Williams and Bennett. All were found guilty of murdering Webb-Bowen, who had died from his wounds several days after the battle, and all were sentenced to be executed. After the Executive Council met, Scott and Rogan's sentences were upheld, but the other boys were given extended prison sentences.

While awaiting his hanging, Scott wrote many letters to people he cared for, including his father and Nesbitt's mother to whom he apologised for what had happened to her son. The letters were suppressed by prison authorities.

Andrew George Scott was executed in Darlinghurst Gaol on 20 January 1880 with Thomas Rogan by his side. Neither made any final statements. His last request was to be buried with James Nesbitt — a request that was eventually granted in 1995 when his remains were transferred from Rookwood Cemetery to Gundagai after agitation from members of the public.

In recent years there has been much discussion of the nature of Scott and Nesbitt's relationship being a homosexual one. It is indisputable that Scott loved Nesbitt very deeply, and it is believed that he wore a ring made from a lock of Nesbitt's hair. Whether this love was romantic or platonic cannot be determined definitively as neither man is alive to state the case. There were many accounts that linked Scott romantically to women, and it has been suggested that Scott's passionate love for Nesbitt may have been an interpretation of his religious beliefs rather than being sexual in nature. In the end we can only speculate. For now, with Scott and Nesbitt presumed to be lovers, it at least helps to create some form of representation for historically repressed members of society.

Though Andrew Scott's bushranging was very minor, and some could reasonably argue he barely qualifies for the term, the impact he had on popular culture of the time was considerable. The sheer volume of fanciful stories about him that were published by papers of the time helped to cement the celebrity status of "Captain Moonlite", which only served to make life more difficult for Scott. It provides us with a cautionary tale about the negative impacts on individuals as a result of how the media portray them, regardless of the validity of the claims being made, and how that shapes the perceptions of others.

Wagga Wagga Advertiser and Riverine Reporter (NSW: 1868 - 1875), Saturday
29 June 1872, page 4

ARREST OF SCOTT BY THE SANDHURST POLICE.
(From the *Bendigo Advertiser*.)

THE public were no doubt considerably surprised yesterday morning upon reading
the account of the capture of Scott which appeared in our columns, and the police of
Ballarat will be as much astounded as anyone. It would have taken a very fertile imagination to suppose that Scott would have ventured so close to the precincts of this
city, whatever he did, for it was so much like putting his head into the lion's mouth.
Notwithstanding the improbabilities of the case, the police authorities of this district
took the precaution of sending scouts into the bush country surrounding Sandhurst,
and on Tuesday afternoon information was received that a strange looking man was
in the neighbourhood of the bone mills.

The alarm was not raised during the day, but at two o'clock yesterday morning
Sergeant Drought, Detectives Alexander and Brown, and Constable James Bradley,
proceeded to Specimen Hill in the police cart. The horse and cart were put up at
Specimen Hill, and the officers crossed the range in the direction of New Zealand
Gully. From what they heard they considered it highly probable that the object of
their search would be in a hut, which they were told was to be found in a thick part
of the scrub.

They came upon the hut very carefully, creeping upon their hands and knees, the
darkness of the night favouring their design. They at first did not know what would
be the best way to commence operations, well knowing the desperate courage of the
man whom they had to deal with, and it almost amounted to. a matter of tossing up
whether they should rush the habitation, which was found to be securely barricaded
and fortified; in case they attempted to storm the hut they felt sure that one of their
lives would be lost, if not that of the prisoner, and they themselves were well armed.
At last they determined to adopt a stratagem. They went to a small machine working
in the gully not far off, where they found a boy who used to live in the hut, and who
was working on the night shift at the machine. They made inquiries of him, and he
described the man whom he had seen in the neighbourhood that evening, from which
description the officers felt sure it was Scott. They asked the boy to accompany them

to the hut, but he said he was frightened of the man, as he seemed a desperate fellow. Ultimately they induced the boy to go to the hut, and ask for a billy inside belonging to himself, they (the officers) following.

When the boy knocked at the door Drought and Alexander crouched down on one side of the door, and Brown and Bradley on the other. Now was the critical moment. The boy called out, "Mate, give me the billy." A man who was inside the hut called out, "What I billy?" He was answered- "The black billy in the chimney." The door, which was securely barred inside, was, then partly and cautiously opened, and the billy thrust out. At this time the door was forcibly pushed open by the detectives, when Sergeant Drought caught the man by the wrists, The detectives and Constable James Bradley all being in front of the hut, then threw themselves upon him. He made a desperate attempt to get to a stretcher where was lying a single-barrelled gun loaded and capped. There was also a six-barrelled revolver fully capped within a few feet of where he was struggling with the officers. He was at once handcuffed, and then said, "I am Scott, it is all up a tree with me." Scott then said, " I am glad there were no lives lost; my intention was not to be taken alive. No one man in the country could arrest me; numbers might have done so. If it were not that you took me so suddenly I would have shot the first man that entered, and if I saw a chance of escape, every other would be done the same to. I have suffered much misery since my escape. If it was in daylight when you came to arrest me, I would have cautioned you to come only a certain distance, and if you ventured to approach I would have shot you and then destroyed himself."

On the way to the lock-up Scott was very anxious to know what the warder's state-ment of the escape was. He was answered that the warder said he bit the thumb of one of them seriously, and that they had used force to silence him. Scott said, "That is correct; we put a blanket in his mouth, and I wonder he did not waken all in the gaol by his crying out. We got the ropes and forms and placed them against the wall; We hoisted each other up; I was the last up. We got down by a rope. The other prisoners were all like children. I was quite cool, and remained to the last. On effecting our escape, we — that is Dermody and I — went to Bacchus Marsh, and afterwards returned to Soldier's Hill, Ballarat, where I left Dermody, and have not heard of him since, nor any of the others; and if I did I would not tell you. I was on my way, when you arrested me, to New South Wales. I thought I was safe, it being my tenth day out. I intended to go to Echuca. I travelled generally through thick country, and was taking the back way to New South Wales. Had I carried out my first intention, I would not have been arrested; my intention was to make to Queenscliff or Geelong, take a cutter, and go to New Zealand."

He was then brought to the Sandhurst lock-up, and on being put into the cell, he looked with contempt at the lining of the cell. "Do you call this lining; I call it nothing but sheet tin or brown paper; I would get out of it in twenty-four hours." Scott states that he is a civil engineer by profession, and that his professional knowledge materially assisted him in his escape.

Whilst waiting in the cell he conversed very freely with the constables and others who were watching him. He was visited by Mr. Martley, the barrister, who said he was requested by one of the photographers in Pall Mall to ask him if he would consent to have his photograph taken. Scott replied, "What do you want my photograph for?" Mr. Martley replied, "Oh, you have such a large number of friends who would like to see how you look,;" to which Scott replied, "Well, I cannot understand why so many people can be found to neglect their business and gather around a lock-up to see a man in trouble." Mr. Martley answered, "You have made yourself quite famous by breaking out of that gingerbread gaol, and so they want to see a man of such celebrity." Scott: "Well, here I am, dressed like a blackguard, and I don't like to have my portrait taken." Mr, Martley: "Oh, if you have any objection to be taken in these clothes a better suit could be got for you. If you do not have your photograph taken, some one will take a sketch of you in the Ballarat Court. As for your appearance, I cannot see why you should object, when you are not particularly a bad-looking man." Scott: "People want me to do this merely for the gratification of morbid curiosity; as I am now, I am quite notorious enough, and I do not want to perpetuate my notoriety. For the present, therefore, I must decline." Scott went on to complain of the Victorian press, which, he said, had described him as a ruffian. He said the charge was false; he had never committed one single act of ruffianism, or anything to justify the press describing him as a ruffian. In breaking out of gaol he had only followed the instincts of human nature, which had a repugnance to being deprived of liberty; but that was not ruffianism.

The prisoner was kept, in the lockup, till near 12 o'clock, when he was taken to the railway station, and was conveyed by train to Ballarat via Melbourne by the mid-day train, in charge of Detective Alexander and other constables.

On Saturday, we learn from the *Evening Mail*, the gaol-breaker, Andrew George Scott, was brought before the visiting justices, Mr. Gaunt, P.M., and Mr. Robert: Lewis, at the Ballarat gaol. The prisoner was charged with the offence of breaking from the gaol, and making his escape from legal custody. The prisoner, who appeared anxious, was nevertheless firm and collected in his demeanour, saluting the justices with military precision, and assuming the attitude of "attention," in which he remained till the close of the proceedings. He admitted the offence, and said that he had been led away by his feelings, which were of a nature utterly beyond his control. He expressed, the deepest sorrow for his offence, and asked the Bench to be as lenient as possible, as he had already suffered both his body and mind. Mr. Gaunt pointed out to the prisoner the gravity of his offence, and remarked that the punishment awarded by the statute was a severe one, He did not think the present a case that called for additional severity, nor yet for particular leniency. Himself and his brother magistrates had determined that a similar sentence to that passed on Plunkett, an old offender, which the prisoner was not, but still, who had been the principal mover in the escapade, would meet all judicial requirements. The prisoner was then sentenced to twelve months' hard labour, the first six months in irons. A slight nervous twitching of the lips was the only sign of recognition of the sentence given by the prisoner, who, having respectfully saluted the Bench, was removed to the quarters allotted him.

IX

⸎

The Stringybark Creek Tragedy

At first light on 25 October 1878, Sergeant Michael Kennedy, And Constables Michael Scanlan and Thomas McIntyre sat mounted with their packhorse, waiting for the arrival of Constable Thomas Lonigan. All men were in plain-clothes, as was the standard for bush work given that police uniforms were too delicate for the rugged outdoors, and too costly to replace on a policeman's meagre wage. Kennedy impatiently looked at his fob watch. It was a handsome gold timepiece with a cover over the face and the back. Under the back cover, near the keyhole where the watch was wound, Kennedy's name had been engraved. It was his most prized possession. It had been gifted to him by the squatters in Doon, his previous placement, for apprehending notorious stock thieves.

Once Lonigan arrived, the troopers headed off towards the Wombat Ranges. Their mission was to apprehend two wanted criminals – Edward and Daniel Kelly. Both were wanted for their role in what was described as the attempted murder of a policeman, a Constable named Alexander Fitzpatrick. Edward, better known as "Ned", being the trigger man that had reportedly shot Fitzpatrick in the wrist, had a reward of one hundred pounds for his capture. Both brothers were believed to be armed and dangerous and given their history it was not hard to imagine that the police were putting themselves in a very dangerous scenario.

The trek out of Mansfield was quite uneventful. The farmers began to start their working day and the party went unnoticed as they rode towards the Wombat Ranges.

A sudden moment of excitement erupted when McIntyre's horse suddenly shied away from the path as a tiger snake slithered past. McIntyre pulled out his revolver and shot the reptile, blowing its head clean off. Lonigan seemed to jump about a foot out of the saddle and quick as lightning had drawn his own Webley from the holster and whirled around towards McIntyre, who smirked at the mangled snake.

"First blood, Lonigan!" McIntyre chuckled.

Lonigan grumbled under his breath. Scanlan sniggered at the pair, but Kennedy was distinctly unamused. "From now on we don't take our weapons out unless we're set upon, is that understood?" he commanded. Everyone nodded. They continued, leaving the mangled serpent behind.

***

When the party reached Holland's Creek, the sun was high above. Kennedy rode slightly ahead of the group and looked around for landmarks.

"What are you looking for, Mick?" asked Scanlan.

"That Martin fellow from Dueran Station showed me a crossing near here the other day."

"Shouldn't we be meeting up with the other party?" asked McIntyre, fidgeting in the saddle nervously.

"We don't want to meet up with them. If we do, we'll find them out of tucker, and they'll eat us out of ours."

After the brief pause, they continued deeper into the forest. It seemed to the men as if the trees stretched on forever. Grey box gums, the strips of bark shedding from the stringybark trees, tussocks of spear-grass bobbing in the breeze and marsupials darting through the undergrowth. Kennedy became aware of a presence just beyond their vision. His ears pricked up and his eyes became extremely active as every instinct told him to be alert. His fingers tightened on the reins.

"Mick, are you alright?" Scanlan asked, riding alongside his mate.

"Aye. Just keep your eyes open."

It was with some relief when they reached a clearing alongside Stringybark Creek and the sergeant elected to establish the camp. Hobbling the horses by some trees, they began to unload the equipment. There was only the one tent between the four of them, and not many provisions.

Unbeknownst to the party, they had been followed for some time by Ned Kelly. Ever since the news of parties heading into the Wombat Ranges had reached Ned through his bush telegraphs he had spent his days patrolling the bush. He had found fresh tracks from the police horses between the lowlands and the boggy area upstream and followed them. It wasn't long before he caught up with the police but gave them a wide berth. One of the men he could have sworn was a Constable Ernest Flood he had a down on, and another looked like it might have been trooper Strahan, who he had heard made threats to his sisters. He immediately turned and headed back to his hideout on Bullock Creek.

When he arrived at the hut, his brother and their mates were stoking the fire. Steve Hart, a nineteen-year-old jockey from Wangaratta, was preparing the billy, while Joe Byrne, a twenty-one-year-old from the Woolshed Valley that had, up until very recently, been horse-stealing with Ned, plonked firewood into the fresh flames. Dan Kelly approached Ned.

"Did you find anything?" he asked.

"There's traps down by Stringybark Creek. From what I saw they look well-armed, just like we were told. I reckon they mean to gun us down rather than arrest us. Flood and Strahan are with them." Ned replied. Dan's face took on a grim aspect.

"We just can't seem to shake those bastards, can we?" he said with exasperation.

"I need to get a closer look at their camp, but can't do it in the light," Ned said, pacing and clenching his fists.

"No, I'll go, you know I can keep quiet and get close." Dan replied. Ned paused for a moment and Dan stood before him expectantly.

"Alright. Head down towards the bogs. You'll know them when you see them."

Dan tucked an old-fashioned horse pistol into his trousers and headed off in the direction of Stringybark Creek. He moved stealthily through the bush until he heard voices. By now the sun was setting and the flicker of flames could be seen through the ferns and tussocks. Dan took cover behind some spear-grass and examined the camp. From his cover he saw five horses, one tent and four bearded men dressed like kangaroo hunters with tweed suits and leather gaiters.

He tried to see what weapons they had. He moved closer and kept low. He spotted a double-barrelled shotgun and a Spencer rifle leaning against a log. No doubt, he surmised, there was more in the tent. He felt something stinging his legs and looked down to see he was kneeling on a nest of jack jumper ants, some of which had ventured into his trouser legs and were biting him. He kept quiet, despite the terrible sting of the insect bites, and tried to make out what was being said by the police, but the stinging was too much, and he began moving swiftly and quietly back to the hut.

***

The next morning, after a breakfast of watery porridge, Kennedy assigned himself and Scanlan as scouts. He took McIntyre aside and informed him of the plan.

"You stay at the camp with Lonigan. We won't be too long, just a scout around the immediate vicinity. See if you can catch some kangaroos or parrots for dinner with the gun and whip up a fresh batch of bread."

Kennedy mounted and smiled at McIntyre who looked grimly back. "Don't be alarmed if we're not back before dusk, Mac."

As Kennedy and Scanlan rode off into the bush, Lonigan busied himself in the tent reading The Vagabond Papers, wherein an investigative journalist had gone undercover in the hospital at Pentridge Prison. Here he had interviewed one Harry Power, the infamous bushranger of eight years previous who was discussing his young offsider – Ned Kelly. Lonigan read with keen interest as Power discussed Kelly's violent inclinations.

As the morning rolled on, McIntyre decided hunt for meat. He took a cartouche of ammunition and the double-barrelled shotgun from the tent and planted his hat on a jaunty angle atop his retreating hairline.

"Where are you going?" Lonigan piped up.

"I'm going to catch some dinner. Kennedy left the shotgun for me," replied McIntyre.

Lonigan sat bolt upright, "Are you mad? They'll hear us!"

"Don't fret, Lonigan. Would Kennedy have instructed me to do it if he thought we'd be at risk?" McIntyre chuckled at Lonigan who frowned in response.

A short walk downstream later McIntyre began searching for signs of the desired marsupials. McIntyre's enthusiasm for shooting was not matched by his competency, however. Unable to procure any kangaroos, he turned his attention to some parrots on a tree branch and fired. The shots missed.

The report of McIntyre's shotgun echoed through the bush to the bushrangers' stronghold on Bullock Creek, and Ned and the others stood to attention.

"What are they shooting at?" asked Steve. Ned stormed into the stronghold and scooped up his carbine. It was a rickety old weapon with the stock and muzzle cut short to allow it to be aimed with one hand, like a pistol. Because the shortened stock meant that the barrel was no longer held in place properly, Ned had tried to repair it with waxed string but the barrel had stubbornly refused to straighten and remained slightly wonky. Ned also grabbed a handful of musket balls he had scored to allow them to split into quarters when fired and his powder horn. He jammed a pocket colt revolver into the back of the crimson sash around his waist and checked over the sawn-off carbine to check it was loaded and primed.

"Come, Dan. Let's go and meet the buggers. We'll bail them up and take their supplies," said Ned. Dan nodded and grabbed his grey woollen sack coat, plunging his sinewy arms into the capacious sleeves.

"We're coming too," said Joe. Ned knew he could either accept the help or risk the others following him into trouble without his consent. He also understood the value of back-up when confronted with four armed troopers.

"Alright. But you do exactly as I say at all times," replied Ned donning a Sydney soft crown hat and pulling the chinstrap under his nose in the fashion of the flash squatters. The others fetched their weapons: Dan collected his hunting rifle, Joe took up an old musket, and Steve grabbed his fowling piece.

***

Almost an hour after setting out McIntyre returned to camp and set about stripping a sheet of bark off a nearby tree with a hatchet. He then gathered water from the creek in the billy and returned to the fire where he began to make a fresh batch of bread using some of the supplies they had brought.

Meanwhile, the Kelly brothers and their mates moved on foot through the sea of blue gums that stretched to the police camp. Ned was a sombre figure in his dark tweeds with the dash of crimson from his sash as almost a warning sign, like a red-bellied black snake. Dan was close by his side in his baggy, rumpled suit and black billycock hat. Behind them Joe Byrne was dressed like a squatter in a handsome blue-grey sack coat and striped tweed trousers, but with the low-crowned hat and high-heeled boots of the larrikin, and Steve Hart was dressed in grey tweed with his lucky red sash peeking out from under his sandy coloured waistcoat, his face covered in patches of downy hair where he was attempting to cultivate a beard.

They worked their way downstream and spread out, using the ferns and spear-grass surrounding the camp as cover. From here they could observe the movements of the police while being unseen themselves. Ned took stock of where everything was positioned. The police horses sensed their presence and began to stir. One of the animals began to snort and dig at the earth with its front hoof.

"The horses seem agitated," said Lonigan. McIntyre barely

acknowledged the comment, focused instead on placing dough into a stockpot and wiping his hands on his oilskin apron.

"I'm going to move them up a bit. I reckon there's something in the bushes spooking them. Keep an eye out, Mac, would you?" Lonigan grumbled. He grabbed his pistol belt and buckled it around his waist, loosening the flap of his holster for easy access.

In the scrub, Dan moved closer to Ned, barely making a sound. "What are we waiting for, Ned?" he whispered.

"I need to make sure that we don't get any surprises. I can only see two of them," Ned replied. He supposed that the other two police were either asleep in the tent or out in the bush as neither of them had made an appearance in the time the bushrangers had been watching the camp.

"Recognise these two?" asked Dan.

"Yeah, I reckon that's Strahan with the horses and Flood by the fire. I'd like to roast him upon it."

They continued to wait for a further fifteen minutes, the tension reaching near to breaking point. Ned scooted around the perimeter of the camp and gestured for the others to come close.

"Alright lads, we're going to take their guns and horses and send 'em back to where they came from with their tails between their legs," Ned whispered, "I want no killing, but if they resist, well, better them than us any day I reckon." The others nodded.

Lonigan sat on a log close to the fire and warmed his hands. McIntyre checked on the bread.

"I suppose it might be a good idea to build this fire up a bit. It can act as a beacon for Kennedy and Scanlan," McIntyre thought aloud.

"I'm sure they know how to get back," Lonigan said. He shifted uncomfortably. He noticed a tussock rustle and whipped his head around.

"McIntyre! There's something in the bushes."

"Don't fret. It's probably a wombat or some such thing," McIntyre replied dismissively, adding fuel to the fire.

There was a flurry of movement in the bush and the bushrangers emerged.

"Bail up, throw up your arms!" bellowed Ned levelling his mangled carbine at McIntyre. The rest of the gang emerged echoing the cry. McIntyre stood up and held his arms out at waist height and dropped his fork.

Lonigan began to run backwards while reaching for his Webley. As quick as thought Ned whipped across and fired. A burst of sparks exploded from the muzzle and the lead ball split into shards of shrapnel and spread like duck shot. Three of the hot pieces of lead struck Lonigan. A huge conical shard went through his exposed left forearm and lodged in his thigh; a smaller shard sliced open his right temple as he looked over his left shoulder. But the most devastating was a jagged shard that pierced his right eye, smashing the orbital bone and driving deep into his brain through the socket, mincing the organ as it went. Lonigan stumbled and tripped backwards over a log, hitting the ground hard with a gasp. McIntyre had winced when the shot went off and was afraid to risk peeking back over his shoulder.

"Oh Christ, I'm shot," Lonigan gasped with his last conscious impulse before he began heaving and writhing on the ground in agony and confusion like a big fish dragged out of a lake. Ned watched him as the thrashing ceased and Lonigan collapsed, the life flickering out of his one remaining eye. The frantic, quavering voice was replaced by a guttural sigh and Thomas Lonigan expired, face-down in a pool of his own blood.

Ned stalked towards the body with a look of grim determination. Behind him the other boys and McIntyre were motionless and aghast. Ned looked down on the bleeding corpse and showed no emotion.

"What a pity. What made the fool run?" he said, rolling the body over. He almost recognised the face.

"Did you see the way he went for his revolver?" said Dan, his body starting to quake. He let out a nervous giggle.

Joe lowered his gun slightly, looking to Ned for some sort of direction as to what came next. Steve was white as a sheet.

McIntyre's heart was in his throat. Ned looked straight at him. It was clear now that this was not Constable Flood, but a stranger.

"Oh, God, my time has come!" McIntyre whimpered in panic.

"Not if you do as I say. What's your name? Where are you from?" said Ned.

"M-McIntyre. From Mansfield."

"Who is he?" Ned continued, pointing at the corpse.

"Tom Lonigan."

"That's not Lonigan. I know Lonigan to see him..." Ned trailed off and inspected the face of the dead man again. Beneath the blood and brain fluid that drenched the face was indeed the features of Lonigan, the broad cheeks and heavy brow, albeit with one eye socket sunken from the shot.

"Ah," Ned allowed the flicker of a smirk to tickle the corner of his mouth imperceptibly, "I thought he was Strahan who blowed about how he'd shoot first then cry surrender." Ned contemplated briefly before continuing. "Lonigan, eh? I had a run in with him one time in Benalla. He nearly ruined me for life."

"Won't be locking any of us poor buggers up again, will he?" Dan said bitterly.

"Where's your revolver then?" Ned asked his prisoner.

"In the tent."

"Keep him covered." Ned instructed Joe.

Ned patted the man down, checking his coat and boots for weapons. Satisfied, he signalled for the man to lower his hands.

Dan paced across the camp and grabbed the shotgun that was resting against a tree stump. He went to the tent and thrust the shotgun barrels in through the flap.

"Out of there you bastards!" Dan shouted.

"There's nobody in there," McIntyre said. Dan lowered the shotgun and stomped towards the horses.

"Where are the others? There was four of you I counted," Ned demanded.

"They're out looking for you."

"When will they be back?"

"Well, I... I don't know. They might not even be back tonight." McIntyre began looking around at the four bushrangers with panic in his eyes.

Dan strode across to Ned waving some handcuffs from the tent.

"Ned, put these on the bugger."

"What use is that?" McIntyre said indignantly.

"He's a trap, he's not to be trusted. Put these on him," Dan repeated. Ned stood stoically with his carbine's muzzle resting on his shoulder.

"I have something here that's better than handcuffs." Ned said tapping the stock menacingly. "If you don't do exactly as I say I will shoot you. If you escape, I will follow you all the way to the police station if necessary and shoot you there. Understand?"

McIntyre nodded his head. Dan pocketed the handcuffs and scowled.

"He'd just as soon have used them on us," he grumbled.

Steve emerged from the tent holding handfuls of rifle rounds. The long brass tubes glinted in the afternoon sun as he rolled them around.

"Look at this – rifle rounds. There's more in the tent besides," Steve said.

"Well, well," Ned turned to McIntyre, "What are you carrying long arms for? You're only allowed revolvers – isn't that true?"

"They're for hunting kangaroos."

"So why do you need so much ammunition? Surely, you're not such bad shots?"

"I swear, they're for catching food."

"Who was shooting before?" Dan interjected.

"I was hunting some birds for dinner."

"What weapons do the others have with them?" Ned continued.

"Just their revolvers."

"What about the repeating rifle?" Dan barked.

"Uh..." McIntyre hesitated. Ned began to lower his gun. "Yes, they have a Spencer rifle with them."

Ned's gaze bored holes into McIntyre. "You came to shoot us."

"No, we came to apprehend you."

"Here, that's enough for now Ned. Let's have some tea, yeah?" Joe interrupted. Ned turned on his heel and stormed off to the far side of the camp. Joe gestured for McIntyre to brew some tea in the billy. The constable complied.

The heat from the fire brought the water to boil quickly. Joe grabbed two pannikins, painted with white enamel that had begun to chip off, and poured the freshly brewed tea from the billy can into the cups. He handed one to McIntyre who grasped the cup with both hands. Joe sat on the log next to the constable and watched him take a drink. McIntyre's hands were shaking violently.

"How is it?" Joe asked.

"Needs a pinch of sugar," McIntyre said attempting to smile. Joe took a sip, staring at McIntyre intensely.

"Mm, you're right. Needs sugar." Joe replied in a monotone. "What's in the pot there?"

"It's bread. I was making a loaf."

"Reckon it might be time for some dinner. May I?" Joe said, walking to the pot where it lay in the dirt. McIntyre nodded as if he had a choice in the matter.

Joe opened the pot and was impressed at the display of bakery. The gang quickly joined him and devoured the bread. Joe offered up a piece for McIntyre to eat but the constable refused. Dan did not take his eyes off McIntyre the whole time.

"Mm, this is good tucker." Steve said, attempting to lighten the mood. McIntyre took quiet pride in the appraisal of his culinary skills.

Joe sat next to McIntyre again, "Here, mate, do you smoke?"

"I do," McIntyre answered.

"Smoke with me," Joe directed, taking out a corncob pipe from his coat. McIntyre took his pipe out of a pouch on his belt and a pinch of cut tobacco. Joe gestured for McIntyre to pass him some tobacco as well.

***

Ned sat by the campfire as he pulled the wadding out of some shotgun cartridges he had found. He tipped out the shot and replaced it with bullets, then replaced the wadding.

"What are the names of the other men in your party?" Ned asked.

"What do you plan to do if they come back? If you're going to shoot them, I'd rather be shot myself than tell you a damned thing," McIntyre protested. Ned smiled.

"Well, I do like to see a brave man. Have no fear; I would not shoot any man who surrenders himself. If they give up their firearms and horses, they'll walk away free."

"What if they don't return? Will you shoot me?"

"I'd have shot you half an hour ago if I wanted that. Just do as you're told, and you'll be fine. But if I do let you go, you will have to leave the force. It's a shame to see such strapping fellows in a lazy, loafing billet like the police."

"I'll do it gladly. My health is bad anyway. I've been thinking of leaving and my life is insured," McIntyre said, his eyes darting around. Ned smiled. He didn't believe the policeman but took a strange amusement in his hostage's nervous ramblings. "But you faithfully promise you won't shoot them, if they surrender? Nor will you let your mates fire at them?" McIntyre begged.

"I promise *I* won't shoot them. The others can please themselves." Ned smirked. Steve and Joe sniggered at Ned's audacity. Despite the gravity of the situation there was still a perverse entertainment to be had by making a trap squirm and all of these young men had their own reasons for wanting to.

"Tell me of your companions," Ned ordered again.

"Their names are Kennedy and Scanlan," McIntyre said with a laboured sigh.

"Kennedy and Scanlan. I'll remember that," Ned said nodding. "Y'know, at first I thought you were Constable Flood. If you were, I'd have roasted you on this fire. There are four men in the police that if ever I lay my hands on, I will roast them alive: Flood, Steele, Strahan and Fitzpatrick. Don't know much of Kennedy, but that Scanlan, I have heard, is a flash fellow."

Ned checked over his weapons and paused in thought. "I suppose, one day, some of you fellows will finally shoot me. But I will make you suffer first, and Constable Fitzpatrick will be the cause of all of it." Ned's countenance took on a sullen appearance.

"You cannot blame us for what Fitzpatrick did to you," McIntyre said, tipping the ashes out of his pipe.

Ned went to reply when he heard something approaching from downstream.

"Lads... quiet – listen!"

All did as Ned said. He noticed movement through the trees ahead. Kennedy and Scanlan were returning after their scouting mission.

"Hist! Take your places!"

The gang scattered into hiding spots. Joe and Dan took up position in the tussocks of spear-grass near the tent. Steve crouched in the tent itself and Ned pressed his finger into McIntyre's chest.

"Remember, you get them to surrender or they're dead men. You warn them or run off, I'll put a hole through you."

McIntyre nodded and sat on a log facing the direction the riders were approaching from. Ned jumped behind the adjacent log, nearly landing in the fire, and kept low. He had the shotgun to hand as well as his carbine. From his hiding spot he was able to watch McIntyre and the arrivals.

Kennedy and Scanlan could smell the campfire and pressed forward. Pushing through the scrub into the clearing they saw McIntyre sitting on a log nervously bouncing his legs. Lonigan, they figured, must have been asleep in the tent. McIntyre cocked his head as if listening for something then nervously rose and approached the two mounted troopers.

"Sergeant, you had better throw down your arms. We're surrounded," McIntyre said with surprising calm. Scanlan chuckled and Kennedy scoped the camp. Behind the log where McIntyre had been seated, he thought he saw Lonigan crouching. He smirked.

212 ~ AIDAN PHELAN

"Oh, well in that case..." said Kennedy opening the flap on his holster. No sooner had the words left his mouth than Ned Kelly rose from cover and fired a warning shot.

"Bail Up! Put down your weapons!" came the thunderous command and the police went for their firearms. The rest of the gang emerged from hiding fully armed and shouting. Kennedy drew his Webley and dismounted, placing the horse between himself and the bushrangers.

Scanlan meanwhile attempted to unsling the Spencer repeater while controlling his terrified horse who shied at the sound of the erupting gunfire and began galloping back the way they had come. As the horse wheeled around Scanlan could see Lonigan's feet on the other side of the log where he fell. He managed to get the Spencer around one shoulder to shoot from the hip, opening fire on Ned who dodged. The horse spun around and as Ned fired back the shot hit Scanlan in the side and tore through his torso, puncturing his lungs. He fell forward onto the horse's neck, and it reared. Scanlan used his failing strength to stop himself from being thrown entirely and dismounted awkwardly. As he did, he was hit in his hip and his shoulder by bullets from Joe and Dan.

He staggered a few paces and tried to run for the cover of the trees but he sunk to his knees after only a few steps, unable to breathe. Blood gushed from the wound in his side.

Kennedy had Ned in his sights as he fired over his horse's rump. The animal was having none of it and took off. McIntyre seized the moment and grasped the reins as the horse shot past him. He flung himself into the saddle.

"Shoot that man!" Dan screamed.

Joe and Steve fired in the direction of the fleeing McIntyre. Kennedy ran to the trees and fired at Dan. The shot hit the teenager in the shoulder and he hit the ground. Joe and Steve didn't notice as they ran into the bush after McIntyre.

Ned exchanged shots with Kennedy who began following McIntyre's trajectory. Ned pursued him, attempting to reload the shotgun as he ran.

Now Dan remained alone in the camp. Scanlan was on the ground in front of him struggling to breathe. Dan kept his pistol trained on him. Scanlan was on all fours and bleeding heavily, a scarlet pool formed under him, dribbling out through the dirt in rivulets. Suddenly Scanlan gurgled and fell face down into the dirt. Dan stood still, his pistol still trained on the dead policeman, too afraid to move. He had never seen so much blood before. Dan began shaking uncontrollably and the world spun around him like he was trapped in a whirlwind. He staggered towards the bush, steadied himself on a Stringybark tree and vomited.

Meanwhile, McIntyre had been dodging bullets on horseback. He had heard Joe and Steve shouting after him but had gotten away. The horse was terrified and rode at full tilt, not taking notice of its rider. McIntyre struggled to remain mounted as branches slapped and scraped his face, lacerating the skin. He turned to look back and a low hanging branch cleaned him up, yanking him out of the saddle. He landed on a tangle of rocks and roots, which knocked the wind out of him. His brain went into panic as he struggled to re-inflate his lungs. For a few seconds he thought he was done for. When he succeeded in regaining his breath, he sucked the air lustily. He staggered inside the trunk of a tree that had been hollowed out by termites and tried to build up some energy to go looking for the chestnut mare.

Elsewhere, Ned was in hot pursuit of Kennedy. The pair were running and ducking behind trees, following the trail of destruction left by the horse. The further along they got the harder it was to follow the trail and Kennedy turned to go deeper into the bush. Kennedy was resolute. He slid down behind a tree and caught his breath. He heard no footfalls; Ned had done the same. He knew that he only had two shots, so he had to make them count.

He emerged from his hiding place as Kennedy did the same. Kennedy was quick on the trigger and fired at Ned. The bullet passed through Ned's beard, just grazing his jaw. He clapped his hand to his face and felt blood on his fingers. A second shot tore through Ned's sleeve, barely touching the skin of his arm. Ned growled and unloaded his shotgun, ripping the bark off the tree by Kennedy's head. Kennedy ran on and hid behind a thick blue gum. Ned stomped through the bush, grimacing.

"Surrender to me and I won't shoot you, you have my word," said Ned as he reloaded the shotgun with his last two cartridges.

"How could I ever trust the word of a God-damned bushranger?" Kennedy spat back.

"I don't want to shoot you."

Kennedy opened the chamber of his Webley and noted that he had one bullet left. He hoped Ned hadn't been counting.

"I have a better idea," Kennedy offered, "you surrender to me, and I'll let you live long enough to hang for what you've done to my mates."

Ned's eyebrows furrowed and met; his beard bristled.

"You're game, I'll grant you that!" Ned shouted. He stood out into the open and Kennedy peered around the tree trunk. He aimed and fired. The shot cut across Ned's ribs, and he clapped his hand on the wound. As Ned reeled, Kennedy stood out from cover and was about to run when Ned jerked the shotgun up and fired at Kennedy, striking him under the right arm.

Kennedy moaned and attempted to run but the pain was overwhelming and he bled freely. After about a metre he dropped his pistol, his fingers too weak from the searing agony in his arm, the weapon useless to him now at any rate. Ned saw that his enemy was wounded and followed at walking pace, like a wolf assured of its next meal but still wary. Kennedy suddenly turned around to face Ned with his arm raised. Impulsively, Ned fired the last shot from his gun. The blast hit Kennedy in the right side of the chest and knocked him off his feet. He hit the ground hard. As Ned moved towards the fallen sergeant his foot knocked something in the undergrowth – Kennedy's pistol. Ned realised too late that Kennedy had been turning to surrender. Ned began to panic, realising that he didn't know how to respond to the situation.

"I'm sorry I shot you," Ned said with almost a whimper. He whipped his hat off and ran his blood-soaked fingers through his hair. Suddenly he became aware of movement behind him. He turned to see the rest of his gang emerging. They halted in shock.

"Ned," said Dan, "what are you doing?"
"He's wounded."
Dan approached the dying man and gave out a nervous giggle.
"I need you to go to the camp and get a horse, yeah? We'll send him back to town and he'll get a doctor," said Ned, by now in deep denial.
"Horse be damned," said Dan, "there's no way he'll survive a trip out of the bush. Look at the mess you've made of him. And even if he survived, he'd only set his mates on us. You know what you've got to do."

Ned sat down in the scrub next to Kennedy. Suddenly he felt a feeble tug on his sleeve. He turned and Kennedy looked up into the bushranger's face. The policeman's eyes were glossy with tears.

216 ~ AIDAN PHELAN

"Take these," he said, his voice little more than a whisper. In his hand was a folded bundle of paper and a gold pocket watch. Ned took the items; they were smeared with blood.

"You must give these to my wife, you must, if there's a single decent bone in your body. Oh, my poor dears..." Kennedy flopped back down, gasping for air, delirious with pain and blood loss.

"My poor Bridget..." Kennedy gurgled as blood pooled in his lung.

Ned frowned and stood. He took Joe's gun, cocked it, and without a word he pressed it to Kennedy's chest and pulled the trigger. There was a flash, a boom and an explosion of gore. All signs of life from the sergeant stopped immediately as blood gushed from a hideous wound big enough to put a fist into, that went straight through the torso. Everyone was motionless and stared at the corpse as blood formed dark red channels in the soft earth.

The gang returned to the camp, dejected. Wordlessly they began to gather anything useful.

Ned searched the tent and found a cloak and bundled it under his arm. He saw Lonigan's body just over the logs. He climbed over the timber and went to the body. He unclipped the policeman's pistol belt and slid it off the corpse. He slung the belt around his own waist over the blood red sash and clipped it. The holster flap was still open, and Ned slid the trooper's Webley in place. He turned to Joe.

"I'm going back to Kennedy. Get them pack horses ready so we can leave when I get back." Ned began to head off. "He was a flash bugger," he mumbled as he passed Scanlan's corpse. He looked around and saw no sign of McIntyre.

"Who took care of McIntyre?"

The group was silent. Ned pressed them.

"Where is McIntyre?"

"He got away." Joe said. Ned was silent with his chest puffed up but he held his tongue as he continued to where Kennedy's corpse lay, carrying the cloak. When he found the body, he noticed the wedding band on Kennedy's finger. He tugged at it and slid the ring off, placing it on his own finger. He draped the cloak over the body. The feet sticking out the bottom made it clear that the obscured lump was a body.

At the camp, Steve loaded the police horses with the weapons and ammunition. Joe searched through Scanlan's and Lonigan's pockets, turning them out to grab any cash or valuables within. He took from Scanlan's finger a gold ring with a blue topaz set in it. From Lonigan he took a gold ring and a cheap pocket watch. Dan claimed Scanlan's watch but quickly realised it had broken when he fell.

Ned reappeared and went to the fire with a broken branch. He set fire to the oily eucalyptus leaves and threw it onto the empty tent.

"Let's go." Ned commanded. Steve followed immediately but Dan and Joe hung back.

"What have we done, Joe?" asked Dan.

"I don't know. I think we're dead men now." replied Joe.

***

Since his fall, Constable McIntyre had found the chestnut mare and sent it off into the bush minus the saddle and bridle. He had then attempted to find his way out of the bush on foot. He crawled for a distance to leave no footprints. Once he felt he was in the clear he attempted to run. His back was in agony, each breath making him feel like his ribs would crack, and the cuts on his face and arms bled heavily. He struggled to put weight on his right foot, his ankle having been wrenched when he was thrown from the saddle. To alleviate some of the discomfort he removed his boots and hobbled. Finally the pain was too much and as he leaned against a tree to catch his breath he noticed a large wombat hole. Getting onto the ground, McIntyre slid feet first into the hole until he could not go further, then bunched up leaves and twigs around himself to create a small, ineffectual camouflage. Reaching into his waistcoat McIntyre withdrew his notebook and pencil and scribbled furiously in it:

> *Ned Kelly, Dan, and two others, stuck us up to-day when were disarmed. Lonigan and Scanlan are shot. I am hiding in a wombat hole until dark. The Lord have mercy on me. Scanlan tried to get his gun out.*

He prayed that in the event the bushrangers should find and kill him there would be some record of what had happened. In the failing daylight he watched as a butcher bird flitted through the canopy above him. He decided he would remain in place until he was sure the bushrangers were gone, then try to make his way back to Mansfield on foot to raise the alarm. As night fell, he felt more alone than he had ever felt in his life, but he had a mission, and he could not afford failure.

Ned Kelly

This, the most well-known bushranger in history, requires no introduction. He has been the subject of innumerable books, plays, films, television programmes, documentaries, musicals, artworks, and on, and on. He has become, for many, an enduring symbol of righteous rebellion or moral degradation. Debate rages over whether he should be viewed as a hero or a villain, though most of the people debating it seem uninterested in the nuances of his story in favour of sweeping generalisation and character assassination. He is known by the masses as "Ned".

Edward Kelly was born, it is believed, somewhere between December 1854 to June 1855 to John Kelly and Ellen Quinn. His birth date is unknown as any records of his birth or baptism have disappeared if they were ever made. His uncles on his mother's side, the Quinns, were often in trouble with the law, as were his Kelly and Lloyd relatives in Australia. The families were all closely knit and when John Kelly died from a form of oedema called "dropsy" in 1866 as a result of alcoholism, Ned found himself dragged deeper into the sphere of influence of his lawless uncles.

Ned's siblings were numerous: Annie, Maggie, Jim, Dan, Kate and Grace. Ned being the eldest son took on more duties and responsibilities around the home. For a time they all lived in an old pub with Ellen's sisters and their children, however Ned's uncle James Kelly burned the building down in a drunken fit of spite one night, nearly killing all of the occupants. Ned took on odd jobs to try and raise money for his family, but it proved to be insufficient. When Ellen took up a selection in Greta, she found it extremely difficult to keep up with the rent. This led to Ned's first dabbling in bushranging.

In 1869 Ned briefly ranged with Harry Power, mostly employed to hold the horses while the older man executed his robberies. Occasionally Ned would be involved in the robberies himself, but Power would later complain about the teenager's impulsiveness and violent urges. When Power was finally caught he blamed Ned, believing he had given him away to police.

Ned had in fact been arrested as Power's suspected accomplice but the charges never stuck in court for one reason or another. Though Ned had in fact given some information to police about Power, it was mostly useless. When he was arrested, Ned was filthy and underfed — an indicator of the way the bushranging life had treated him.

Ned's first brush with the law actually came in between stints of working for Power, when he assaulted a Chinese man called Ah Fook for allegedly threatening his sister. Ned avoided gaol for the incident, but he would shortly thereafter land in Beechworth Gaol for three months for assaulting a hawker named Jeremiah McCormack after he got mixed up in a rivalry between the McCormacks and another hawker named Ben Gould.

When he got out of gaol he was soon back in to do three years after being tried for receiving a stolen horse and found guilty. The horse had been taken by a family friend named Isaiah "Wild" Wright, but had been lost. Wright had borrowed one of Ned's horses to get home, and when Ned found the missing animal he rode it into Greta where the local policeman, Senior-Constable Edward Hall, spotted him. Hall suspected the horse was stolen and attempted to arrest Ned. There was a scuffle and Ned was only taken after being held down and beaten severely over the head with Hall's revolver.

Ned served his sentence at Beechworth Gaol, Pentridge Prison and the hulks at Point Gellibrand. When he was released he went straight for a short while, but in 1877 he undertook a well-organised horse and cattle stealing operation with his stepfather – George King – and two Beechworth lads named Aaron Sherritt and Joe Byrne. The operation mostly targeted squatters and selectors Kelly and his associates had something of a grudge against. Likely other members of Ned's family and friends assisted in various capacities as well to shift the stolen animals. The operation was successful, but did result in two German brothers named Baumgarten being gaoled for buying and selling the stolen animals.

On 15 April 1878, Constable Alexander Fitzpatrick was sent by Sergeant Whelan at Benalla to take charge of the police station at Greta. Fitzpatrick had heard there was a warrant out for the arrest of Dan Kelly, Ned's teenage brother, for his suspected involvement in horse stealing and made it known to Whelan that he intended to arrest Dan *en route* to his assignment. Despite popular belief, Fitzpatrick was not required by law to carry a copy of a warrant with him.

When Fitzpatrick arrived at the Kelly selection, Dan was not at home so he lingered in the area until dusk and returned to the Kelly selection in case Dan had returned, rather than cutting his losses and proceeding as ordered. When the trooper returned to the Kelly homestead he was greeted by Dan Kelly who had just returned from riding. Dan agreed to go quietly with Fitzpatrick to the station on condition that he could finish his dinner first as he had been riding all day. He denied having stolen any horses and it would later be revealed that he had been in gaol when the animals in question were stolen, corroborating his assertions.

What happened next is hotly debated, even after more than a century has passed, due to conflicting evidence but was the inciting incident for the lawlessness that followed. According to popular understanding, Fitzpatrick possibly made an unwanted sexual advance on fifteen year-old Kate Kelly and a fight broke out. Fitzpatrick claimed that Ellen Kelly hit him in the head with a coal shovel, and that Ned Kelly entered the house and shot him in the wrist, accompanied by Brickey Williamson and Ellen Kelly's son-in-law Bill Skillion, who were both brandishing revolvers. Ned Kelly would claim he was never there, and Ellen would indicate in a later interview that Fitzpatrick was drunk and had fought with Ned and Dan. Another version of the story states that Fitzpatrick injured his arm on a door latch and claimed it was a bullet wound, cutting himself with a penknife to make it look like he had removed a bullet. Regardless of what story is the more accurate one, Fitzpatrick returned to Benalla and lodged a report after stopping for a drink at the pub to steady his nerves.

The following day Ellen Kelly, Brickey Williamson and Bill Skillion were arrested and charged with aiding an attempted murder. Ned and Dan, meanwhile, had gone into hiding at Dan's hut in the Wombat Ranges, and a £100 reward was posted for the capture of Ned Kelly for attempted murder. While the brothers were hiding, Ellen Kelly, Williamson and Skillion were sentenced: Ellen received three years hard labour, the two men were given six years each. Ned would repeatedly state afterwards that this perceived injustice was a key motivation for his lawless behaviour.

Days later a search party was sent from Mansfield to find the Kelly brothers. Word soon reached the bushrangers that they were being hunted and they tracked the police as they ventured into the bush from Mansfield on 25 October 1878. Despite the fact they had constructed a fortified hut with huge logs for walls and an armoured door made of sheet metal to protect them in an ambush, the bushrangers remained on edge. The police party consisted of Sergeant Michael Kennedy and Constables Thomas McIntyre from Mansfield, Michael Scanlan of Mooroopna and Thomas Lonigan of Violet Town. They set up camp on the banks of Stringybark Creek, unaware they were close to the bushrangers' hideout.

The following day Kennedy and Scanlan headed off to scout for the brothers, leaving McIntyre and Lonigan to tend the camp. McIntyre shot some parrots with a shotgun Kennedy had left him for the task of hunting something for supper. He returned to camp and began cooking bread. Unknown to them, the sound of McIntyre shooting had been heard and Ned Kelly decided to bail up the police camp. He and Dan were joined by Joe Byrne and Dan's mate Steve Hart, a jockey from Wangaratta. Ned claimed his intention was simply to rob the police of their food and weapons then send them home.

In the afternoon the Kelly Gang emerged from the bush and ordered McIntyre and Lonigan to bail up. McIntyre did as instructed but Lonigan ran and was shot by Ned Kelly with a quartered bullet. A piece of shrapnel pierced Lonigan's eye and entered his brain, killing him. Ned insisted that Lonigan had gotten behind a log and was about to shoot him. McIntyre would refute this, stating that there was not enough time for Lonigan to have done so.

The bushrangers raided the camp, gathering what they could of value. Dan Kelly insisted McIntyre be handcuffed but Ned refused. He interrogated McIntyre and ordered him to get the other police to surrender when they returned. When Kennedy and Scanlan returned, McIntyre attempted to get the police to surrender but very suddenly shots were fired. Ned shot Scanlan in the torso as his horse tried to bolt. Kennedy jumped out of the saddle and began shooting with his pistol, engaging Ned in a firefight. McIntyre escaped on Kennedy's horse and rode into the bush.
After a chase, Kennedy was wounded and fell a distance from the camp. Ned, by his own account, had injured him and finished him off by shooting him in the chest at close range as he lay dying. He would claim it was a mercy killing.
Constable McIntyre, meanwhile, had been badly injured when he was knocked off the horse by a branch, and hid in a wombat hole overnight. The following day he

walked to a farm and raised the alarm. For over a century the killings at Stringybark Creek remained the worst singular incident of police fatalities while on duty in Victoria's history.

Almost immediately parliament passed the Felons Apprehension Act, which gave them the power to Proclaim people as "outlaws". This was based on the legislation of the same name passed in New South Wales. It meant that the outlaws were not protected by the law and could be murdered without provocation and the killer would not only be exempt from any legal repercussions, they would receive a reward for it. Ned Kelly, Dan Kelly and their two accomplices — Joe Byrne and Steve Hart had not yet been identified — were officially declared outlaws in the colony of Victoria with £1000 reward for Ned's capture, and another £1000 offered for the other three.

On 9 December 1878, the bushrangers stuck up Younghusband's Station at Faithfull's Creek and imprisoned the staff in a storeroom, where they were kept overnight. That evening a hawker arrived to camp at the station and he was bailed up as well, and he outlaws took new outfits from the wagon and spruced themselves up with perfume. The next morning they destroyed the telegraph lines and added to the prisoners in the shed by bailing up anyone that came past.

In the afternoon Ned, Dan and Steve rode to Euroa to rob the bank. They bailed up the bank staff and robbed the bank, then took the staff and the manager's family with them back to the station where Joe had been guarding the prisoners. The gang stayed until night time and then left, ordering the prisoners to wait until they were long gone before leaving themselves. The gang escaped with over £1500 in gold and money. In response the reward was raised to £4000.

With all four gang members now officially identified, it was harder for them to move around, so Joe Byrne's best friend Aaron Sherritt kept the police distracted by giving them false information. In early 1879 he informed police that the Kelly Gang would be going to Goulburn. The police immediately headed for Goulburn, but the outlaws were actually heading for Jerilderie.

At midnight on 7 February, 1879, the Kelly Gang bailed the Jerilderie police up and imprisoned them in their own lock-up. Over the next couple of days they disguised themselves as police in order to scope out the town. On 10 February, the bushrangers started rounding people up in the pub, then went into the bank next door and bailed up the staff. They robbed the bank and Ned destroyed records of the bank's debtors. Afterwards, Ned gave a speech in the pub to all his prisoners.

Ned and Joe had written a letter that was to be published in the local newspaper, but the local news editor had run out of town once he realised the Kelly Gang were robbing the bank. Ned gave the letter to one of the bankers to be passed onto the press and the gang headed off with £2000 pounds of stolen money and gold. This caused the New South Wales government to double the reward to £8000.

The gang were reliant on their sympathisers for fresh horses, food, occasional shelter and up-to-date information. In return, the gang gave the majority of the money they stole from banks to their supporters. In a widely criticised move by police, many suspected sympathisers were arrested and held for remand for an indefinite period, thus cutting off the gang's access to their support network.

For the next few months Aaron Sherritt kept the police distracted by hosting watch parties at the Byrne selection every night, and a party of Native Police was sent from Queensland to hunt for the outlaws. At this time the outlaws were mostly hiding in the Strathbogie Ranges or the Warby Ranges, and had begun to collect steel plates, mostly plough mouldboards, in order to craft bulletproof armour. Ned Kelly would claim his original intention was to wear the armour during bank robberies as the banks were now all guarded by armed soldiers. Each gang member had their own suit, but mystery still surrounds who made the armour and how they did it. Many believe it was made by local blacksmiths or by the gang themselves.

Though Aaron Sherritt was a sympathiser too, many of the gang's other supporters thought he was working for the police and had urged the gang to murder him. Meanwhile, Ned Kelly had decided to escalate the conflict with the police and take out as many of them in a single strike as possible. He planned to lure them out on a special train and derail it. A commotion at Aaron Sherritt's hut would cause the police, who were based in Benalla, to go by train to Beechworth and resume the hunt with a fresh trail. In order to get to Beechworth they had to pass through Glenrowan, where the train line would be broken on a treacherous bend, causing the train to fly off the tracks. The intention seems to have been to murder the police on board in order to force the government to stop pursuing the gang out of fear, and potentially take survivors hostage as leverage to make the government give in to their demands.

On 26 June 1880, Dan Kelly and Joe Byrne bailed up a neighbour of Aaron Sherritt named Anton Wick. They took him to Sherritt's hut and used him to lure Aaron to the back door. When Aaron opened the door Joe murdered him, shooting him twice with a shotgun. Aaron died instantly. The four police constables that had been assigned to protect Aaron had no way to escape the hut and hid in the bedroom. Joe and Dan tried to force the police out of the bedroom for several hours before giving up and riding off to join Ned and Steve at Glenrowan.

At Glenrowan, Ned and Steve bailed up many locals as prisoners and forced a team of quarrymen and some platelayers to pull up a section of the train track. At daybreak the prisoners were split into two groups: women and children were kept in the gatehouse to be guarded by Steve, everyone else was taken to The Glenrowan Inn. Throughout the day more prisoners were captured as Ned waited for the police train. To keep the prisoners occupied there were sporting games held at the inn, card games were played inside, drinks flowed freely and there was even a dance in the bar room.

As it was a Sunday, no civilian trains would be running and Ned expected the police to arrive as soon as they heard the news of what had happened at Aaron's hut. What Ned had not discovered was that the news of Aaron's murder did not reach the police in Benalla until after lunchtime.

That evening Ned agreed to let the local schoolteacher, Thomas Curnow, take his sick wife home when they went to capture the local policeman, Constable Bracken. As soon as he got home, Curnow gathered a candle and a red scarf and went to the train line so that he could signal the police train to stop.

Back at the inn, as Ned was giving a speech the police train finally arrived and stopped at the station, having been warned by Curnow about the sabotaged track. The outlaws donned their bulletproof armour and when the police reached the inn a siege commenced.

During the battle, Ned escaped into the bush and fell unconscious while the rest of the gang remained in the inn. Most of the women and children escaped though the crossfire, and Joe Byrne was killed by a police bullet as he had a drink at the bar. Police reinforcements continued to arrive throughout the early hours of the morning and just before sunrise Ned Kelly reappeared behind the police lines. He briefly fought the police on his own before a blast to his unprotected knee brought him down. He was captured alive but badly wounded.

At ten o'clock in the morning the rest of the prisoners were let out. By this time people from all around had descended upon Glenrowan to watch the siege and a portable telegraph had been set up to broadcast news of the siege live to Melbourne. In the afternoon the police decided to burn the inn down to flush Dan and Steve out, but they were already dead.

Ned Kelly was sent to Melbourne Gaol to be treated for his wounds but was not expected to survive. Here he was able to be visited by his mother, who was serving her sentence in the same gaol. When he was deemed fit, he was sent to Beechworth for a committal hearing. Authorities were worried that having a trial in Beechworth would mean there was a strong likelihood of there being sympathisers in the jury so in order to have the best chance at convicting him, he was transferred back to Melbourne for his murder trial.

In the Supreme Court, Ned Kelly was found guilty of murdering Constable Thomas Lonigan then sentenced to death by Sir Redmond Barry. While he was held in Melbourne Gaol to await his execution, his sympathisers tried to get a reprieve but it was to no avail. On 11 November 1880, Ned Kelly was hanged in Melbourne Gaol. After his execution, his body was taken to the dead house, his head was shaved and a death mask made, then his body was removed to be dissected by university students. The remains were buried in the gaol but were later transferred to Pentridge when Melbourne Gaol closed permanently in the 1920s. They have since been reburied in Greta near most of his family.

Burrowa News (NSW: 1874 - 1951), Friday 1 November 1878, page 2

BUSHRANGING AND MURDER OF THREE POLICEMEN.

MELBOURNE, Sunday.

News was received this evening from Mansfield that constables Lonergon and Scanlon have been shot dead by four bushrangers at Stringy Bark Creek, about 20 miles from Mansfield. Constable McIntyre escaped, but his horse was shot under him. Sergeant Kennedy is also missing. The police have started in search to scour the country, and to bring home the dead bodies. The bushrangers are supposed to be the notorious Kelly's party for whom the constables were in search.

MELBOURNE, Tuesday.

A search party of seven or eight constables, with a number of towns-people, started out from Mansfield to-day, all fully armed, and with provisions for four or five days. There is an impression that Kennedy may be still alive, and hiding away from the bushrangers. Kelly and his companions have now got eight days' provisions, and abundance of ammunition and weapons; and, in such a country, may elude capture some time. They have connections all about, and were fully aware of the movements of the police from the remarks Kelly made to Macintyre. Kelly also asked for the news of the murderer of sergeant Wallings, and was told that he had been shot. Great excitement exists in the country all around, and at one time an attack on Mansfield was apprehended.

The inquest on the bodies of the murdered constables commenced to-day, and was adjourned. It appears that the Mansfield district is alive with notorious characters, who express sympathy with the bushrangers and act as their confederates, as the movements of the police would seem to have been known to the gang. Two men, known as Dummy Wright and Wild Wright, were arrested to-day for endeavouring to intimidate the search party. They behaved like infuriated animals, and threatened that if they were not released the police camp at Mansfield would be attacked by bushrangers. The police of the district appeared to have been badly arranged and mounted.

The following particulars are by telegraph from a Special Reporter to the Melbourne "Argus." :—

MANSFIELD, Monday Night.

The police heard privately that the Kellys, for whom they had been looking for months past, were in the ranges at the head of the King River. The Kelly family live at Greta, 50 miles from here, and the brothers were understood to be in concealment where Power once hid himself. Two parties of police were secretly despatched last week — one from Greta, consisting of five men, with sergeant Steele in command, and one of four from Mansfield. Though the movements of the Mansfield party were supposed to be dark, the object of the expedition leaked out, and, no doubt, was rapidly telegraphed across the bush to Edward Kelly. The ranges are infested with a brotherhood of Kellys, Lloyds, Quinns, &c. They occupy land amongst the hills, and ostensibly carry on the operations of cattle-breeders. From the account given by constable McIntyre, it appears that the Mansfield party started on Friday, equipped with revolvers, one Spencer rifle, and a double-barrelled gun, lent by a resident of the township. They had a tent and a fortnight's provisions. They reached Stringybark Creek, 20 miles from here, on Friday evening, and camped on an open space on the creek. It was the site of some old diggings. They pitched the tent near the ruins of two old huts. They were about 15 miles from the head of the King. No special precautions were thought necessary, because the party supposed they were a long way from Kelly's whereabouts. The ranges round about were almost uninhabited, and the party were not quite sure whether they were on the watershed of the King or the Broken River; but both Kennedy and Scanlan knew the locality intimately. It was Kennedy's intention to camp for a few days, patrol backwards into the ranges, and then shift the camp in About 6 a.m. on Saturday Scanlan went down the creek to explore, and they stayed away nearly all day. It was McIntyre's duty to cook, and he attended closely to camp duty. During the forenoon some noise was heard, and McIntyre went out to have a look, but found nothing. He fired two shots out of his gun at a pair of parrots. This gunshot, he subsequently learned, was heard by Kelly, who must have been on the lookout for the police for days past. About 5 p.m. McIntyre was at the fire making the afternoon tea, and Lonergon by him, when they were suddenly surprised with the cry, "Bale up; throw up your arms!" They looked up, and saw four armed men close to them. Three carried guns, and Edward Kelly two rifles. Two of the men they did not know, but the fourth was the younger Kelly. The four were on foot. They had approached up the rises, and some flags or rushes had provided them with excellent cover until they got into the camp. McIntyre had left his revolver at the tent door, and was totally unarmed. He, therefore, held up his hands as directed, and faced round. Lonergon started for shelter behind a tree, and at the same time put his hand upon his revolver; but before he had moved two paces Edward Kelly shot him in the temple. He fell at once, and as he laid on the ground said, "Oh, Christ, I am shot." He died in a few seconds. Kelly had McIntyre searched, and when they found he was unarmed they let him drop his hands. They got possession of Lonergon's and McIntyre's revolvers. Kelly remarked when he saw Lonergon had been killed, "What a pity; what made the fool run!" The men helped themselves to several articles in the tent. Kelly talked to McIntyre, and expressed his wonder that the police should have been so foolhardy as to look for him in the ranges. He made inquiries about four different men, and said he would roast each of them alive if he caught them. Steele and Flood were two of the four named. He asked McIntyre what he fired at in the forenoon, and said they must have been fools not to suppose he was ready for them. It was evident that he knew the exact state of the camp, the number of men, and the description of the horses. He asked where the other two were, and said he would put a hole through McIntyre if he told a lie. McIntyre told him who the two absent men were, and hoped they would not be shot in cold blood. Kelly replied, "No, I am not a coward. I'll shoot no man if he holds up his hands." He told McIntyre that the best thing he could do was to advise Kennedy and Scanlan to surrender, for if they showed fight or tried to run away they would be shot. McIntyre asked what they would do if he induced his comrades to surrender. Kelly said he would detain them all night, as he wanted a sleep, and let them go next morning without their arms or their horses. McIntyre told Kelly that he would induce his comrades to surrender, if he would keep his word, but he would rather be shot a thousand times than sell them. He added that one of the two was a father of a large family. Kelly said, "You can depend on us." Kelly stated that Fitzpatrick, the man who tried to arrest his brother in April, was the cause of all this; that his (Kelly's) mother and the rest had been unjustly "lagged" at Beechworth. Kelly then caught sound of the approach of Kennedy and Scanlan, and the four men concealed themselves, some behind logs, and one in the tent. They made McIntyre sit on a log, and Kelly said, "Mind I have a rifle for you if you give any alarm." Kennedy and Scanlan rode into the camp. McIntyre went forward, and said, "Sergeant, I think you had better dismonnt and surrender, as you are surrounded." Kelly at the same time called out, "Put up your hands." Kennedy appeared to think it was Lonergon who called out, and that a jest was intended, for he smiled and put his hand on his revolver case. He was instantly fired at, but not hit; and Kennedy then realised the hopelessness of his position, jumped off his horse, and said, "It's all right; stop it, stop it." Scanlan, who carried the Spencer rifle, jumped down and tried to make for a tree, but before he could unsling his rifle he was shot down and never spoke. A number of shots were fired. McIntyre found that the men intended to shoot the whole of the party, so he jumped on Kennedy's horse, and dashed down the creek. Several shots were fired, but none reached him. Apparently the rifles were empty, and only the revolvers available, or he must have been hit. He galloped through the scrub for two miles, and then his horse became exhausted. It had evidently been wounded. He took off the saddle and bridle, and concealed himself in a wombat hole until dark. He then started on foot across country, and walked until 3 p.m. on Sunday, when he reached McColl's place, near Mansfield.

Two hours or so after McIntyre reported the murder of the troopers, Inspector Pewtress set out, accompanied by McIntyre and seven or eight towns-people, for the camp. The police station was so empty of weapons that all the arms they could take were one revolver and one gun. They reached the camp with the assistance of a guide, at half-past 2 this morning. They found the bodies of Scanlan and Lonergon. They searched at day-light for the sergeant, but met with no traces of him. The tent had been burnt and everything taken away or destroyed. There were four bullet wounds on Lonergon and five on Scanlan. Three additional shots had been fired into Lonergon's dead body before the men left the camp. The extra shots were fired so that all might be equally implicated. McIntyre is certain that Kennedy was not hit, but no one here at present ventures to do more than hope that the brave fellow has not been since murdered. It is McIntyre's belief that Kelly meant to spare none, but dispose of them in a way to render their fate a mystery. Now that they know McIntyre has escaped, they may possibly let Kennedy live. A large party will be despatched at 7 o'clock to-morrow morning to succour Kennedy if alive, and run down the murderers. They will provide themselves with food for several days. McIntyre is weak from bruises and from 48 hours' severe exertion. The sorrow felt for the death of Scanlan is universal throughout the district. He seems to have been a brave, cool, amiable, excellent man. Kennedy was an efficient bushman and a resolute officer. He has a wife and five children, and, fortunately for them, should he be killed, his circumstances are good. Scanlan was unmarried, and his station was Benalla. Lonergon was from Violet Town. He has left a widow and four children, badly off.

[Sergeant Kennedy has since been found murdered. Further particulars in our Melbourne telegram.]

MELBOURNE.

Thursday.

News has just arrived from Mansfield that the body of Sergeant Kennedy was found near the camp at 8 o'clock this morning. He had been shot. There were three bullet wounds in his body.

The Government have increased the reward for the capture of each of the Kelly gang to £500. The widows of the constables shot will draw their husbands' pay.

In the Assembly, the Sydney Outlawry Bill was introduced, under which bush-rangers will be shot down if they fail to surrender to justice, and passed through all its stages.

Hobart Town in Howe's Day

Sketch by Lieutenant C. H. Jeffreys of Hobart Town in 1817 and Government Schooner 'Kangaroo'.

Courtesy: Libraries Tasmania, LPIC147/3/141

"The Last and Worst..."

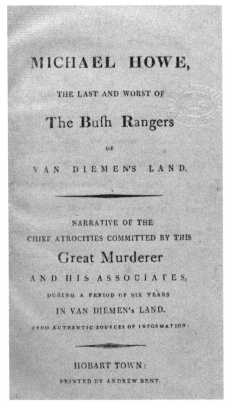

The title page of the first text about Australian
bushranging, printed only months after
Michael Howe's death, from a manuscript
supposedly written by Thomas Wells.

Courtesy: National Library of Australia, SR 343.94
WEL

Brady and Company in the Dock

James McCabe, Matthew Brady, and Patrick Bryant sketched by Thomas Bock, 1843.
Courtesy: State Library of New South Wales, FL1077003 - DL PX 5; IE1076928

It is worth noting that at the time this sketch was made, James McCabe had already been captured, tried and hanged. Bock was referring to his previous sketches of McCabe to place him with his former accomplices while they were on trial.

Valleyfield

'Valleyfield', by John Richardson Glover (c.1850-59)
Courtesy: National Library of Australia, PIC Volume 1112 #PIC/5235/11

Port Arthur in the time of Cash & Co.

Port Arthur, Tasmania, 1843
Courtesy: State Library of New South Wales. FL3267708

'Martin Cash', by Thomas Bock (1843)

Courtesy: State Library of New South Wales, FL1076998 - DL PX 5; IE1076928

MORGAN, THE BUSHRANGER. — SEE PAGE 10.

Morgan, the bushranger, by Samuel Calvert (1864)
Courtesy: State Library Victoria; 1645936;

Morgan at the Round Hill Station

MORGAN AT THE ROUND HILL STATION—SEE PAGE 12.

Morgan at the Round Hill Station, by Frederick Grosse (1864)
Courtesy: State Library Victoria; 1688096; mp000779

Hall, Gilbert, and Dunn sticking up the Mail at the Black Springs

Hall, Gilbert, and Dunn sticking up the Mail at the Black Springs, by Robert Stewart (1865)
Courtesy: State Library Victoria; 1647175; b48916

John Gilbert, the Bushranger.—SEE PAGE 87.

John Gilbert, the Bushranger, by Eugene Montagu Scott (1865)
Courtesy: State Library Victoria; 1648892; b48953

Power the Bushranger, by Charles Nettleton (1870)
Courtesy: State Library Victoria; 1801790; cc000767

"Power Country" in the 1860s

Alpine landscape near Beechworth, by Alfred Eustace (c.1865)
Courtesy: State Library Victoria; 1797014; is013875

Bush Travelling: Crossing the Creek, by Samuel Calvert (1860)

Courtesy: State Library Victoria; 1788846; mp016953

Cadaver of Frederick Ward, the bushranger Captain Thunderbolt, by
Andrew Cunningham (1870)

Constable Alexander Binning Walker, who killed the bushranger
Thunderbolt, by Andrew Cunningham (1870)
Courtesy: State Library New South Wales; IE3283327; FL3283336

JUNE 4, 1870.]   SYDNEY PUNCH.

THE LAST OF THE BUSHRANGERS.

A TRIBUTE TO THE AUSTRALIAN POLICE FORCE.

"THE LAST OF THE BUSHRANGERS. A Tribute to the Police Force."

Source: Sydney Punch (NSW: 1864 - 1888), Saturday 4 June 1870, page 9

In this press cartoon, the crowned feminine figure representing New South Wales wields her sword over the prostrated body of Captain Thunderbolt to land a final, fatal blow. The visual style and the monogram on the stone by Thunderbolt's head indicates the work of Sir John Tenniel, who is best known for his work on Lewis Carroll's "Alice" books. Tenniel was a cartoonist with the satirical magazine *London Punch*, which was published worldwide, usually portraying conservative ideas in his trademark whimsical style. This illustration clearly reflects the attitude of the people - and most importantly, the establishment - of New South Wales that bushranging had been dealt a killing strike with the death of Thunderbolt. However, as was typical (and some might argue is still the case) this view was only upheld by ignoring what was still happening in neighbouring colonies - specifically Victoria (as seen below).

BUSHRANGING IN VICTORIA.—SULLIVAN FIRING AT TROOPER MAYS.—(SEE NEXT PAGE.)

Source: Weekly Times (Melbourne, Vic.: 1869 - 1954), Saturday 17 December 1870,

page 9

Prison portrait of Andrew George Scott, prisoner #10124 (c.1872)
*Courtesy: Public Records Office, Victoria; VPRS 515/P0000, Central Register for
Male Prisoners 9706 - 10160 (1872)*

Ballarat Gaol in its Heyday

H. M. Gaol Ballarat, by Solomon & Bardwell, photographers (1861)
Courtesy: State Library Victoria; 1642993; mp000489

This is the gaol as it would have looked to Scott, Plunkett, Taylor, Dermoody, Stapleton and Marshall. The prison was still in operation until 1965 when it was closed to allow the School of Mines to expand, and what remains now houses Federation University.

The Police Camp at Stringybark Creek

Scene of the Wombat Police murders (1878)
Courtesy: State Library Victoria; 1806777; nc001201

In this photograph, stand-ins assume the positions of McIntyre and Kelly on the left and Kennedy on the right at the actual crime scene. Another photograph in this series shows the same men replicating the finding of Kennedy's body.

"The Bushranging Tragedy"

THE BUSHRANGING TRAGEDY: PORTRAITS OF THE FOUR CONSTABLES AND THE TWO KELLYS.
1—CONSTABLE LONIGON.   2—EDWARD KELLY.   3—CONSTABLE SCANLAN.   4—SERGEANT KENNEDY.   5—CONSTABLE M'INTYRE.   6—DANIEL KELLY.

The Bushranging tragedy: portraits of the four constables and the two Kellys (1878)

Courtesy: State Library Victoria; 1656251; b50579

Acknowledgements

It has been exactly five years since I began *A Guide to Australian Bushranging*, so this book seemed to be a fitting anniversary commemoration. What began as a website where I could share my research into the history of bushranging has continued to grow and grow into other areas, which now includes - obviously - publishing books.

It would be remiss of me not to acknowledge the people that helped me reach this point. Firstly, there's the people that have followed me all the way through this journey to date via social media and my website. Knowing there are people out there who eagerly follow what I do is humbling and gratifying.

But perhaps the most important individuals in getting me to this point are my late father, Keith Phelan, who actively encouraged my fascination with history and Ned Kelly in particular through excursions, activities and countless conversations; Matthew Holmes, whose film *The Legend of Ben Hall* reinvigorated my passion for these stories at a time when I was feeling completely disconnected, and who on a personal level has been a great friend and supporter of my work; Noeleen Lloyd, who continues to provide me with sage wisdom and push me towards bettering my craft and getting myself out there; and my fiancée Georgina Stones who continues to motivate me every day to engage with this history and push myself to following through with my plans, and whose own incredible research has profoundly impacted on my own research and understanding.

I could not possibly go without pointing to the many biographers and historians, living and dearly departed, whose work has shaped this volume and to whom I am deeply indebted: James Erskine Calder, Karl Rawdon von Steiglitz, Margaret Carnegie, Edgar Penzig, Peter Bradley, Gary Dean, Kevin Passey, Allan M. Nixon, Gregory Powell, Bob Cummins, Carol Baxter, Jane Smith, Paul Terry, Matthew Grubits, Ian Jones, John Malony, and Alex Castles. This is not an exhaustive list, but it does cover the people whose work had the most impact on my research for this particular volume of *Bushranging Tales*.

I hope this book goes some way towards preserving these stories for posterity, and motivates others to dig deeper into history to find more stories. I am but one man, and though I am doing my bit to collect, catalogue and share this history, I cannot do it alone - my brain is already too full of tales, dates, names and trivia to learn it all to the point of infallible expertise.

I thank you for taking the time to procure this book and read it. It is people like you who make this all worthwhile.

- Aidan Phelan, December 2022

About the Author

Aidan Phelan is the writer and historian for the website *A Guide to Australian Bushranging*, which has been bringing Australia's outlaw heritage to a worldwide audience since 2017. In 2021 he was featured in a series of interviews on ABC Radio Hobart and Northern Tasmania discussing the history of bushrangers in Tasmania, and was interviewed for The Hobart Magazine about bushranger "Rocky" Whelan.

In 2020 he self-published his first novel, *Glenrowan*, which dramatised the final months of the Kelly Outbreak. He is also developing *Glenrowan* as a television miniseries with filmmaker Matthew Holmes (*The Legend of Ben Hall.*)

In 2022, he published his book *Aaron Sherritt: Persona non Grata*, which examined the life of Aaron Sherritt and his involvement in the Kelly Outbreak of 1878-1880. It is the first time a book focused on Sherritt has been published.

He has also worked as an illustrator, contributing work for Judy Lawson's *The Clarke Bushrangers: A Clash of Cultures* in 2020, and regularly provides illustrations for *An Outlaw's Journal* by Georgina Stones, including her books *Joe and Maggie* (2020) and *Ah Nam* (2022).

WHAT ARE PEOPLE SAYING ABOUT A GUIDE TO AUSTRALIAN BUSHRANGING?

"A truly fantastic resource for bushranger enthusiasts!"

- MATTHEW HOLMES (WRITER/DIRECTOR, *THE LEGEND OF BEN HALL*)

Great site. Very informative and reliable. Highly recommended it to anyone wanting to learn more about Australia's bushranging history.

- NATHAN M.

See for yourself:— *www.aguidetoaustralianbushranging.com*
Or find us on social media:— *www.facebook.com/AustralianBushranging*

Also available from Australian Bushranging

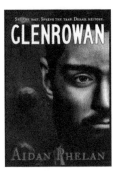

Glenrowan by Aidan Phelan

The Kelly Gang have been on the run for months and are the most wanted men in the British Empire. No expense has been spared in the hunt to bring them to justice. With the introduction of highly specialised trackers to hunt them and rumours of treachery amongst their supporters, the outlaws are desperate. Soon their leader, Ned Kelly, will hatch a plan that will not only bring an end to the pursuit, but will leave an indelible mark on the history of Australia. Glenrowan is the story of how one man's burning obsession can have far reaching consequences, and how a tiny town between towns became as iconic as Gettysburg or Waterloo.

The true story of Aaron Sherritt's involvement in the Kelly saga is revealed. Was he truly the traitor he has been accused of being?

From his poverty-stricken childhood, to his lawless youth, we see Aaron's life reflecting the society around him and the emerging Australian identity. His close friendship with Joe Byrne sees them both in and out of mischief until Ned Kelly enters their lives and things spiral out of control.

Aaron Sherritt:
Persona non Grata by
Aidan Phelan

William Westwood: In
His Own Words

William Westwood was only sixteen when he was transported from Essex as a convict for stealing a coat. After landing in New South Wales and being assigned to a cruel master who would have him flogged at any opportunity, he decided that he would reclaim his freedom by any means necessary. Years later, as an inmate on Norfolk Island, a place known as the Isle of Despair, William Westwood immortalised his life in written word, and it is reproduced here in full, along with transcriptions of his letters. Contemporary news reports and a collection of images help to fill the gaps and more fully immerse the reader in the world of the notorious "Jackey Jackey".

Joe Byrne was a widow's teenage son with dreams of something better than life on a dairy farm. Ah Nam was a miner with a taste for booze, women, gambling and fighting. By a twist of fate their paths would cross and Joe's life would never be the same again.

In Ah Nam, Georgina Stones shines a light on a forgotten chapter in the early life of one of Australia's most infamous outlaws, with original illustrations by Aidan Phelan, as well as essays, contemporary images and articles bringing life to the frontier town of Beechworth and its larger than life denizens.

Ah Nam by Georgina Stones

Available online now from most reputable bookstores including Booktopia, Book Depository, Amazon, Dymocks, Angus and Robertson, Barnes and Noble, Waterstones and Fishpond.

Ingram Content Group UK Ltd.
Milton Keynes UK
UKHW020055280323
419243UK00002B/34